SCHOOL ADMINISTRATOR'S COMPLETE LETTER BOOK

SCHOOL ADMINISTRATOR'S COMPLETE LETTER BOOK

Compiled and Edited by GERALD TOMLINSON

PRENTICE HALL
Englewood Cliffs, New Jersey 07632

Prentice-Hall International, Inc., *London*
Prentice-Hall of Australia, Pty. Ltd., *Sydney*
Prentice-Hall Canada, Inc., *Toronto*
Prentice-Hall of India Private Ltd., *New Delhi*
Prentice-Hall of Japan, Inc., *Tokyo*
Prentice-Hall of Southeast Asia Pte. Ltd., *Singapore*
Whitehall Books, Ltd., Wellington, *New Zealand*
Editora Prentice-Hall do Brasil Ltda., *Rio de Janeiro*

20 19 18 17 16 15

Library of Congress Cataloging in Publication Data

Main entry under title:

School administrator's complete letter book.

Includes index.
1. Schools—Records and correspondence. 2. School
management and organization. 3. Letters. I. Tomlinson,
Gerald
LB2845.7.S36 1984   651.7′5′024379   83-24409

ISBN 0-13-792367-8

9 780137 923670

90000>

PRENTICE HALL
Career & Personal Development
Englewood Cliffs, NJ 07632
A Simon & Schuster Company

On the World Wide Web at http://www.phdirect.com

Printed in the United States of America

Dedication

To Mary Usakowski, whose way with children,
teachers, administrators, and in-laws is an
enduring legacy and a continuing inspiration.

ABOUT THE EDITOR

A full-time freelance writer, editor, and consultant specializing in the field of education, Gerald Tomlinson began his career as a teacher of English. He has for the past 20 years held various editorial positions, including that of Executive Editor, in textbook and trade book publishing. Mr. Tomlinson has edited many well-known high school grammar and composition textbooks as well as books on education, law, business, and sports. Listed in *Who's Who in the East, Contemporary Authors,* and *The International Authors and Writers Who's Who,* he is a long-time member of the National Council of Teachers of English, the Society for American Baseball Research, and the Mystery Writers of America.

ACKNOWLEDGMENTS

A great many people helped in the nationwide search for outstanding examples of school correspondence. Among those who made valuable suggestions and recommendations were Cal Adamson, Atlanta, Georgia; M. Virginia Biggy, Concord, Massachusetts; John C. Board, Helena, Montana; Ralph Brewer, Jackson, Mississippi; Weston H. Caswell, Scotia, New York; Mary E. Cole, Warwick, Rhode Island; Donald F. Day, Concord, New Hampshire; Verne A. Duncan, Salem, Oregon; Pascal D. Forgione, Jr., Hartford, Connecticut; James O. Hansen, Pierre, South Dakota; Dennis J. Kane, Cheyenne, Wyoming; Terry Ley, Auburn, Alabama; Arthur Linneman, Portland, Oregon; Douglas McConkey, Newark, Delaware; Jerry B. Murphy, Phoenix, Arizona; Caroline H. Sturtevant, Augusta, Maine; Donnis H. Thompson, Honolulu, Hawaii; Mrs. Ronald H. Warner, Phoenix, Arizona; and Robin C. Young, Columbia, South Carolina.

CONTRIBUTORS

This book was assembled with the invaluable, indeed indispensable, assistance of the following contributors. The letters and memos in it are their letters and memos. Sometimes the material has been edited for consistency or excerpted for conciseness. Usually the actual names, titles, and addresses in the letters have been changed to ensure privacy. Yet the letters are real ones, written in response to real circumstances.

The original letters were typed in a variety of styles—full block, semiblock, and so on. In this book they all appear in a standard format, semiblock with indented paragraphs. That is only one of many acceptable formats, and its use here should not be construed as a special recommendation. Any traditional format is equally good.

Aberdeen, Maryland
J. Walter Potter, Principal, Aberdeen High School

Anniston, Alabama
Neva M. Griffin, Director of Curriculum, Anniston City Board of Education

Augusta, Maine
Raymond G. Taylor, Jr., Superintendent of Schools, City of Augusta

Averill Park, New York
John J. Thero, Principal, Algonquin Middle School

Baltimore, Maryland
Sandra L. Wighton, Principal, Western High School

Barrow, Alaska
Don Renfroe, Superintendent of Schools, North Slope Borough School District

Bismarck, North Dakota
Larry Otterson, Principal, Century High School
Emeroy Swanson, Principal, Bismarck Senior High School

Bowie, Maryland
John M. Hagan, Principal, Bowie High School

Brandon, South Dakota
Carleton Holt, Superintendent, Brandon Valley School District No. 49-2

Brunswick, Georgia
Kermit Keenum, Superintendent, Glynn County Schools

Bucks County, Pennsylvania
C. Meade Beers, District Superintendent, Pennsbury School District
Norman L. Haider, Assistant to the Superintendent, Pennsbury School District

Carson City, Nevada
Robert Slaby, Principal, Carson City High School

Chicago, Illinois
Very Rev. Richard J. Ehrens, Vicar for Catholic Education, Archdiocese of Chicago

Cincinnati, Ohio
Roberta E. Glaser, Principal, Deer Park High School

Copley, Ohio
Dianna M. Lindsay, Superintendent, Copley-Fairlawn City Schools

Cranston, Rhode Island
Joseph J. Picano, Superintendent, City of Cranston Public Schools

East Providence, Rhode Island
Myron J. Francis, Superintendent of Schools, East Providence Public Schools

Ellensburg, Washington
Eugene B. Jump, Principal, Morgan Middle School

Elmira, New York
Jerome R. O'Dell, Principal, Southside High School

Elwood, Iowa
Larry Shay, Principal, Delwood Junior-Senior High School

Flagstaff, Arizona
David A. Williams, Superintendent of Schools, Flagstaff Public Schools

Grand Forks, North Dakota
Everett C. Knudsvig, Principal, Red River High School

Great Falls, Montana
Larry D. Williams, Music Supervisor, Great Falls Public Schools

Greenwich, Connecticut
Ernest B. Fleishman, Superintendent, Greenwich Public Schools

Greenville, South Carolina
J. F. Hall, Superintendent, The School District of Greenville County

Hilo, Hawaii
Kiyoto Mizuba, District Superintendent, Hawaii District, Department of Education

Jacksonville, Florida
Nathaniel Davis, Principal, Northside Skills Center

Jacksonville Beach, Florida
Lois F. Johnson, Principal, Duncan U. Fletcher Junior High School

Jefferson City, Missouri
Therese M. Fenney, Assistant Superintendent of Schools, Diocese of Jefferson City

Jonesboro, Arkansas
Rodger Callahan, Principal, Jonesboro Senior High School

Kansas City, Kansas
Bill B. Todd, Principal, Washington High School

Lake Charles, Louisiana
Deidre R. Foreman, Social Studies Supervisor, Calcasieu Parish School Board

Lewistown, Montana
Ronald B. Mattson, Superintendent of Schools, Lewistown Public Schools

Littleton, Colorado
Robert Tschirki, Superintendent, Littleton Public Schools

Lubbock, Texas
Knox Williams, Principal, Lubbock High School

Madison, Maine
James W. Hennigar, Superintendent of Schools, School Administrative District No. 59

Madison, Wisconsin
Robert T. Reif, Principal, LaFollette High School

Minnetonka, Minnesota
Robert St. Clair, Principal, West Junior High School

Nashua, New Hampshire
Berard Masse, Superintendent of Schools, Nashua School District

New Haven, Connecticut
Gerald N. Tirozzi, Superintendent of Schools, New Haven Public Schools

New York, New York
Samuel Kostman, Principal, George Washington High School

North Platte, Nebraska
Don Holscher, Guidance Department, Madison High School

Oakland, California
Harold Zuckerman, Principal, Fremont High School

Oak Ridge, Tennessee
Thomas W. Hayes, Principal, Robertsville Junior High School

Oklahoma City, Oklahoma
Jimmy V. Scales, Principal, Millwood Junior-Senior High School

Omaha, Nebraska
Evelyn Montgomery, Director, Elementary Education, Omaha Public Schools

Oxford, Alabama
Herbert E. Griffin, Assistant Superintendent, Oxford City Board of Education

Oxford, Ohio
Raymond C. Kley, Principal, Stewart School

Philadelphia, Pennsylvania
Herbert A. Levin, Principal, Alvin A. Swenson Skills Center
Harry C. Silcox, Principal, Abraham Lincoln High School

Pocatello, Idaho
Gaylord Flicker, Principal, Grace Lutheran School

Richford, Vermont
Carroll G. Hull, Principal, Richford Junior-Senior High School

Roanoke, Virginia
Garland R. Life, Principal, Cave Springs High School

Seattle, Washington
Robert Christian, Principal, Seattle Lutheran High School

Spencer, Oklahoma
Leon Edd, Principal, Star-Spencer High School

Springfield, Oregon
Stephen M. Barrett, Assistant to the Superintendent, Springfield Public Schools

Tacoma, Washington
Connie Rickman, Assistant Principal, Lincoln High School

Tucson, Arizona
William K. Poston, Jr., Superintendent, Flowing Wells Schools

Tupelo, Mississippi
Julian D. Prince, Superintendent, Tupelo Municipal Separate School District

Wayland, Massachusetts
William G. Zimmerman, Jr., Superintendent of Schools, Wayland Public Schools

Williamsport, Pennsylvania
Jay F. Livziey, Principal, Theodore Roosevelt Middle School

Wilmington, Delaware
Rev. James W. O'Neill, Principal, Salesianum School

HOW YOU WILL BENEFIT
FROM THIS BOOK

As a professional educator, you are a professional communicator. You write and speak on many occasions. It is part of your job. Although the public appearances may be manageable and often enjoyable, the amount of paperwork—the sheer volume of written communication—is likely to be overwhelming at times.

If it is, this book can help you. *School Administrator's Complete Letter Book* will help you to cut down on the paper load. It does this in the most practical way—by example. It offers you a large and carefully chosen selection of model letters and memos for a wide variety of educational purposes and circumstances.

This is more than a valuable source book on school communication. It is a gold mine of tested, usable letters and other communiques, some of which can be used practically word-for-word from the book, while others can be adapted to your specific needs. It contains letters to be used and letters to be emulated.

If your office has word processing equipment, you will find countless individual paragraphs here that can be stored as boilerplate on magnetic disks. These paragraphs can then be arranged and rearranged as needed to produce original and responsive letters for common, recurring situations. Word processing equipment also permits the easy substitution of names and addresses.

By using this book as a ready reference guide—as a source of both ideas and of specific phrasing—you can save time and produce correspondence of true distinction.

The letters and memos you will draw on in the pages that follow are models of both style and content. They represent the contributions of more than 60 outstanding school administrators throughout the United States. Contributors include superintendents, principals, supervisors, guidance counselors, and others, all of them with well-earned reputations for solid, professional communication. Their geographic distribution is broad, literally from Maine to Florida and from New York to California, Alaska, and Hawaii.

Every kind of letter is included. There are letters addressed to parents, teachers, students, teacher applicants, other school administrators, businesspeople, and the community at large.

The letters reflect the diversity of American life and the many facets of American education. Some are from inner-city schools. Others are from rural schools or districts. Still others are from small-city schools or suburban districts. Vocational schools are represented, as are private and parochial schools.

There are letters of appreciation, reprimand, congratulation, evaluation, and sympathy. There are letters that deal with curriculum, school budgets, public relations, busing, dress codes, textbook selection, contracts, work-study programs, discipline, expulsion, resignation, special days, and much more. The book is filled with both standard topics and original, usable ideas.

Included are first-rate models of many kinds of memos. In fact, you will find examples of all sorts of school paper work, including the kind of routine internal correspondence that is as necessary as it is time-consuming. *School Administrator's Complete Letter Book* is an indispensable aid to nearly every type of administrative writing task. Its hundreds of model letters and memos can save you untold hours—hours you can apply to your vital work as an active, visible administrator.

Here are a few examples of how specific pieces of correspondence were created to solve unusual, difficult, or sensitive problems:

Problem: A teachers' strike had just ended, with some residual hard feelings on both sides.

Remedy: The principal wrote a conciliatory memo, appealing to the teachers' pride and professionalism, striking exactly the right note. (Pages 27–28)

Problem: For reasons that were not clear, vandalism rose sharply throughout the entire school system.

Remedy: The superintendent wrote a letter—a copy of which went to every student—in which he explained the serious consequences of vandalism and asked students to help in stamping it out. (Page 40)

Problem: A student had a continuing history of behavior problems. Individually, the incidents were not very serious. But the pattern itself was disturbing.

Remedy: The principal wrote an explanatory letter to the child's parents, explaining the background difficulties, describing the most recent incident, and asking for a meeting to discuss the situation. (Page 118)

Problem: A teacher left his class unattended, and a fight, resulting in injuries, broke out before the teacher returned.

Remedy: The principal sent the teacher a formal reprimand, a copy of which went into the teacher's permanent file. (Pages 211–212)

Problem: A newspaper editorial had perpetuated a misunderstanding about the cost of education and the burden being borne by local taxpayers.

Remedy: The superintendent wrote a clear, factual letter to the editor in which he explained the misunderstanding, thus putting the school system's financial affairs in a more favorable light. (Pages 225–226)

Problem: Tuition for a nonresident student was in arrears, with no reason or excuses given.

Remedy: The superintendent wrote a letter, requesting payment, to which he attached a copy of the policy statement regarding out-of-district tuition. (Pages 269–270)

These are just a few examples. Actually, every letter in this book responds to a specific need in a way that is courteous, thoughtful, and professional. The letters vary, but the differences are often based as much on the writer's awareness of audience and circumstance as they are on personal style.

Each chapter begins with a letter that appears on the letterhead stationery of a school or district. It is signed by the administrator who wrote it. These letters act as chapter dividers, and they also serve as examples of good business-letter format. Although they are excellent models, there is no implication that they are somehow the best letters in each chapter. Rather, they are the ones that seemed to work best as chapter dividers and chapter openers.

Every letter in the book is timely. Many of the problems you have to deal with in your correspondence are up-to-the-minute ones. Innovations and new policies require careful explanation. Because of this, you will find models here on such topics as computer technology, PSAT/SAT scores, censorship problems, and main-streaming.

In short, *School Administrator's Complete Letter Book* is just what its name promises, a complete model-and-reference book for school administrators on the subject of school correspondence. It is clearly organized, designed for easy use, and filled with the best letters of the best communicators in modern American education. It can make your daily life smoother and your professional image sharper. It will be a valued companion in the days and years ahead.

Gerald Tomlinson

Contents

When school opens in the fall, there are a number of letters and memos for the administrator to write. This chapter includes 15 of them.

In this chapter are 15 model letters dealing with school facilities and their use, with an emphasis on the physical plant and on buses.

These 13 letters cover a broad range of topics. In general, they represent the individual views of school administrators, although some deal with district policy.

Curriculum is the substance of education, and good communications are especially important in the area of curriculum. Here are 17 exemplary letters.

If a program is new or unusual, it will probably have to be described or explained in writing. This chapter contains 15 such descriptions.

Pleasant but not easy to write, these kinds of letters are a part of every administrator's responsibility. Included here are 18 that have succeeded.

The flip side of the coin—the letters in this chapter are anything but pleasant, but they may be necessary. These 19 letters are good examples.

The 13 letters, memos, and forms in this chapter have to do with the evaluation of personnel—always a topic of concern, both to the profession and to the public.

Everyone likes to say yes, but the actual written process of doing it is not always easy. These 14 effective models show the way.

Most of the letters in this book illustrate the empathy and compassion that one expects from professional educators. That is particularly true of these 10 letters.

Happily, congratulatory letters are one of the largest categories in the school administrator's letter-writing repertoire. No fewer than 20 models convey the good news.

People inside and outside the school often work hard on behalf of the educational enterprise. They deserve praise. In these 22 letters they receive it warmly.

Nothing is harder to write than a sympathy letter. Words seem trivial in the face of tragedy—yet they are needed. This group of 9 letters can help.

The school administrator's lot, like the policeman's, is not always a happy one. Verbal hand-slapping may be required, and these 14 letters do it well.

No one is immune to criticism, certainly no one in a position of educational leadership. Answering criticism persuasively, as these 14 letters do, is an art worth mastering.

School is an adventure. Variety is . . . well, you know. These 16 letters and memos explain what the recipients need to know about upcoming special events.

Whole books have been written on public relations. The 10 letters in this chapter illustrate a few of the ways in which schools can make a good impression on the public.

Without money, nothing. The writers of these 13 letters have a knack of explaining money matters in a way that makes sense and should also make friends.

After many a letter comes the wrap-up. But even the wrap-up usually requires a good letter. The 9 included here show a variety of successful approaches.

START OF SCHOOL YEAR AND WELCOME

1

CHAPTER 1

The letters in this chapter do not all bear September dates, but a number of them do. Basically, they deal with school opening in the fall. There are two main exceptions. One letter concerns the aftermath of a strike. The second welcomes a transfer student who could be arriving at any time during the school year.

The chapter's theme might be called "beginnings," but a further characteristic that the letters have in common is this: they are all well-written.

They are excellent in a number of specific ways. One of them is clarity. The reader knows exactly what the writer is saying. While that may sound like a modest virtue, every letter writer knows how hard it is to produce clear, unambiguous prose. In these letters, the writers have produced it.

Each letter achieves its purpose. It communicates. No parent is left in doubt concerning his or her child's activities at the start of the school year. No teacher is left in doubt as to the principal's plans and wishes. No principal is left in doubt as to what the superintendent expects.

NORTH OLMSTED JUNIOR HIGH SCHOOL
27351 BUTTERNUT RIDGE ROAD
NORTH OLMSTED, OHIO 44070
(216) 777-7700

August 19xx

Dear Student:

Welcome to North Olmsted Junior High School. We hope that your two years with us will be educationally profitable for you.

Junior high school is a time of change. The work load and social adjustments are greater here than at the elementary level. You will be expected to attend school regularly, complete all assignments, and behave appropriately. Your year will be exciting and filled with many new opportunities.

Enclosed you will find five very important sources of information: (1) parent-teacher handbook, (2) homeroom assignment, (3) first quarter's calendar of school events, (4) daily schedule, and (5) emergency medical form. Your parent or guardian must complete the emergency medical form, and you must bring it with you on the first day of school. This is imperative. Completion of the form is required by state law.

Read all items carefully. Students are responsible for knowing the contents of their handbooks. In addition, you will be expected to go directly to your homeroom on the first day of school to receive individual class schedules.

Bus schedules are printed in the School Zone and in local newspapers. Eighth graders are to ride the yellow school buses.

Good luck in your first year at North Olmsted Junior High School. We hope it will be your most successful year ever.

Cordially,

Dr. Dianna M. Lindsay

Dr. Dianna M. Lindsay
Principal

INVITATION TO ORIENTATION PROGRAM

A good invitation letter is like a good news story in that it tells who, what, when, where, and why. Notice that the following letter covers the "five W's" clearly and concisely.

Dear Parents:

You are cordially invited to attend a high school orientation session with your son or daughter on Monday, May 10, 19xx, at 7:30 p.m. The meeting will be held in the Van Allen High School cafeteria.

At this meeting we will introduce you to the teachers and curriculum of the high school. Much of our time will be spent explaining the class schedule for next year, but we will also discuss how you should plan for the following high school years.

School personnel will be open to suggestions from parents and students regarding the curriculum and extracurricular activities.

Please mark your calendar: Monday, May 10, at 7:30 p.m. This is an important meeting for both parents and students. Refreshments will be served.

EXPLANATION OF COOPERATIVE EFFORT WITH UNIVERSITY

Many schools and districts have made arrangements of one kind or another with local colleges and universities. The next letter introduces one such cooperative effort to parents. It was signed by both the superintendent of schools and the president of the university.

A Message to the Parents of the Class of 19xx

Congratulations! This fall your son or daughter will become a member of the Class of 19xx. You as parents and we as teachers have a mutual obligation to help the members of the Class of 19xx prepare themselves for a successful future.

This year, for the first time, the Wright School District is being joined by Lowell University in a cooperative effort to improve the quality of your child's high school education, especially in the basic skills of reading, writing, mathematics, and science.

Recent trends indicate that employers will demand ever higher levels of competence in the basic skills. Students entering the job market after high school will find that only the most highly qualified graduates are hired. A carefully planned high school program will be essential to future success in the world of work.

Many members of the Class of 19xx will choose to attend Lowell University, while some will select other fine colleges and universities. Regardless of their choice, they will discover when they apply that, just as competition for jobs has increased, so has competition for entrance into college.

The best opportunity for acceptance by the school of their choice is the successful completion of a strong, well-planned academic program in high school.

The Wright Public Schools offer complete academic programs with the flexibility to meet your student's individual needs. The schools cannot do it all, however. Your interest, your involvement, your support, and your parental guidance have never been more important than they will be over the next four years.

You can begin your involvement by studying the accompanying booklet and emphasizing to your child the importance of his or her high school years. Working together, we can make certain that the members of the Class of 19xx will meet their educational objectives.

INTRODUCTION OF NEW TEACHERS

There are various ways for a principal to introduce new faculty members to parents. One is by means of a newsletter. The following introduction of new teachers takes about one-third the length of the entire newsletter.

Dear Parents:

It seems as if it takes almost no time for the first semester to move into high gear. Barely two weeks have passed, and yet we are already well into the 19xx–19xx school year.

This newsletter is the first of what I hope will be an informal monthly review that will give me an opportunity to let you know what is happening here at Holy Name Academy.

This year, as some of you know, we have had a few changes in personnel. Two lay teachers are new to the faculty. *Mr. Del Slaughter* has assumed the responsibility for the Christian Service Program. Del graduated in June from St. Georges University and has his degree in religious education. From the Catholic University in Washington, D.C., comes *Miss Roxana Lewes*. Roxana has her A.B. degree in Choral Music, and she will be working with Mr. Chris McDonough in the music program.

Two Oblates have also been added to the faculty. *Rev. Mr. Bob Massi,* who recently graduated from Rehobeth College, is teaching Social Studies. *Fr. John McKenton,* who will be teaching English, is ill and is recuperating at home. Taking his place for the first few weeks of the semester is Mr. George Redden, an experienced substitute teacher, who has his A.B. in Religious Studies from Leipsic College.

We are happy to welcome these new members to our faculty. All four are well qualified in their particular teaching disciplines, and I am sure they will further enhance our exceptionally fine faculty.

INVITATION TO PARENT-TEACHER CONFERENCES

Here is another cordial and persuasive invitation. Note that the writer stresses the importance of the parent-teacher conferences and underlines their importance by noting that teachers will remain in the gym until 8:00 p.m.

Dear Parents:

The teachers at Wood Junior High School are looking forward to meeting you at our fall Parent-Teacher conferences that will take place on Monday, November 8.

We will conduct these meetings in the same way as last year, with all teachers having assigned locations in the gym. The conferences will begin at noon and continue into the early evening.

Each conference is scheduled for a specific time. Your time or times are listed below. If for some reason this schedule poses a problem, please call 663-2886 so that we can work out a more agreeable one.

It is important that you attend these conferences. They represent the best way we have found to let you know how your son or daughter is doing in school.

To accommodate as many parents as possible, our teachers will stay in the gym through 8:00 p.m. on November 8. You will notice on the schedule below that time has been allowed between conferences for you to visit nonscheduled teachers, if you wish.

Refréshments will be served in the cafeteria, and the gym and hallways will feature some Art and Industrial Art displays.

Sincerely,

Milton Spencer
Principal

November 8, 19xx:

Time	*Student*	*Teacher*

BACK-TO-SCHOOL MEMO AFTER STRIKE

Letters on touchy subjects are the most difficult ones to write. Exactly the right tone must be struck. The writer of the following letter, by appealing to the teachers' pride and professionalism, achieves that tone admirably.

TO: All Staff
FROM: Robert Hayward, Principal
SUBJECT: Return to School

This is a difficult memo to write, even though I realize that much of what I want to say is already understood and accepted by many of you on an individual basis. Naturally, I am delighted that we are all together again at Muir High School. We have been through a difficult period—so difficult, in fact, that I suppose the word "together" can apply only in the physical sense at this time.

Nevertheless, the nature of our job demands unity. Whatever the feelings we may have about individuals and issues, our job at Muir High is to help educate students, and that job requires a team effort. We are honor-bound to work together with mutual respect, despite our personal differences.

Little is to be gained from an atmosphere hostile to learning or personal growth. Muir's faculty and staff have always enjoyed a reputation for being "together." The days and weeks ahead can enhance that reputation. Let us help each other heal the wounds as quickly as possible and get down to the business at hand of educating our students.

FIRST NEWSLETTER TO PARENTS

The reader of this newsletter to parents would almost certainly receive a favorable impression of the school and be convinced that his or her children are being thoughtfully cared for and taught.

Dear Parents:

By now you have received the most important word about how this school year has begun—the informal reports given to you by your son or daughter. The faculty and staff at Melville Middle School hope those reports are positive. We hope you feel that the school year has begun well for your child.

It seems to us at Melville that classes began smoothly and that these first few weeks have been a fine beginning of what should be a productive school year. The boys and girls have been most cooperative.

The sixth graders adjusted easily to their new surroundings and their schedules, and are a friendly presence in the school. The seventh graders enjoy having grown up from being the youngest in the school. The eighth graders have made an excellent start in terms of academic work and overall behavior.

Chorus and band have been organized, and, now that students have settled into their class routine, student activities, intramural football and soccer, and various organizations are moving into operation. As you may know we have just completed a spirited election campaign for Student Council.

If you have any concerns about any aspect of your son's or daughter's schooling, feel free to contact the teacher concerned, a guidance counselor, or me. We welcome your inquiries.

WELCOME TO TRANSFER STUDENT

This letter is so cheerful and friendly you might miss the fact that the main substance of it could have made it seem abrupt: "You will find enclosed a copy of our student handbook. We will need your health records and a transcript of your grades. . . "

Dear Jason,

Welcome to Farragut Junior High School! We are looking forward to your arrival. We know how hard it is to leave your friends and acquaintances, but we also know that you will have the opportunity to get to know many of our fine students.

The staff at Farragut Junior High School is available to assist you and your parents as you make plans for enrolling. We will need your health records and a transcript of your grades, which should be fowarded to us by your present school.

You will find enclosed a copy of our student handbook. It will answer many of the questions you may have about Farragut.

Please accept my best wishes for a continued happy and successful school year.

WELCOME TO PARENTS OF NEW STUDENT

Informality can be a real plus in a letter to parents if it is not overdone. The writer of the following letter conveys an informal tone perfectly. In addition, the letter is filled with information useful to parents.

Dear Mr. and Mrs. Everett:

Welcome to Crosby!

Your daughter Marie may already have filled you in on some of the details of life at Crosby Middle School—whether the other kids are friendly, what the teachers are like here, the quality of the lunches served, and whether Crosby is easier or harder than the school she last attended. We like to think that after the first ten days all new students feel like veterans.

We are pleased to have you as partners in this educational year. As the year progresses, and as you become either more informed or more puzzled, we encourage you to call the school and talk with those who might be of help. If your question deals with in-class events, please ask to speak with the teacher. If it deals with the overall program, curriculum, or activities, please contact me directly.

One of our goals is to see that the parents and guardians of students— like the students themselves—feel at home at Crosby. To accomplish that, Parent Newsletters are mailed to all students' homes throughout the school year, providing you with information about events and activities.

You will also want to look at Marie's copy of the Crosby Student Handbook. It does a good job of explaining a typical year at our school. By reading it, you will have a better idea of what to expect.

We are glad to have you with us this year, and we want to assure you that we will do our best to help your child experience academic, social, and emotional growth. With your help and cooperation, this should be an excellent school year.

MEMO ON IMPROVING APPEARANCE OF SCHOOLS

An effective memo makes it absolutely clear what action is desired. In this memo, the writer numbers the two items that require action—a good device for giving them visual emphasis. In fact, the whole memo is a model of clear expression.

TO: Principals
FROM: Thomas Fitzgerald, Superintendent
SUBJECT: Appearance of Schools for Opening Day

Many changes were made during the past 18 months regarding custodial services. I appreciate the efforts that you and your custodians have made to improve the cleanliness of schools, both inside and out.

Last year I requested and received approval for the purchase of grounds equipment to be placed on each school campus. This purchase allowed the local school principal to be responsible for weekly maintenance of shrubbery and grass around the school buildings. The major grass cutting is still a responsibility of the Maintenance Department, and all areas that can be properly cut with large equipment will continue to be maintained by the central crew.

During the past two weeks, I have visited school campuses as part of the review for opening school. I am requesting that the following action be taken by each principal.

1. All cleaning inside the building should be completed before we begin the Leadership Workshop on August 3. If you have a special condition that prohibits the inside work from being finished on this date, please notify my office before August 2.

2. All shrubbery should be appropriately trimmed, all raking around the buildings should be complete, all areas of grass to be cut with a small mower should be taken care of, and all trimming with the weed-cutter or other equipment should be done by Friday, August 6.

I am sure you will join me in making a commitment to the board and to the public that on the opening day of school our schools will be better inside and out than ever before. I am prepared to wear appropriate clothes and join you and other administrators within the school and custodial staff, if necessary, to achieve this objective.

Please remember that we serve a public that demands not only a good education program for the children but also expects our schools to be an attractive part of the community. They want the schools to look as good as any other public buildings.

Again, thank you for your efforts toward improvement. If you need assistance in reaching the objectives stated in this memo, please notify my office immediately.

LETTER AND FORM ON SPORTS PARTICIPATION

A letter that is attached to a form should be as brief as possible, and this one is. It contains all the necessary information, but not a bit extra.

Dear Parents:

Your child will be participating in an interscholastic sport at Cather High School this fall. By now, he or she should have brought home a copy of the Handbook for Athletics adopted by the Bryan City Board of Education.

If you received this handbook, please sign the form below. To be eligible to participate in interscholastic athletics, your child must return this form to his or her coach within the next five days. The coach must also receive a completed Physical Condition form signed by you.

We appreciate your cooperation. If you have any questions concerning our policy on athletics, please feel free to call.

CATHER HIGH SCHOOL

19xx–19xx

We have received a copy of the Bryan Public Schools' Handbook for Athletics. We understand the policies, rules, and regulations stated therein and intend to abide by them.

I give permission for _____
(student's name)

to participate in _____,
(sport)

_____   _____
Signature of Parent or Guardian   Date

_____   _____
Signature of Student   Date

EARLY REPORT ON STUDENT'S PROGRESS

Here is an example of a kind of pre-report-card report: a letter. While it requires the effort and cooperation of all teachers, its value is indisputable.

Concerning ——————————————————————————
                          [student's name]

Dear Parents:

Our teachers have prepared this written report early in the school year in the hope that it will provide you with useful information about the adjustment and progress of your son or daughter at Melville Middle School.

The first report card period ends on November 12. Since that is three weeks from now, please bear in mind that the progress indicated below may change by then. With your encouragement and support, we hope that your son or daughter will achieve the kind of progress you consider acceptable or commendable.

If you are not satisfied with the progress shown on this report, there is still time for needed improvement prior to the end of the first report card period.

English Teacher ———————————— Approximate mark ———

Comments ——————————————————————

————————————————————————————————

————————————————————————————————

[Similar blanks follow for teachers of mathematics, reading, science, social studies, health, and other subjects.]

Please sign this report and have your son or daughter return it to the homeroom teacher. Feel free to contact individual teachers (567-9876) or guidance counselors (234-7654) if you have questions or concerns about the progress described in this report. Rose Dundee is the guidance counselor for grades six and seven; Leroy Otto is the counselor for grade eight.

Sincerely,

James Gowanda
Principal

Parent's Signature _____

Parent's Comments _____

_____

BACK-TO-SCHOOL MEMO TO STAFF

Inspiration and motivation demand considerable skill with words. The writer of the following memo shows that kind of skill. It is clear that he has written his memo carefully, then revised it, seeking the best possible words and the best possible order of words.

TO: All Staff
FROM: Chester Downing, District Superintendent
SUBJECT: Return to School

A new school year presents opportunities for various beginnings—new classes, new faces, sometimes new courses, and often new materials. Summer and vacation can be great healers; and as we approach the opening day of a new school year, the end-of-year pressures that plagued us in June seem quite remote and inconsequential.

Newness alone, however, cannot produce transformation. We ourselves must be willing to be caught up in the rebirth that is possible with each new year. Starting a new year gives us the opportunity to make new plans, design new strategies, and implement new ideas. There is a special kind of joy and satisfaction in planning lessons and activities for a new class; for although the subject or grade level is the same, the students are new, and they appreciate the planning that is done for them. Whether one's responsibility is administrating, supervising, teaching, preparing lunches, maintaining a building, or managing an office, there is always room for improvement and for new ways to do a good job even better.

We can be proud of what we achieve in Fosterville—in our classrooms, in our offices, and on our playing fields and stages—but our achievements are not due to complacency and satisfaction with the status quo. Our program is what it is because a staff of dedicated, aspiring men and women have a common goal—to do what is best for students—and are always looking for ways to achieve that goal.

This year, as in the past, we must concentrate on the processes that spur continuing advancement: evaluating what we have, determining what we can do to improve, and identifying what we need to make those improvements.

Let us make 19xx our best year yet!

INVITATION TO BACK-TO-SCHOOL NIGHT

This is basically a covering letter, attached to each student's schedule of classes for Back-to-School Night. As a covering letter, it needs to be brief, and it is.

Dear Parents:

You are cordially invited to attend Westside High School's Back-to-School Night, October 18, at 7:30 p.m.

Along with this note, your son or daughter will give you a personal schedule that he or she has prepared for the evening. This schedule is the same as your student's daily schedule—except that each of these Back-to-School classes will last only ten minutes.

Teachers will explain briefly the content of each course and tell you their requirements and expectations of students. You will be free to ask questions at the end of each teacher's talk, if time permits.

We look forward to meeting you on October 18.

LETTER TO PARENTS OF KINDERGARTNER

In a sense, the next letter is one of reassurance at a trying time. The writer must give necessary advice and counsel, while not seeming to be either patronizing or alarmist. It presents the letter-writer with something of a tightrope, and this writer succeeds in walking it well.

Dear Parents:

Your child has reached an important milestone. On Tuesday, September 9, 19xx, he or she will start kindergarten at the Port Freedom Elementary School. It is an exciting experience, and it should be a very enjoyable one if a few simple suggestions are followed.

1. Try to bring your child to the school playground a day or two before school opens. Explore the playground area. As you will see from this visit, we have an exceptionally attractive and well-equipped playground. It is likely to appeal to your child.

2. In discussing the start of school with your child, be positive. Tell him or her how much fun school can be. Your child will almost surely like kindergarten—especially if you present it in an enthusiastic way.

3. When your child first gets on the school bus, it can be a rather traumatic time for both of you. Try to stay calm and cheerful. Say goodbye with a smile. Remember, this is an adventure for your child, a fascinating beginning.

We believe that your child's first day of kindergarten will be an enjoyable one. We intend to do everything in our power to make sure that it is. Our kindergarten teachers are looking forward with great enthusiasm to September 9. It is a day we are sure you will look back on with fond memories.

❧ A Word on Style ❧

REFER TO PRIOR EVENTS

If you are answering a letter or a phone call, it is always a good idea to say so immediately: "Thank you for your letter of January 14." An opening like that informs the reader of your reason for writing and also creates a continuing record.

Usually, it pays to add something about the subject of the previous letter or phone call: "Thank you for your phone call yesterday in which you inquired about the reasons for your son's failing grades in English, Spanish, and American History."

You may want to refresh your reader's memory about a sequence of events: "We have corresponded in the past about your daughter's unexcused absences from school." That opening sets the stage for the specific content of this letter—another unexcused absence.

If you refer to prior events in this way, your letters, when looked at in the future, will be self-explanatory. A person reviewing your files will be able to make sense of nearly every letter, without requiring a briefing about the events leading up to each one.

❧ A Word on Style ❧

CHOOSE AND USE A DICTIONARY

Your secretary needs a dictionary, and so do you. No matter how talented and efficient your secretary is, you will find that an occasional misspelling or mishyphenation is likely to slip through. It is very hard for a typist to proofread his or her own work. Even if you are the rare administrator whose secretary-typist can do it, you still should read letters carefully before signing them.

If something looks wrong, check it in your dictionary. Stay with the same dictionary. For instance, this hyphenation of the word *En-gland* may look wrong to you. If you use an American Heritage dictionary, it *is* wrong. It should be *Eng-land.* However, if you use a Merriam-Webster dictionary, the hyphenation *En-gland* is correct.

Dictionaries vary. Their recommended hyphenations may be different. Their preferred spellings may be different. Their advice on usage may be different. Choose and use a good college dictionary—and be sure your secretary uses the same one. The following college dictionaries are all excellent:

The American Heritage Dictionary of the English Language
Funk and Wagnalls Standard College Dictionary
The Random House College Dictionary
Webster's New Collegiate Dictionary
Webster's New World Dictionary of the American Language

BUILDINGS AND BUSES

2

CHAPTER 2

In this chapter the letters have to do with school facilities and their use, which is to say, mainly with buildings and buses. They range from a principal's response to parents' concerns with lighting to a superintendent's letters to staff concerning reorganization, school closings, and staff reductions.

These letters, like all good business letters, have a number of distinct virtues. One of them is conciseness. The letters are no longer than they need to be.

This does not mean that every letter in this chapter is short. Some kinds of correspondence have to be longer than other kinds. What it means is that none of the letters contain extra words or superfluous information. Even if they contain many paragraphs, they are only as long as necessary.

A covering letter for a report on recommended school closings, a letter suspending a student from a school bus, a statement of permission policy for long bus trips—these are basically short letters. The writers in this chapter have produced letters on those topics, and others, that are appropriately, and admirably, concise.

ANSWER TO PARENT'S QUESTION ABOUT BUSING

DUNCAN U. FLETCHER JUNIOR HIGH SCHOOL
2000 NORTH THIRD STREET
JACKSONVILLE BEACH, FLORIDA 32250

October 29, 19xx

Mrs. Anthony Bostwick
10770 Stilwell Drive
Jacksonville Beach, Florida 32050

Dear Mrs. Bostwick:

Following your phone call, I have been in touch with the transportation office of the school system. The enclosed card is a list of students carried each day on Bus #118. The numbers circled in red are those that exceed the legal limit of 66 students per bus.

The transportation office is troubled, as you are, by the large fluctuation in the number of students carried on this bus—from 41 to 72—and we cannot account for it. All of us are concerned about the safety of students at all times and have looked for alternatives. At the present time, the only option open to us is to "double-trip" the bus, sending one half of the students at one time and one half of them a half-hour later. Both morning and afternoon schedules would have to be adjusted.

I think the question we need to answer is whether the disease warrants the cure. I would appreciate your thoughts on this matter and look forward to hearing from you.

Sincerely,

Lois D. Johnson

Lois D. Johnson
Principal

LETTER TO STUDENTS ON VANDALISM

Dear Students:

The Saguaro schools have experienced an unusually large amount of vandalism this year. The results of such acts go far beyond the cost of repairing the damage and replacing the broken or stolen equipment.

Our regular maintenance schedule is disrupted. General repair work has to be delayed for all schools until the damage is repaired. There is an actual loss of school time because of missing materials and equipment plus the time required for cleanup and repair.

Unfortunately, one act of vandalism, or simple carelessness, seems to lead to another. A note written on the restroom wall is soon answered by another note. A set of initials cut into a desk soon becomes two sets of initials. One soda can or sack thrown on the floor becomes a reason for someone else to throw litter on the floor.

We need your help. We ask you to help by showing an interest and concern for your school. If each of you sets an example of helping and caring, other students will follow your lead. School pride is contagious. You can catch it and give it to a friend. You can cause an epidemic of pride!

Your interest and support will do more to stop vandalism and careless damage to the schools than all the watchmen we can employ.

Please help.

FOLLOW-UP ON RENAMING OF SCHOOL BUILDING

This letter deals with something that is hardly an everyday occurrence, the renaming of a school when a new building has been constructed for it. However, it is a fine example of a thank-you letter—appreciative, specific, and sincere.

Dear Dr. Watkins:

When the new Eastman High School was built, I recall that you, as an active and dedicated Board member, led the move to have it given the name "Eastman Community Educational and Recreational Facility."

The appropriateness of that name was never more evident than last Saturday. We had approximately 250 boys and a large crowd watching them at a regional wrestling contest. At the same time we had nearly 300 Girl Scouts from the area using the facility for an annual meeting. On the same day at the school, Tom Robbins enrolled 390 young people in our upcoming Super Saturday program, and, finally, we administered the College Board ACH test to 23 students.

I know how proud you must be to see the community getting this fine educational and recreational use of the building that you envisioned. Eastman has been, and continues to be, a true community educational and recreational facility.

Thank you for spearheading the drive to rename the school—and thank you for the new name itself.

REQUEST TO CONTRACTOR FOR HELP ON LIGHTING PROBLEM

Although this is not quite a letter of complaint, there is an unmistakable note of tension in it. The writer, handling the problem well, does not charge the subcontractor with providing insufficient light, but he strongly suggests that the contractor must prove the school's light to be sufficient.

Dear Mr. Seeley:

Recently I have received calls from four parents indicating that their children are having eye problems. The parents attribute some of these problems to improper lighting at the school. I have tried to assure them that this building was designed with proper candlepower, but further assurances will be necessary.

Our custodians are checking all individual rooms to make sure the lights are in good working order. As far as we know, they are. The level of lighting, not defective lamps, has been the specific complaint.

Does your company have a machine that will spot-check the candlepower in some of the classrooms? If so, I think that you, as the subcontractor responsible for the electrical work in the new building, should be the one to run such tests.

Please let me know if you will be able to do this, and when it can be done, so that I can get in touch with these concerned parents.

USE OF SCHOOL FACILITIES BY OUTSIDE GROUP

This is a good example of a letter that incorporates district policy into its contents without directly quoting that policy. Notice how the restated request in the first paragraph is matched against the district policy in the second paragraph, with the third paragraph then drawing the appropriate conclusion.

Dear Mrs. Allard:

Thank you for your letter concerning the possible use of Fillmore High School's gymnasium for a hobby show to be sponsored by the Women's Club of Elm City. You state that you plan to charge admission to this event but not to offer for sale any of the items displayed.

According to our district rules, you may use the facility and charge admission when the proceeds thereof are to be expended for educational or charitable purposes, when nothing is to be sold, and when your group meets the requirements outlined in Section 414 of the New York State Education Law.

Since your club intends to donate the proceeds from this event to the American Heart Association, since nothing is to be sold, and since your club meets the requirements of Section 414, you are welcome to use our gymnasium if it is available when you need it.

Enclosed are an application form and a list of rules for the use of school facilities.

SCHOOL CLOSINGS AND STAFF REDUCTIONS

Here is a matter-of-fact covering letter for a superintendent's report that makes unpopular recommendations. The report calls for some schools to be closed and the staff reduced. Anticipating his readers' response, the superintendent uses the last paragraph to try to forestall immediate outcries.

Dear Staff Member:

Attached is a copy of the report that I presented to the Board of Education at last night's regular monthly meeting. I have also sent copies of the ten-year enrollment projections and school-capacity data to each school. These reports are too voluminous to allow making copies for each staff member.

My major effort is to see that we not only maintain an outstanding school system but that we continue to improve where necessary. I am convinced that in order to do so we must shrink our facilities, and ultimately our staff, if we are to provide a full range of fine programs and services. I am also convinced that we must have an intelligent long-range plan to accomplish this, if we are to avoid the annual attempts to "nickel and dime" our allocations and programs by annual budget cuts.

The recommendations I have made will create anxiety in the community and among our staff. Shortly, I plan to meet individually with every school staff in order to speak directly to those concerned and to discuss our planning procedures. I know that principals will be scheduling meetings as well.

STAFF MEETING ON REORGANIZATION

This memo is a follow-up to the preceding one. It makes good on the super-intendent's promise to meet personally with the people involved in a painful reor-ganization of the schools. Again, it is straightforward and nonapologetic. At the same time, it clearly indicates the seriousness of the situation.

Dear Staff Member:

Please accept this invitation to meet with me in the Edwards High School auditorium on Monday, December 11, at 3:15 p.m. At that meeting, I want to talk with our entire Edwards Public School Staff about the issues of grade reorganization, school closings, and staff reductions.

This subject, understandably, produces tension and anxiety. My pur-pose is to provide you with as much information as I possibly can about these matters. You deserve to hear information firsthand rather than through the newspapers or by way of rumors.

My second purpose is to let you know, personally, that we will do everything within our means to deal with staff decline in a sensitive and supportive manner. Our personnel office is preparing some historical data on leaves, retirements, and resignations, so that we can share with you our realistic assessment of employment opportunities.

I look forward to this opportunity of meeting with you. The session is not mandatory, but I do urge you to attend.

COORDINATION OF PRIVATE AND PUBLIC SCHOOL BUS SCHEDULES

A polite appeal for cooperation, this letter gets right to the point, stating exactly what is being requested. The writer gives a good reason for his request, asks for early action, and, finally, thanks the private school principal for cooperating.

Mr. Frederick Telford
Principal
Grace Lutheran School
Fosterville, Pennsylvania 19100

Dear Mr. Telford:

Enclosed is a copy of the Fosterville School District calendar for 19xx–19xx which the Board of Education approved at its March meeting.

As you prepare your own calendar for next year, we would appreciate it if you would keep in mind the days we have scheduled as days off. By keeping your calendar and ours reasonably compatible, we can reduce transportation costs for the district and realize some energy savings.

We hope you will forward your school's approved calendar to our Director of Transportation as soon as it is available.

Thank you for your cooperation.

NOTE OF THANKS FOR OFFER OF COOPERATIVE BUSING

This is basically a courtesy note, making the point that the writer is willing to provide the same busing assistance he is thanking the reader for offering.

Mr. Paul Morris
Director
Vo-Tech District 87 Service Center
Mantle, Oklahoma 74600

Dear Mr. Morris:

Let me take this opportunity to thank you for the prompt and positive manner in which you responded to the request of Ms. Ada Pernell, our Director of Transportation, for assistance in transporting Mantle High School students to Rogers-Jansky Vo-Tech School.

We appreciate the assistance you have offered. For our part, we will cooperate in every way we can to make this new plan work. We will also reciprocate in whatever way possible.

Thanks again. You have helped us out considerably. Just let us know when and how we can help you.

LETTER TO PARENTS ABOUT STUDENT'S BUS BEHAVIOR

The most impressive thing about this letter is its specific detail. The writer does not just state school busing policy, he explains what happened on the bus in this particular instance. The letter is personal and, as such, is more likely to result in change than a form letter would be.

Dear Mr. and Mrs. Verrazano:

This letter is to let you know that your son Vincent left his assigned school bus at the high school yesterday without approval and later went home on another bus.

Because most parents want to know the whereabouts of their children, and do not want their children getting off the bus except at home, we have a policy that students may not switch buses or bus stops without a note from parents approved by school officials.

What apparently happened was that Vincent got into a fight with another boy on his assigned bus, and this fight continued outside until both boys were restrained by Mr. Dobbs, the Vice Principal. Vincent then boarded a bus to which he was not assigned and rode home on it.

I have spoken to Vincent about this situation. Your follow-up at home to impress on him that he should always take his regular bus, unless you write a note otherwise, will be appreciated.

SUSPENSION FROM SCHOOL BUS: PERSONAL LETTER

A succinct, no-nonsense letter, this says in two paragraphs all that needs to be said.

Dear Mrs. Brookfield:

Your son Andrew has been reported for misbehavior on the school bus three times this year. Three such referrals result in suspension from the school bus. Thus, Andrew is suspended from riding the school bus as of Monday, November 29, 19xx.

In accordance with Melville School District procedures, it will be necessary for you to meet with Mr. Kenmore, the bus driver, and me before bus riding privileges can be restored. Please contact me to arrange a meeting time convenient for the three of us.

SUSPENSION FROM SCHOOL BUS: FORM

Note that even though this is a form, the tone is courteous. No one reading it would suppose that the suspension was imposed arbitrarily. Also, note that all necessary information is supplied. The reader knows why the suspension occurred, how long it will last, and what to do in the meantime.

Dear _____:

We regret to tell you that the bus riding privileges of your son/daughter, _____, have been suspended from _____ to _____.

When a situation develops that endangers the safety or well-being of other students on the bus, it is necessary for the school to take the necessary steps to correct it.

The reason or reasons for this suspension of bus privileges are as follows: _____

_____

_____

If you have any questions about what occurred on the bus, please feel free to call me at school. The phone number is 635-2103, extension 209.

It is the responsibility of the parents to provide transportation during this period of suspension.

During this time, I would appreciate your having a talk with your son or daughter about the responsibilities involved in riding the school bus. Thank you.

Sincerely,

Troy Muncy
Principal

The bus driver's name is _____

REFUSAL TO TAKE STUDENT ON FIELD TRIP

One very effective device is to refer to relevant prior events, as the writer of this letter does. Here it puts the writer's decision into context, implying that it is the culmination of a series of incidents rather than a single, harsh act.

Dear Mr. and Mrs. Malone:

As you know, Clyde has had behavior problems throughout the school year. We have discussed them, and I know you have been concerned about them, but as yet there has been no significant improvement.

I do not feel that teachers can be asked to take the responsibility of a full-day field trip, involving extensive bus travel, for students who are potential behavior problems or who we believe could act irresponsibly. For that reason, your son may not go on the eighth grade field trip to Burlington on May 17, 19xx.

There will be regular classes on May 17 for students who will not be going on the field trip.

PERMISSION POLICY FOR LONG BUS TRIPS

Every good letter sticks to the point, and this one is no exception. The writer states general policy only. Even though this letter might be attached to a permission form for the first bus trip of the school year, the writer does not go into the specific trip, just the general policy.

Dear Parents:

This year your son or daughter will have the opportunity to take a number of field trips. Because of this, from time to time you will receive a form to fill out, granting permission for your child to participate in the trip.

It is important that these forms be filled out, signed, and returned to the school at least one day prior to the trip. No student will be allowed on any trip without this signed and completed form. Teachers will not be permitted to make exceptions to this rule for any reason.

Field trips are an important part of your son's or daughter's education, and I hope you will attend to these permission forms as promptly as possible. Thank you.

CHOICE OF CHAPERON FOR LONG BUS TRIP

At first glance a congratulatory note, this is actually an informational letter for newly chosen chaperons. Unlike the previous letter, this one covers a number of distinct points, but it does so paragraph by paragraph, with each paragraph making its own point clearly.

Dear Miss Campbell:

Congratulations! You have been chosen by your principal to be one of the chaperons on the annual Barkley Public Schools' eighth grade bus trip to Washington, D.C., in May. This trip is as popular with teachers as it is with students. More than three times as many teachers as needed volunteered to be chaperons. I am pleased that you were one of those selected.

Please complete the enclosed acceptance/insurance/medical form and return it to my office as soon as possible.

We will be having a meeting on December 4 at 1:00 p.m. in the auditorium of Barkley Community College for the parents of all eighth grade students who expect to go to Washington. Details of the trip will be given at that time. You are invited to attend.

A fund-raising electronic Game-A-Thon will be held on Friday, November 24, and Saturday, November 25, at the Barkley High School gym, beginning at 6:00 p.m. each evening. Although plans are by now in place for it, we can always use another set of hands.

Once again, I congratulate you on becoming a chaperon. The staff and I are looking forward to working with you as we prepare for our journey to the nation's capital.

≋ A Word on Style ≋

CHECK UNFAMILIAR FORMS OF ADDRESS

Most forms of address cause no difficulty. You know whether the person you are writing to is a *Mr.*, a *Mrs.*, or a *Dr.* But some titles, particularly those of people in government, the military, and the clergy, can be tricky.

How do you address an archbishop, for example? In the inside address of the letter (and on the envelope) he is *The Most Reverend.* The salutation reads *Your Excellency.*

How do you address the Chief Justice of the U.S. Supreme Court? A member of the President's cabinet? A lieutenant colonel in the U.S. Army?

Unless you are dealing with such titles on any everyday basis, you will probably have to look them up. A chart showing some frequently used forms of address is included on pages 284–286.

POLICY AND PHILOSOPHY

3

CHAPTER 3

This chapter contains a group of letters and memos, often motivational, dealing with school and district policy and individual and administrative philosophy. Some are directed at students, some at parents, some at teachers, and some at other administrators. A few of them are statements of policy. Others quote preexisting policy.

Since the letters are aimed at different audiences, they do not all sound alike. Different audiences require different word choice and sentence structure. Writing that is aimed at students is necessarily less complex than that aimed, say, at other administrators.

The letters in this chapter show a keen awareness of audience. The letters to students are clearly intended for children. Without talking down to youngsters, the writers manage to communicate with them. On the other hand, the letters to parents, teachers, and other administrators are clearly directed at adults.

This awareness of, and consideration for, one's audience characterize the excellent letters that follow.

PRINCIPAL'S LETTER TO STUDENT NEWSPAPER

OAKLAND UNIFIED SCHOOL DISTRICT
1025 SECOND AVENUE, OAKLAND, CALIFORNIA 94606

November 5, 19xx

Dear Students:

Some of you have talked to me about how I should change this school. There is no easy way to change schools or people unless they want to change. A school is people. It takes its personality from what they do for, with, or against each other.

If you want to change Fremont, then start now. Drop one less paper or can on the floor or grounds. Pick up one piece of litter. Be nice to one more person. Do one more assignment. Say hello to someone you don't know. Pay someone a compliment. Say thanks to someone who did something for you. Learn something new in class every day. Show respect for yourself and for others.

Fremont will always be a part of your life when you leave here. Take pride in it now. Help make it a better place, day by day, through the better ways you do things, the better ways you act.

Our school should be a community where people offer strength and support to each other. It should be a community that offers personal growth to everyone, a good place to learn, to work, to be.

Sincerely,

Harold F. Zuckerman

Harold F. Zuckerman
Principal

WORKSHOP FOR PROMOTING GOOD CITIZENSHIP

A good memo, like a good letter, takes the feelings of the reader into account. Notice that in this excellent memo the superintendent compliments his staff in each of the last two paragraphs. Appreciativeness of this kind, whenever possible, is likely to make the reader receptive to the memo as a whole.

TO: All Principals
FROM: Chester Downing, District Superintendent
SUBJECT: Inservice Workshops, September 21 and 28

The enthusiasm of the staff about continuing the work on good citizenship begun in June has led to our setting up these two workshops. One-hour early dismissals on the next two Wednesdays will give us adequate time, I believe, to conduct these additional workshops.

Once again, the emphasis will be on discussing problems relating to citizenship that exist in the schools. We will try to make plans for promoting good citizenship among students and for increasing students' interest in school and learning.

My review of the reports on the June meeting indicates that many suggestions made by the staff have already been incorporated into the procedures and practices of the schools. The smooth opening of schools this fall and the continued harmony are proof of the effectiveness of the work done by you and your staffs. The positive attitude of teachers and students cannot be denied.

All of us want this period of good feeling to continue. The time provided for these workshops, and possibly for future inservice sessions, is evidence of our interest and concern.

IMPORTANCE OF STUDENT DISCUSSIONS

This particular letter to students was posted throughout the school and was well received by students, parents, and teachers.

Dear Students:

It goes without saying that everyone wants you to get good grades. I. would like to add something to that. I would like to ask each student to *participate*.

There is academic value in a student's being present in class, in hearing the explanations of teachers, in discussing subjects with other students.

Although a student may be able to read a textbook and pass an examination, if he or she has not participated—has not become involved in classroom discussions—that student has missed a valuable part of the education offered in our school.

STUDENT CONTRACT FOR CLASSROOM PARTICIPATION

Since schools differ so widely, there is always the possibility that what is needed in one school is less important in another. The following contract was prepared for students in a large-city school with continuing discipline problems.

TO THE STUDENT: You have a right to know what is expected of you from the beginning of the semester. You also have a right to accept, or not accept, other people's expectations of you. If you sign this contract, it means you agree that the rules stated below are reasonable, and you will follow them.

1. I understand that I am my own master. Whatever I say or do is my own choice. Therefore, I am responsible for the consequences of my words and actions.

2. Since I am a human being, I am not perfect. I have my bad days. I make mistakes. I get confused. I get angry, sad, and restless. When this happens, I realize that I must act in a way that does not make others feel uncomfortable or resentful. If I want help, I will ask for it directly and honestly.

3. I know that I am unique. I have my own special talents, ideas, and skills. I am capable of success and expect to be treated as a person who can take care of herself or himself.

4. Since not everything in school is perfect, I have a right not to be satisfied. When that happens, I will tell the teacher truthfully, clearly, and calmly what my complaints or resentments are. Then I will give the teacher a fair chance to listen to me and to give me a reasonable response. If I am still not satisfied, I will ask another responsible person of my choice to help me get my message across.

5. I like feeling secure and relaxed. I have a right to learn in a quiet, orderly classroom. I will help keep the class peaceful by respecting myself and all other persons in the room.

6. Since I dislike pollution and waste, I will not litter; I will not abuse anyone else's property; and I will replace what I use, and use only what I need. I will help keep the room neat.

7. I am proud of what I create. I will write so that people can read my work easily. I will put my name on my paper in a way that says, "I did this and I am proud."

8. Since I like to be favorably noticed, I will act so that people will recognize me in a positive way. I will also let other students know when I like them or feel good about what they do.

9. I will try always to come to class on time. Because I am not perfect, I may occasionally be late. When I am, I will come into class in a quiet, non-attention-getting manner and make an extra effort to catch up what I missed. I understand that if the teacher feels I am coming late too often, I must accept whatever decision the teacher makes.

10. I enjoy helping people. When a substitute comes into class, I will make an extra effort to help that person feel happy he or she came to our school. I will cooperate with the substitute teacher or guest.

11. Since I like people to trust me with their possessions, I will take care of what I borrow.

12. I want to learn, grow, succeed, and be happy. I understand that the best way to begin doing this is by being totally honest with myself.

Signed: _____ Date: _____

Classroom: _____

POLICY STATEMENT TO BE READ TO STUDENTS

Like the preceding contract, this statement was designed to improve school citizenship. It is a straightforward, common-sense list of rules and requirements.

TEACHING STAFF: Please read this bulletin with care to your homeroom class on Monday, September 12.

Because Muir High School is attended by people who are capable of taking responsibility, it should not be necessary for us to have a large number of do's and don't's for the safe operation of the school. There are a few rules, however, where the need is obvious, some that are legal restrictions, and others that are just plain common sense. The thinking student will know what is right and what is wrong, what is appropriate and what is inappropriate for our school.

Attendance at Muir High School is for the purpose of obtaining an education. This requires full attendance at all classes, coming to class on time, and using every minute productively. Always have the tools, books, pencils, and notebooks required for class. Leave radios at home. Radios played indiscriminately around the school are a disturbing factor. Therefore, you are not to bring radios or tape recorders to school. If they are brought to school, they will be taken and kept in the dean's office for the rest of the day.

There are legal restrictions on smoking in school or on the school grounds. There are also restrictions on using drugs, including alcoholic beverages. None of these activities helps your learning, and they often cause behavior that is not helpful to receiving a good education. On a practical basis, we ask you not to bring food or drink into the classrooms. You are there to recite, to write, to learn, to listen. Finish your food before you go on. Plenty of time is allowed for lunch. You should not be late to class because of lunch period or snacks between classes.

Above all, everyone at Muir High School has a right to be secure in his or her mind, body, and property. We should respect each other and each other's property. There is to be no fighting in the school or on the grounds. Nothing can happen between two people at this school that cannot be settled in a rational, peaceful, adult, productive way. We have counselors, deans, administrators, teachers, and other people willing to help. Violence and vandalism are illegal, impractical, and inhuman. Let us do unto others as we would have others do unto us.

Have a good year. We appreciate your efforts and hope you find the days ahead to be your best ones you have had at school so far. Good luck.

HANDBOOK STATEMENT ON SCHOOL CITIZENSHIP

Every letter writer knows that it is important to keep one's audience in mind. When writing for children, that means keeping one's prose simple and basic. The following handbook statement is a good example of this.

SCHOOL CITIZENSHIP: No matter where you go or what you do, you will find certain regulations to guide you. Naturally, there are rules and regulations at McClellan Middle School. They are meant for your benefit.

Your conduct at all times should reflect the good upbringing you have had. You should show respect for the property, rights, and privileges of others, just as you expect and appreciate this respect when others show it to you. You are responsible to the school authorities and teachers for your conduct while you are a school citizen. Good behavior can help make your school life a happy and rewarding one.

Your conduct at all McClellan Middle School activities is a reflection on your school. We expect you to be worthy of the respect of others at all times.

We want you to be proud of your school and your fellow students, and we want others to be proud of them. Each of you has a responsibility for the school's reputation.

LETTER ON DRESS CODE POLICY

Letters, like all other writing, have a beginning, a middle, and an end. In this letter, the beginning states the problem, the middle quotes policy regarding it, and the end calls for action. That formula works for many letters.

Dear Mr. and Mrs. Valentine:

Yesterday morning your son Ted wore a T-shirt to school containing a picture and slogan that the teachers and I do not regard as appropriate for the classroom.

Please ask Ted to show you the shirt, and see if you don't agree with us that it should not be worn to school. Ask him also to show you page 7 of his Student Handbook, where it states, ". . . students should dress . . . in a manner conducive to good behavior and to the creation of a good educational atmosphere in the school."

Ted's T-shirt caused some disruption of classroom teaching and activities. Please make sure he does not wear it again. Thank you.

SUPERINTENDENT'S COLUMN IN NEWSLETTER

This exceptionally well-written and persuasive column makes use of an effective technique: noticing something in one's surroundings and using it in an analogy. Here a message posted for workers in a business establishment is applied to students. Observe how well it succeeds.

Next to the quest for peace, our nation's most important goal is the development of a high-quality educational enterprise that will prepare all youngsters for life in a fast-changing and complex world. Indeed, few people disagree with the belief of Clifton Fadiman: "There is an intimate connection between the survival of democracy and the quality of our public education system."

With this thought in mind, the philosophy and the attitude of district officials become rather important. I was reminded of this during a recent visit to a thriving business establishment.

While waiting in line, I noticed an interesting philosophy posted on a wall. It was especially stimulating because the employees obviously subscribed to the message. I believe the philosophy is as appropriate to schools as it is to businesses, and I have chosen to substitute the word *student* for *customer:*

A *student* is the most important person in any school.

A *student* is not an interruption of our work—he or she is the purpose of it.

A *student* is not just a statistic. He or she is a flesh-and-blood human being with feelings and emotions like ourselves.

A *student* is one who comes to us with needs and/or wants. It is our job to fill them.

A *student* is deserving of the most courteous and attentive treatment that we can provide.

A *student* is the lifeblood of this and every other school. Without him or her, we would have to close our doors.

The focus of the future should be on service and excellence. We are pleased, as employees of the Littleton Public Schools, to have the opportunity to serve and work with your students. The importance of teaching and learning was well stated by a late President of the United States:

"From the desk where I sit, the answer to all world problems is found in a single word. That word is *education.*"

Those words inspire and support the challenge and commitment we educators have for quality education in the Littleton Public Schools.

SURVEY OF CHANGES IN COMMUNITY

This is one of the more ambitious letters in the book. It reports on a survey showing the changes that have taken place in a community over a ten-year period. Implicitly, it answers the parents' questions, "Why aren't our schools the same today as they were a few years ago?" It is a thoughtful, reasoned answer.

Dear Parents:

One of the problems with surveys is that they often apply to so large a group. On the other hand, when we attempt to collect meaningful data within the community, it is often viewed as an invasion of privacy. In understanding your school, however, I think it is important for you to know what we mean when we talk about changes that are taking place.

In 19xx I selected a random sample of 100 seventh graders from our student body at Humphrey Junior High. Hoping to get a better idea of what our community was like, I compiled information supplied by parents on such items as occupation, level of education, number of children, and marital status. Last spring I took a look at the 19xx variety of seventh grader to get some idea of what changes had taken place here in Gilberton over the past ten years.

Some of our data are clouded by changes in terminology. In 19xx 58 percent of the mothers in the survey listed their occupation as *homemaker*. In 19xx the number had dropped to 47 percent. This information may not represent a significant shift, however, since some of the women may simply be rejecting the term *homemaker*. What can be concluded is that slightly over one-half of the mothers of today's seventh graders at Humphrey are working outside the home.

Both men and women significantly increased their level of education in the decade just past. Twenty women reported holding college degrees as compared with nine in 19xx. A similar increase occurred with men—from 25 to 35 over the ten-year period. The number of men who did not finish high school was reduced from ten to five.

Marital status is a more delicate issue to deal with and harder to tally. During 19xx only one of the 100 students was from a home with divorced parents. By 19xx the figure had risen to nine. We confirmed this notable change—1 percent to 9 percent—by checking through our other grade levels. Again, a part of the increase could be a greater willingness by people to share this kind of information with the school, but it is safe to conclude that the divorce rate has risen here in Gilberton just as it has in other parts of the country.

This information was collected to help us understand our community better. It helps us get a clearer idea of what we are like collectively and what educational decisions should stem from the profile. The information was given voluntarily, and everyone had, and currently has, the right to have (or not have) the information included in the school files. In any case, individual names are not available, and people who have access to these files are under solemn instructions to keep individual data strictly confidential.

Unquestionably, the changes noted above have had effects upon our school and the students in it. Sometimes when both parents in a family work, a youngster becomes more responsible and independent. Sometimes the opposite happens. In some cases where a husband and wife are divorced or separated, the children and both parents make an excellent adjustment. In other cases, the result is open warfare over the children.

One effect seems clear: We are beset with rapid and dramatic change, not only in technology but in a very basic institution like the family. Rapid change is stressful, and there is little question that we at Humphrey have youngsters and their families who are in need of help and support. We are also fortunate in having large numbers of students and parents who are handling stress and change very well and who provide models for the kind of good citizenship that we hope virtually all our students will ultimately attain.

MEMO ON RACIAL BALANCE

All books on letter writing advise using the word *you* whenever possible, in preference to *I*. The writer of the following memo does that very well, switching from *you* to *I* at the very end so as to emphasize his personal commitment and responsibility.

TO: Area Assistant Superintendents
FROM: H. C. Lyman, Superintendent
SUBJECT: Compliance with Court Order

As you know, the board of trustees voted to accept our recommendation to change the schedule regarding student assignments. You will now need to be ready for a meeting with the board in January regarding any proposed boundary changes you wish to submit in order to keep your schools in compliance with the court order.

Following that initial meeting, it will be the responsibility of you and the appropriate board members in your area to schedule meetings that will give parents sufficient opportunity to make suggestions and voice opinions regarding any proposed changes. You then will be expected to work through your appropriate board members and prepare a final recommendation for the total board at their April meeting. Assignments can then go out in May as usual.

It is most important for the future of this school district that you look closely at any of your schools that are out of balance and that you plan to recommend the necessary changes this year to bring those schools back into compliance.

I will expect you to organize yourselves and take whatever preliminary steps are needed in order to get ready for the January board meeting.

ADMISSION GUIDELINES FOR CATHOLIC SCHOOLS

This is a fairly long, effectively written covering letter for the listed guidelines that follow. It is an important letter, because it puts the guidelines into their educational and social context.

Dear Pastor, Principal, and School Board Chairperson:

As Catholic educators, we have a deep and abiding bond and feel sympathy with all co-educators (parents, teachers, and administrators) in both the public and private educational sectors. A deep concern for the welfare of children is at the heart of our common bond and permeates our relationship at all times.

During any difficulty, including the present situation, we are convinced there can be a solution when sincere, talented, and good-willed persons focus their efforts on finding an answer.

Catholic school authorities wish to fulfill a supportive role in the current situation. To that end, I am calling to the attention of the Catholic educational community (pastors, principals, local school board chairpersons and members, teachers, parents, and students) the guidelines for admission recently sent to guide local enrollment decision-making.

As Vicar for Catholic Education, I am reminding everyone concerned that the members of the Catholic School Office support the enrollment-transfer guidelines, and also I am encouraging local administrators to assume responsibility for leadership in implementing these directives.

The spirit of the Catholic School guidelines is based upon a longstanding policy. We Catholic educators cannot allow our schools to become havens or refuges for those who would encourage the transfer of children to Catholic schools for the purpose of avoiding a current problem in another school system.

I anticipate full cooperation with the guidelines because I believe all will realize they are an important witness to our faith and to the bond which exists rightfully among educators whose primary concern is the child.

<u>Suggested Priorities for Admission</u>
<u>of Students to Elementary Schools</u>
<u>in the Archdiocese</u>

In the admission of students to elementary schools in the archdiocese, the order of priority shall be as follows:

1. Children of parishioners
   a. children from families with children already enrolled
   b. children now reaching school age
2. Transfer students from other Catholic schools
   a. from schools that are merging or consolidating
   b. from schools not offering full programs 1–8

3. Children of non-parishioners
    a. children from families with children already enrolled
    b. children from families newly moved into the parish and whose children have been in Catholic schools where such were available or from public schools where Catholic schools were not available.
    c. children now reaching school age
4. Transfer students from public schools. Parents who live within parish boundaries and have children who have been students in public schools can make application for admittance into the Catholic school, but such admission should be delayed for at least one year after the first application.

Parish school authorities are authorized to make discretionary exceptions to these priorities in favor of fostering values of social justice and personal spiritual development.

PARENTAL VIEWS ON LUTHERAN EDUCATION

Certain kinds of correspondence from church-related schools may require a different approach and different tone from that used in the public schools. Here is an excellent example of a letter to Lutheran parents.

Dear Mr. and Mrs. Caldwell:

The academic and Christian education of your daughter Hope is important to all of us as participants in Trinity Lutheran Church and School.

Often parents have special concerns and joys in regard to the education of their child. The expression of these concerns and joys to me as principal can help Trinity Lutheran School do a better job for the benefit of your child.

If you feel so inclined, please express your concerns and joys on this paper and return it to me. Also, if you feel the need for a consultation in regard to these matters, just place a check mark in the space indicated, and I will call you to set up an appointment.

This letter is not being sent to all parents at once. However, each family will receive a copy as the year continues. Of course, I hope you will feel free to contact me at any time in regard to your child.

Sincerely,

Rex Moreland
Principal

Concerns to share:

Joys to share:

—— Please call us to set up an appointment for a consultation.

                                                                                    _____
                                                                                    Phone number

PRINCIPAL'S NEWSLETTER TO STAFF

A letter that motivates without seeming either self-serving or patronizing is a challenge to write. The writer of this letter successfully met that challenge.

Purpose

This is the first in a series of letters from the principal. The subjects will range from educational philosophy and teaching techniques to information and ideas I am interested in sharing with you. The raison d'etre for *Musings* is a simple one. Through it I hope to help bridge our communications-information gap. It is another way of reaching out.

A Teacher's Right to Fail

It has always been my feeling that a teacher has the right to fail. Since teaching is, as it has often been described, an art rather than a science, our successes can seem fleeting or far away, while our failures are glaring, obvious, and immediate. My own outlook has always been that a teacher's, as well as a man's, reach should exceed his grasp. If a teacher's efforts, predicated upon his or her careful preparation, intelligent conception, and solid execution do not meet with hoped-for success, something is still gained through the experience. In the process of stretching, growth inevitably takes place for both the teacher and the class. Without that extra stretch, not only is our personal and professional growth arrested, we are almost inevitably consigned to a fate of vegetation and deterioration.

Consider for a moment the examples of our colleagues who have just recently risked the prospect of failure, whose reach stretched them to their utmost. Without their courage and adventurousness, we would not have been granted a $175,000 Title VII bilingual program, would not have become involved in the Teachers College project for high school students on Youth Guidance and Research, would not have been given a grant from the Coordinating Council for Criminal Justice for developing student leadership, would not have mounted an extraordinary Dominican Relief Fund campaign. These are but a few recent examples of triumphs that resulted from people's reaching and stretching.

That capacity to take risks, to face up to difficult and complex issues, will help us to meet the enormous challenges represented by the Lora decision, the basic competency tests, and the need to improve student attendance—to name but a few. We may fail; we may achieve only partial success; but at least we will not be prisoners of cynicism or hostages to despair.

❧ A Word on Style ❧

WATCH OUT FOR ELEGANT VARIATION

H.W. Fowler, that old arbiter of prose style, warned against what he called "elegant variation." It bothered him that many writers seemed compelled to choose synonyms rather than repeat the same word over and over. A *committee* would become a *group* and then a *panel* and then a *team*—all to avoid repeating the original word.

The problem is that elegant variation is more likely to confuse the reader than to inspire him. The reader may assume that subtle distinctions are being hinted at, when none in fact exist. The committee does not change its nature from sentence to sentence. It is the same old committee—but overzealous reference to a thesaurus may cloud that fact.

It usually pays to stick with your original (and best) word, particularly if that word is vital to your reader's understanding of an entire letter.

❧A Word on Style❧

KNOW THE TWO-LETTER STATE ABBREVIATIONS

As part of its ZIP code system, the U.S. Postal Service introduced two-letter abbreviations for all 50 states. They are in widespread use, especially in business correspondence. The letters of educators still tend to carry spelled-out state names. If you opt for the two-letter abbreviations, you will find that most of them are easy to remember. But the M's, because there are so many of them, can cause trouble. Here they are:

Maine	ME	Minnesota	MN
Maryland	MD	Mississippi	MS
Massachusetts	MA	Missouri	MO
Michigan	MI	Montana	MT

You will find a complete list of abbreviations recommended by the U.S. Postal Service on page 283 of this book.

CURRICULUM, TESTS, AND INSTRUCTIONAL MATERIALS

4

CHAPTER 4

Letters and memos dealing with curriculum, tests, and instructional materials are the substance of this chapter. A few specific courses and a few specific tests are mentioned, but mainly the letters are general: guidelines for proposing course changes, a report on achievement test results, a memo on textbook adoptions.

As in all the chapters, the letters are good examples of their kind. A distinct characteristic they share is that they begin effectively. The critical opening sentence is strong, which means that the letter (or memo) has been carefully structured. It has been thought out in advance. The first sentence gets directly to the point.

It is all too easy to beat around the bush, especially if the topic is unpleasant. The writers in this chapter avoid that pitfall. They go straight to the heart of the matter. A reader does not finish the first sentence and think, "So what?" The reason for the correspondence comes through immediately.

Every good letter starts well. The first sentence in each letter in this chapter shows the truth of that proven letter-writing principle.

OFFICE OF
THE SUPERINTENDENT

July 26, 19xx

Mr. Jack Hanna
Instructional Television and Radio
2712 Millwood Road
Columbia, South Carolina 29250

Dear Mr. Hanna:

This letter is to inform you of our interest in the Law-Related Education Project. We support your application for a block grant being submitted through the U.S. Department of Education. We will make a special effort to have one or more representatives present at the training session that will result from your being awarded this grant.

As I understand it, this will be a joint effort between the states of North Carolina and South Carolina with the goal of implementing law-related education materials into existing curricula.

Please understand that this letter of support does not represent a financial commitment on the part of The School District of Greenville County.

Sincerely,

J. F. Hall

J. F. Hall
Superintendent

The School District of Greenville County
301 Camperdown Way · Box 2848 · Greenville, South Carolina · 29602 · 803/242-6450

GUIDELINES FOR PROPOSING COURSE CHANGES

Whenever a step-by-step procedure is to be followed, the use of numbering makes sense. Here the memo writer has kept a fairly complicated procedure simple by using numbers and letters under the heading "New Course."

TO: Staff Members
FROM: Luther Kitchell, Principal
SUBJECT: Curriculum

In order to modify existing curricular offerings at Willkie High School, you must follow certain procedures:

New Course
1. Write a proposal that includes the following:
   a. Statement of need
   b. Targeted students
   c. Course objectives
   d. Facilities
   e. Materials
   f. Staff
   g. Budget
   h. Implications
   i. Evaluation (of course, materials, students).
2. Submit this proposal by October 15 of the year prior to the intended implementation of the course.
3. Meet with the WHS curriculum committee, when requested, to present your proposal. Be ready to answer questions.
4. Be willing to meet with the curriculum committee a second time, if necessary, to answer further questions and supply additional explanations.
5. After approval by the curriculum committee, meet with Dr. Rush and Dr. Gowdy to discuss the proposal.
6. If the proposal has been approved thus far, present it to the curriculum committee of the Fayette County Public Schools.

As of this moment, these steps apply to a course for the 19xx–19xx school year. Anything submitted after October 15 will have to be considered as an adoption proposal for the following school year.

Deletion of old course
Submit your recommendation to the WHS curriculum committee for review. This must be done by October 15 for the coming school year; by February 15 for the following school year.

Change in course prerequisites
Submit your recommendations to the WHS curriculum committee for action. Have a written rationale. Dates are the same as those for course deletion.

TASK FORCE TO REVISE CURRICULUM GUIDE

The best possible way to start many letters is with "Thank You." Here the thanks are for agreeing to serve on a curriculum task force. But many occasions warrant thanks. One of the most common letter openings is, "Thank you for your letter of March xx."

Dear Mrs. Winnfield:

Thank you very much for agreeing to serve on the task force to expand and revise the curriculum guide for Louisiana Culture (11–12). Upon completion of the work, you will be awarded six (6) PIP points.

The task force will meet from 1:00 p.m. to 3:00 p.m. each afternoon during the week of July 19–23, 19xx, at Beauregard High School, 620 Eunice Street, Polksville. You must attend each of the five (5) sessions from 1:00–3:00 to receive the six PIP points.

All materials will be provided, and I will keep you up-to-date as we progress toward the meeting dates.

Enclosed you will find a list of the units of study that will be included in the guide. If you have any materials, plans, resources, or ideas that will be useful in these areas, please bring them to the workshop.

Thank you again for your interest, support, and cooperation.

Sincerely,

Elizabeth Ruston
Social Studies Supervisor

SUGGESTED DAILY LESSON PLAN FORMAT

It is always a good idea to get to the point quickly. This memo makes its purpose clear in the first sentence.

TO: Secondary Social Studies Teachers
FROM: Elizabeth Ruston, Social Studies Supervisor
SUBJECT: Suggested Daily Lesson Plan Format

A number of teachers have suggested that I send them a copy of an ideal daily lesson plan format. I have enclosed a sample lesson plan. You should bear in mind, however, that there is no single, standard format that everyone is supposed to follow. Daily lesson plans usually include the following: (1) objectives, (2) activities to be carried out in class—procedures, (3) materials to be used, (4) minimum skills to be taught, and (5) form of evaluation to be employed.

This year's lesson planning is a useful reference tool for next year's teaching. While few teachers want to teach the same lessons year after year, it is always helpful to look back on what you have done, and to learn from successes as well as from mistakes. Lesson plans present a valuable day-by-day record of your teaching. They offer a means of adjusting future methods of teaching and evaluation.

If you have any questions, do not hesitate to let me know. I appreciate your interest and cooperation.

KEYS TO A GOOD SECONDARY READING PROGRAM

Here the superintendent has not merely sent out photocopies of an important professional article, he has written a memo of his own, summarizing the content of the article. It is much more likely to be read carefully than Xerox copies of the article would have been.

TO: Intermediate and High School Principals
FROM: George Kahana, District Superintendent
SUBJECT: Keys to a Good Secondary Reading Program

In a recent article in the NAASP Bulletin, John N. Mangieri presented some good pointers on how to develop a successful secondary reading program. I would like to summarize his advice on this subject, because it is of vital concern to all of us.

1. Teacher support of a secondary reading program is essential. As with any other content program, proper planning is crucial, and this planning must involve teachers.

2. A strong teaching staff is a must. Provide the training needed, and ask teachers to seek professional improvement on their own.

3. Since teachers cannot fully determine the necessary teaching materials at the outset, use the 60–40 formula. Allot 60 percent of the program budget for materials before the program starts, then 20 percent in November, and the last 20 percent in April.

4. Evaluate the program at least quarterly, and preferably once a month. Check reading achievement, library circulation, achievement in content areas, frequency of use of content reading strategies by subject

teachers, and other criteria that the teachers and principal consider important. Pre- and post-test results should be discussed by all teachers.

5. Keep the faculty regularly and publicly informed of the program's intent, scope, and progress. Stress the degree of each department's involvement.

6. Provide support and leadership through weekly contacts with teachers and students. A successful secondary reading program requires strong administrative commitment.

MEMO ON USE OF MICROCOMPUTERS

It would be hard to find a clearer, more informative memo than this one on the establishment of an advisory council.

TO: All Staff
FROM: Harvey Larimore, Assistant Superintendent for Secondary Education
SUBJECT: Computer Council for Stefansson Public Schools

The Stefansson Public Schools' use of microcomputers has expanded dramatically over the past year. Many staff members involved in daily work with microcomputers have felt a need to share their ideas with one another as well as to discuss thoroughly the direction this district should take in regard to computer use.

We propose to create a Computer Council to provide leadership for this district regarding future use of computers in the instructional program. The Computer Council will consist of one teacher representative from each of the six secondary schools, plus two elementary principals and/or teachers. The business manager of the school district will also serve on the council in order to provide information on the district's business use of computers.

The council will be chaired by Burt Mott, Director of the Instructional Services Center, and will be an advisory arm of the Instructional Services Center.

We expect the council to meet once a month during the school year. We hope the school principals will be able to provide council members with a free period at the end of the day to facilitate these monthly meetings.

Some areas in which the council can offer guidance, direction, and coordination are these:
1. Development of a philosophy of computer use for the school district

2. Development of computer-literacy curricula at the elementary, junior high, and senior high levels
3. Development of senior high computer elective courses and independent study programs
4. Review of administrative and other district uses of computers
5. Advice on district purchases of computer hardware and software
6. Inservice teacher training on computer literacy

Mr. Mott intends to convene this council in the fall of 19xx, with members to serve throughout the 19xx–19xx school year.

PRINCIPAL'S REVIEW OF STUDENT'S WORK

Any parent would be impressed by the following letter. It is tactful but at the same time firm. The principal has obviously made a point of uncovering the kind of specifics the parent wants to know.

Dear Mr. Houghton:

Thank you for your inquiry about Dan's progress in fifth grade. The following information may help you to understand Dan's present scholastic situation.

English: Dan seems a bit improved. His grade at the moment is between 75 and 80.

Social Studies: Dan's test scores show an erratic pattern, averaging out to about 70. Your son seems to daydream in class. He may not fully realize that school is hard work.

Mathematics: Again, Dan sometimes appears to be a dreamer. His grade, however, is approximately 80.

Science: Dan likes science especially well, and his average shows it: 95.

Reading: Dan is in the top fifth-grade reading section. His grade is approximately 85.

A few samples of Dan's written work in social studies are attached. The three homework papers seem to indicate that Dan is very careless and not especially concerned about the quality of work he turns in to us.

Note the two copies of the same social studies test that are attached They are testimony to his erratic performance. On the first he earned 49; on the second 96. No formal teaching of subject matter occurred between the two tests—only a review of Dan's work, a warning to him on his carelessness, and a lecture on his need to work harder. Apparently he did work harder. He must be made to realize that his hard work should have preceded the first test so that a grade of 49 could have been avoided.

Dan has the ability to do better and more careful work in all subject areas, even science. I hope that a study of the attached papers will add to your insight into Dan's problem.

If you wish further information about his progress in school, please call me or any of his teachers.

LETTER EXPRESSING CONCERN ABOUT CLASSWORK

This letter might be called a reprimand couched in terms of a plea. It is a model of diplomacy. Note that it has the added purpose of forewarning parents about low grades in the first marking period.

Dear Parent:

As chairwoman of the Foreign Language Department, I would like to ask your help. Many of the freshmen and sophomores are having difficulty adjusting to the new school year, especially in French and German, but to some extent in Spanish and Italian, too. They are having difficulty recalling what they learned last year, which makes it hard for them to adjust to this year's routine. This year's work demands considerable homework and responsiveness to drill in class. So far the results have not been up to our expectations.

You should be aware of this situation so that you can help the students by encouraging them to do their foreign language homework every night and expecting them to respond in class. Perhaps you can also sympathize with your child after a marking period that may show some disappointly low grades. I hope, as I know you do, that these grades will improve as teachers and students adjust better to one another.

For further information, I encourage you to join me and the other teachers for an open house on October 14.

Optional P.S.

Happily, the problem described in this letter does not apply to your son or daughter, whose present grade average is above 80. However, the classroom climate does make a difference, and I am sure you will want to ask your child to continue the good work and to encourage other students along the same lines. The teachers and I hope to see you and discuss the situation further at our open house.

GUIDANCE COUNSELOR'S LETTER ON ACHIEVEMENT TESTS

In general, it is easier to read short paragraphs than long ones. The journalistic model of one or two sentences per paragraph is often a good one to follow for letters sent to readers of varying abilities. The following letter is a good example.

Dear Parents:

Last October the SRA Achievement Series Test was administered to your son or daughter at Eiseley Junior High School.

This test is used as a tool to help us measure the academic progress of your child and possibly to discover strengths and weaknesses that could help us in meeting your child's educational needs.

Students will be given the results of this test during their regularly scheduled English class on Wednesday, January 27, and on Thursday, January 28.

We would like to invite you, as concerned parents, to attend this session and participate in interpreting the results of the test.

Each session will be held in the library at Eiseley Junior High School during your child's assigned English period. The time of that class is indicated below. If you cannot attend, you will still see the general results of the test, since a test profile will be sent home with your child.

We hope to see you on January 27 or 28.

Sincerely,

David Arnold
Guidance Counselor

January 27	*January 28*
1st Period 8:30– 9:19 _____	4th Period 11:36–12:29_____
2nd Period 9:23–10:11 _____	5th Period 12:33– 1:31_____
3rd Period 10:15–11:02 _____	7th Period 2:17– 3:05_____

REPORT ON ACHIEVEMENT TEST RESULTS

This covering memo is a persuasive plea on a critical topic. It relies on the report for its backing, but it notes the favorable results so that the Board of Finance chairman will be aware of them whether he reads the full report or not.

TO: Seymour Shelton, Chairman, Coltsboro Board of Finance
FROM: Kent Windsor, Superintendent of Schools
SUBJECT: Report on Achievement Test Results (19xx)

Enclosed you will find a copy of our district's Report on Achievement Test Results, which basically represents a summary of the results for all grade 4–8 students on the Iowa Tests of Basic Skills (ITBS). Aslo enclosed is an Executive Summary relating to this report.

In reviewing the results, you will note that for the fourth consecutive year our students have shown continuous, system-wide academic gains and improvement in each of the grades tested.

I sincerely hope you will have the time to study the report carefully and, in turn, share the optimism of the Superintendent and Board of Education that the school district is in fact improving. Without question, there is need for further improvement, but the fact that the scores have been consistently getting better represents a positive, significant trend.

Often when a budget presentation is made to the Board of Finance, questions are raised concerning outcomes and the specific progress that students in our public schools are making. The enclosed report provides a comprehensive, in-depth analysis of both outcomes and growth trends. It should help to provide the board of Finance members with an increased awareness and understanding of the school district's accomplishments.

Having made this point, I am extremely hopeful that when we discuss budget matters in the future, it will be with a clear understanding that the school district is improving and that it rightfully deserves the necessary financial support to continue that improvement. Our ultimate goal, of course, is to ensure that every student realizes his or her educational potential.

Should the members of the Board of Finance have any questions regarding the results of the achievement tests, I would be happy to discuss the report with them.

LETTER REGARDING MATH COMPETENCY TEST

Here is a short, clear letter that gets to the point quickly, gives all the facts needed, and leaves no question about what action the reader is to take.

Dear Parent:

Your son or daughter must complete the 35 objectives on the Math Competency Test to graduate. As of this date, your youngster has completed _____ objectives.

Because of the importance of this requirement, we want to meet with you to explain the program. W have included a note indicating the date, time, and place for the meeting. In view of the cost of transportation, we have made arrangements to meet in an elementary school near your home.

If you are unable to attend the scheduled conference, please call Benton High School. The number is 921-5678, and office hours are 7:00 a.m. to 3:00 p.m.

CONFERENCES WITH COUNSELOR AFTER IOWA TEST

Sometimes, as here, a brief explanation provides a good opening for a letter.

Dear Parents:

This year your ninth grade son or daughter took the Iowa Test of Educational Development. The purpose of this test is twofold: (1) to measure academic progress and (2) to find out more about the abilities and interests of students.

The results of the test will be explained to students in small group conferences between the counselor and several students.

We are inviting you, as parents, to be involved in the conferences if you would like to do so and if you are able to attend. They will be held at Eiseley Junior High School. Each will be approximately 30 minutes long.

Your assigned time is _____ on _____
The conference will be in the nurse's office at Eiseley.

If you are unable to come at the scheduled time, you may call and arrange a special conference. Special conferences will begin a week or so after the regular conferences are completed. If you have any questions, please feel free to call me at 234-0987.

PLANNING FOR LOCAL TEXTBOOK ADOPTIONS

Adopting a basal reading series is a matter of crucial importance, and the writer of this memo says so. The seriousness of his tone matches the seriousness of the decision to be made.

TO: Middle School Reading Teachers
FROM: Jack Brantley
SUBJECT: Reading Textbook Adoption

As you know, school systems throughout Alabama will be adopting new reading texts during this school year, and those new texts will be in use for the next six years.

Mr. Montgomery is calling a meeting of all reading teachers for tomorrow afternoon so that we can plan the process we will follow in making our local reading adoptions. It is critically important that we make a good selection of reading materials. Our current basal reading series, published by Bokern-Clark, has been in use for 12 years, and I feel that it must be replaced. Of course we have been using the Caswell books as a supplementary series for the past six years.

Before the meeting, please take time to review the booklet that you recently received, entitled *Minimum Standards and Competencies for Alabama Schools.* Pages 3, 4, and 5 contain the third grade competencies that we will want to be sure our new reading series reinforces.

I look forward to meeting with you tomorrow afternoon in the library immediately after bus duty ends.

MEMO ON TEXTBOOK SELECTION PROCESS

The writer's method of structuring this memo, with numbered and underlined major points, is a familiar and effective one.

TO: Dr. J. V. Sailors, Superintendent
FROM: Neva Griffin, Director, Curriculum and Instruction
SUBJECT: Textbook Selection Process

Because textbooks play such a major role in determining what is taught in our classrooms, I believe we are obligated to provide our teachers with as much information as they need to make the best selections possible. After having observed our textbook selection process from start to finish this year, I believe there are some ways it can be strengthened from an instructional point of view. Suggestions for strengthening the process and the rationale for the suggestions follow:

1. *Begin the process earlier in the year.* There were seven weeks between the organizational meeting of the textbook committee and the meeting for submitting final decisions. This is not time to give adequate review to such a large number of textbooks while fulfilling regular teaching responsibilities. Publishing house representatives tell me the books can be shipped earlier if requested by the LEA.

2. *Return to the practice of receiving one set of elementary books for each school.* Several committee members stated they had not gone to Johnston to review

all the books; others stated they were the only ones from their schools to go to Johnston. I believe the inconvenience to us in the central office is warranted if it helps bring about a more thorough appraisal of books before making a choice. (If we provide each publisher with a list of school addresses, UPS can deliver the books—a move that will cut our transportation problems in half.)

3. *Structure the review and evaluation process* by developing an appraisal form to be used when examining textbooks. We might begin with forms used by the State Textbook Committee and adapt them to our purposes.

4. *Consider having local presentations after the area meeting.* The presentations made at the area meeting should help our committee members narrow the selection field. If the members agree on two, maybe three, top choices, representatives from those publishers could be invited to meet with the members for question-and-answer sessions. Such sessions could be planned for 2:30–3:30 p.m. (one session per publisher) and would cause very little absence from the classroom.

LIST OF TEXTBOOKS ADOPTED

This combination thank-you note and informative memo saves the main news for last—a good way to keep a reader's attention until the end.

TO: Textbook Committee Members, Teachers, Principals
FROM: Jack Brantley
SUBJECT: English/Speech/Spelling Textbook Adoptions

Our textbook adoptions for English, Speech, and Spelling have now been completed. This means that we know the textbook series we will be using in these subject areas for the next six years.

I want to express my thanks to each of you who worked on this year's adoption. Selecting a new textbook series is never easy, and there will always be disagreements. However, I believe you have done an outstanding job and made excellent choices.

The new books will be ordered soon and should be available by the opening of school next fall. We will also order enough teacher materials to give each teacher a copy or copies of them. These materials should arrive before the end of school or shortly after summer vacation begins.

Here are the books and series we have adopted:

ENGLISH:	Grades 4–6	Bodmer Book Company
	Grades 7-12	Robinson-Boles, Inc.
SPELLING:	Grades 4–8	Ligon Book Company
SPEECH:	Grade 10	Knodel & LaPlante

MEMO ON TEXTBOOK ORDERS

The beginning of this memo—"As we discussed earlier"—is often an appropriate start. "As you know" is also a common opening and frequently works well.

TO: All High School Principals
FROM: Eunice Hodge, Mathematics Supervisor
SUBJECT: Textbook Orders for 19xx–19xx School Year

As we discussed earlier, new textbooks have been adopted by the state in all areas of mathematics. You have received some but not all of the books in each area.

If your school is interested in ordering new math textbooks, please get in touch with me to see if you have all the samples you need for previewing purposes. Then or later, if you have any questions on the listed books, please do not hesitate to call. Having served on the State Textbook Adoption Committee, I have detailed information on each of them.

Thank you for your cooperation.

LETTER IN RESPONSE TO CHALLENGED TEXTBOOK

In this letter, the writer's technique is to isolate the problem. The complainant has only one specific concern—"The Lottery"—which the writer focuses on and deals with. This is an excellent example of a "defusing" letter.

Dear Mr. Uehling:

This is to acknowledge receipt of your written complaint about the ninth grade literature anthology, Knodel & LaPlante's *Exploring Modern Literature,* that your daughter Beatrice has been using in Mrs. York's English class.

My understanding is that your objection concerns only the short story "The Lottery," written by Shirley Jackson, and not the anthology as a whole.

Your daughter is hereby excused from reading "The Lottery." Mrs. York has been asked to provide Beatrice with an alternate short story of equal merit but on a different theme, one that you and she will not find objectionable.

As you point out in your complaint, the textbook in question is on the whole an excellent one, and I am sure you will want your daughter to continue using it. Our textbook selection committees take pains to select materials that are appropriate and valuable for student use. Naturally, a literature anthology is one of the most difficult kinds of books to choose, partly because of its diversity of content, partly because of the varying backgrounds of our students at Lloyd High School.

Let me commend you on your taking an active and caring interest in Beatrice's education.

❧ A Word on Style ❧

REWRITE

The person has not yet been born who can write a perfect first draft of anything much longer than a bank check. Every original letter needs editing. Some need much more than what is commonly thought of as editing. They need rewriting.

There is nothing wrong with crossing out sentences and even whole paragraphs if they don't work. Why tinker with a lemon when it needs rebuilding? Somewhere back in creative writing courses the notion was instilled in a lot of people that one's written prose is close to sacred, that maybe a little proofreading would be tolerable—but that major repairs are not in order.

Nonsense. Major repairs are usually in order. English teachers should make that point firmly and often, at least in the high school grades. Simple prose is hard work. A good letter, a letter that says what it is supposed to say, and says it clearly, concisely, and persuasively, is often the one that has been rewritten, and rewritten, and rewritten.

SPECIAL PROGRAMS

5

CHAPTER 5

The letters in this chapter deal with various kinds of special programs, such as elective courses, programs for the gifted and talented, remedial programs, bilingual education, adult education, work-study programs, Title I, and more. Some letters explain the programs. Others are aimed at enrolling students.

All the letters in the chapter show evidence of having been carefully planned and organized. A letter explaining a course of study cannot be written as quickly, or with as little revision, as a short memo or friendly letter sometimes can be.

Of course it pays to plan every letter to some extent. It also pays to revise. Nearly every letter can be improved and sharpened by careful revision. Unnecessary words can often be cut. Sentence structure can usually be improved. A second or third draft of a letter—when time permits and the occasion warrants—is almost certain to be better than the first draft.

If the letter is a form letter, as some of the ones in this chapter are, it especially needs careful planning and thoughtful revision. The letters that follow underline this fact.

LETTER TO PARENTS ON PEER COUNSELING

NORTH PLATTE SCHOOLS

NORTH PLATTE. NEBRASKA
69101

January 15, 19xx

Dear Parents:

The Guidance Department at Madison Junior High School is in the process of establishing a Peer Counseling Program. We believe that such a program can and will be a positive influence in our school.

Your child is one of 14 ninth graders who have been selected as Peer Counselors. They were chosen on the basis of their leadership qualities, their ability to communicate well with other students, and their concerned and caring attitude toward the problems of others.

Training sessions will be held during the school day, usually one period per week. The amount of time devoted to counseling will depend on each student's class load and his or her desire to participate.

Some time ago, we in the Guidance Department had a conference with your child and discussed our plans for a Peer Counseling Program. We are most happy that your son or daughter agreed to help us and become a part of this program.

If you have any questions about the Peer Counseling Program, I hope you will call me at Madison Junior High School or, better yet, come and visit me at the school.

Thank you

Sincerely,

Don Holscher

Don Holscher
Guidance Department

WELCOME TO EXCHANGE STUDENT

Here is a warm and friendly letter of welcome. The writer's choice of adjectives contributes much to the tone: *rewarding, happy, pleasant, fulfilling, delighted.*

Dear Georgette,

As you begin your school year at Woolcott High School, I want to say hello and welcome. This should be an exciting, rewarding year for you, one that will be both a learning experience and an adventure. I believe you will like your classmates at Woolcott High as you become acquainted with them and join in their activities. The juniors are happy to have an exchange student among them, and I am sure they will do whatever they can to make your stay pleasant and fulfilling.

You will be learning about the United States at first hand—surely the best way—and, because of your presence here, we hope and expect to learn more about France. Our French classes are delighted, of course, that they will have a native speaker at school. Mr. James's class in European History is also looking forward to your contributions.

Indeed, all of us at Woolcott High are pleased that you can spend this year with us. If we can be of service in any way, please call on any of us—the students, the teachers, or the administrators. My own office is open to you at all times.

Best wishes for a successful school year.

NEWSLETTER DESCRIPTION OF NEW COURSES

This excerpt from a newsletter for alumni describes briefly a number of new high school programs, ranging from first-aid lifesaving to agronomy and soil testing.

Dear Alumni:

Lincoln High School has undergone many changes in the last few years. We are no longer a neighborhood school, since 600 students attend Lincoln from outside our boundaries. The school population has dropped from a high of about 5,000 students to our present 2,800. We now have one bell schedule of 8:10 a.m. to 2:00 p.m. This has led to much smoother operation of the school.

Perhaps the most notable and positive improvement in the school has been the creation of a number of new programs. We finally have the swimming pool promised the school in 1951. It is used throughout the day for gym classes and after school for the swimming teams of Frankford,

Northeast, Washington, and Lincoln High Schools. First-aid lifesaving courses are offered for Lincoln students. This gives our students an edge in getting summer employment as lifeguards.

A computer room will be dedicated in November. In all, the room has fifteen microcomputers. Course offerings include a Computer Math I course, which is an introduction to computers, and a Computer Math II course, which includes the teaching of programming.

The influence of our Horticulture Program can now be seen throughout the school. The courtyards have become a colonial garden, a nineteenth-century rose garden with a gazebo, and a pond setting with a rustic waterfall. In the near future, a Shakespearian garden will be added. Students in this program compete every year in the Flower Show against Penn State, Temple, Delaware Valley, and the University of Pennsylvania.

A new program was begun in September in the area of Environmental Studies. Special courses in agronomy and soil testing will be offered as part of this program. Our hope is that the closeness of Pennypack Park and our own 84-acre site will provide the kind of setting to permit the development of this new program.

Clearly, Lincoln High School is not the same school many of you attended years ago. It is not necessarily becoming better or worse, but rather is adjusting, as most schools have had to do, in order to meet the demands of the present and the educational needs of the students we serve.

LETTER TO PARENTS ON ELECTIVES

The beginning of the third paragraph in this letter shows an excellent way to avoid (actually, to avoid overusing) the word *I*. The sentence begins, "Let me urge you. . . ." Variants could include, "Let me suggest . . . ," "Let me take this opportunity . . . ," "Let me say. . . ."

Dear Parents:

Although your son or daughter has had some choice of courses in the freshman and sophomore years, it is in the junior year that electives become most important. For that reason, I am writing to you now, shortly before your son or daughter begins selecting courses for the junior year.

Hamilton High School offers a wide variety of elective courses, most of them for either a semester or a full school year. Your son's or daughter's guidance counselor has a good picture of your youngster's capabilities and interests and will undoubtedly make excellent course suggestions. Still, it is your son or daughter who has to make the actual choices. They are important choices.

Let me urge you to go over with your son or daughter the courses listed and described on the attached pages. They are the ones available next semester. Please note that some have prerequisites, others do not. In making choices, your child should be guided to some extent by his or her present occupational goals. I believe you can help in this area by providing an adult perspective to complement that offered by the guidance counselor. Certainly, we want you to be satisfied that your son or daughter has made the best possible choices from among those offered by Hamilton High's exceptionally rich curriculum.

Should you have any questions about the elective program in the junior and senior years, please call me or your child's guidance counselor. We will do our best to answer them.

PILOT PROJECT ON GIFTED AND TALENTED

This is a good, clear memo with no wasted words.

TO: Members of Gifted and Talented Committee
FROM: A. L. Dundee, Principal
SUBJECT: Update on Pilot Project

We have identified 22 students who are likely candidates for our pilot program this spring for the gifted and talented.

Tomorrow morning during second period we will hold an orientation program in the auditorium with these 22 students to go over what our gifted and talented program will be like and what we expect to accomplish in it. Perry Morris, Marion Walworth, and I will conduct the orientation.

Attached is a letter we will be sending home with each potential candidate.

Students who decide to take part in the pilot program will be scheduled into it, provided that their regular schedule is not severely disrupted.

ESTABLISHMENT OF REMEDIAL PROGRAM

Here is a letter that should lead to improved coordination between a junior high and a senior high school.

Mr. Kirby Van Wert
Principal
Sherman High School
Sherman, Ohio 43400

Dear Mr. Van Wert:

After a detailed analysis of several diagnostic tests, we have determined that there is a need at Dunbar Junior High School for additional instruction if our ninth grade students are to be fully prepared for high school. The tests we analyzed include the Iowa Tests of Basic Skills, Differential Aptitude Tests, and the Ohio Vocational Interest Survey.

We identified four major areas for concentration: (1) mathematics, (2) reading, (3) media skills, and (4) social awareness. After several staff discussions, I approved the following four-phase program for students in grade nine:

1. Nine weeks of a mathematics laboratory designed to pretest and place students in appropriate sections.

2. Nine weeks of a reading laboratory designed to meet individual reading needs.

3. Nine weeks of work on library skills with a pretest for placement.

4. Nine weeks of guidance instruction to increase students' social maturity, drug-abuse understanding, and career awareness.

Fourteen faculty members have been assigned to this new program. Also, for the 19xx–19xx school year we are scheduling every ninth grader to the Basic Life Skills Course.

In short, we are doing everything we can to ensure that the tenth graders who enter Sherman High will be equipped to do high school work.

LETTER TO COMMUNITY ON ADULT EDUCATION

In a way this is a sales letter—and a very effective one. It has a strong opening, a good conclusion, and a brisk pace throughout.

Dear Resident of Coolidge Township:

Learning is a lifelong process. In this fast-changing world, there are always new skills to be acquired, new subjects to be mastered, new insights to be gained. That is why our adult education courses are so popular and why we have been adding to our offerings every year.

Within the next week or two, you will receive our spring adult-education bulletin describing nearly 80 courses that we will offer in evening classes at the high school this semester. These courses are designed for you, the adult resident of Coolidge Township.

Please look through the bulletin, read the course descriptions, and decide on the course or courses that seem right for you. We look forward to seeing you at the high school this fall.

LETTER TO PARENTS ON SUMMER SCHOOL

Brief as the following letter is, it contains all the specifics. As a kind of invitation (not the most pleasant kind) it covers the five W's—who, what, when, where, and why.

Lee Shelby

Dear Mr. and Mrs. Shelby:

On at least one previous occasion we have discussed the possibility of Lee's having to repeat the sixth grade. If a student does not make sufficient progress academically, repeating becomes mandatory. That is the situation we now face.

The only alternative I can offer is for your child to attend a concentrated summer school session in mathematics and reading skills. Successful completion of that course will result in promotion to seventh grade.

This program employs a highly trained and skilled teacher. It will meet five days a week for four weeks in Room 132 at the Bierce School. The hours are 8:30 to 10:30 daily. Cost of the course is $20.00.

Should you choose this option, please complete the enclosed registration form at your earliest convenience. If you have any problems or questions, feel free to call Mrs. Caldwell or me at the Bierce School.

NOTICE TO PARENTS ON BILINGUAL EDUCATION

This letter must be translated into the proper foreign language since parents of the students involved will not be fluent in English.

Dear Parents:

Kilmer High School has a program that we think is appropriate for your son or daughter. It is called bilingual education, and its purpose is to provide most of your child's content-area instruction in   [language]   .

At the same time this instruction is being given in _____, we will concentrate on teaching your child the skills of English. As soon as he or she is ready to receive instruction in all classes in English, we will recommend the changeover.

Our intent is to try to reduce the importance of the language barrier in school at a critical stage in your child's education.

This program will be explained in detail at a meeting in the Kilmer High School auditorium on Monday evening, March 28, at 8:00 p.m. Mr. _____, who is fluent in _____, will conduct the meeting in that language. You are urged to attend. I am sure you realize that this is a very important decision for your child's future.

Please come. We will do our best to answer any questions you have.

LETTER TO PARENTS ON WORK-STUDY PROGRAM

The writer of this letter gets to the point immediately, then explains the benefits of the work-study program and the background of the student's possible involvement in it.

Dear Mr. and Mrs. Linden:

We would like to enroll your son Tom in our work-study program at Coolidge Township High School.

As a student in the work-study program, Tom would spend approximately one half of the school day in classroom instruction and the other half working for a local employer in a salaried position.

The work-study program is of great benefit to many students. It gives them an opportunity to work at a real job, earn money while they are learning, and, at the same time, continue their schooling in order to receive needed academic credits.

We have discussed this program with Tom, and he would like to participate. Now we would like to meet and talk with you about it. If you will call me at 5678-321, we can set up an appointment at which we will explain the program further and try to answer any questions you may have.

Please let me hear from you.

PROGRAM ON EMPLOYMENT FOR NON-COLLEGE-BOUND STUDENTS

One standard and excellent opening for a letter of response is, "Thank you for your letter of May 29, 19xx. . . ." The following letter uses an equally appropriate one: "This is in response to your letter of May 29, 19xx. . . ."

Mr. Chester Newberry
Executive Vice President
Greater Rutledge Chamber of Commerce
Rutledge, South Carolina 29700

Dear Chet:

This is in response to your letter of May 29, 19xx, concerning the Greater Rutledge Employment Program. We are very pleased to cooperate with the Chamber of Commerce and the private sector of our community regarding employment opportunities for non-college-bound students.

It is my understanding that Mr. Anderson and Ms. McColl have discussed with your staff some of the details that will need to be worked out as this program proceeds.

At this point, I see no need to present this program to our Board of Trustees for approval since, in reality, it is no different from a number of other arrangements we have with organizations throughout the school district. Mr. Anderson, Ms. McColl, and our other school district representatives have the authority to make the necessary decisions for the district.

Please be assured that you have our full support and cooperation in this endeavor.

EXPLANATION OF NEIGHBORHOOD YOUTH CORPS

The longer the letter, the more revision is likely to be necessary. For a letter as long and important as the following one, a number of drafts were probably required. The care spent in organizing, drafting, and revising it shows clearly in the finished version, which went out under the signature of the Assistant Director, Neighborhood Youth Corps.

Ms. Elma Kelso
Personnel Director
Adams-Whitman Construction Company
Astoria, Washington 98100

Dear Ms. Kelso:

This letter contains a brief outline of the Neighborhood Youth Corps program along with samples of the forms we use, general information on procedures, and special features of our local program.

Introduction. The employment problems encountered by youth have consistently been more severe than those met by other workers. The

Neighborhood Youth Corps program, administered by the Manpower Administration of the U.S. Department of Labor, attempts to deal with the high unemployment and educational deficiencies of many youths.

The program consists of three main components: in-school, summer, and out-of-school. For in-school youths, the program provides part-time jobs during the school year. In the summer, jobs are available to youths enrolled in in-school projects. For youths who have dropped out of school, the program offers full-time work and training experiences.

Purpose. The in-school program provides work experience and supportive services to low-income youths to enable them to continue or to resume their education. The program stresses raising the educational attainment of youths and increasing their employability through paid work experience. Program sponsors are urged to develop flexible projects to meet the individual needs of their enrollees.

Objectives
a. To provide gainful employment and other benefits to disadvantaged youths with high potential for delinquency
b. To increase the potential employability of disadvantaged youths through meaningful work experience and academic training
c. To provide additional income to youths from poor families
d. To provide incentives for enrollees to complete their high school training and to improve their academic achievement
e. To assist disadvantaged youths to develop responsible attitudes and to overcome problems of social adjustment

Our office will assign a project counselor to follow up on the students assigned to you. This person will be available to the student worker as well as to his or her immediate supervisors to work out any problems that arise at the work site. Please feel free to contact the counselor at any time during the project. The counselor will visit the work site at intervals, pick up time sheets, deliver checks, keep written progress reports on the enrollees, and answer any questions.

Enrollees are covered by State Industrial Insurance. In case of injury, notify our office immediately. If medical services are necessary, the proper forms must be filled out. Again, the project counselor will be able to assist you.

In the past, enrollees have not been allowed to work more than 234 hours during the summer. Because of that, we suggest placing one work crew from June 10 to July 19 and another from July 22 to the end of August. This approach allows a full eight-hour day plus vacation time for the enrollees, and it offers more jobs for qualified students.

Included are sample forms the immediate supervisor will need to be familiar with. If you have any questions about our procedures, please call our office.

LETTER TO TEACHER CONCERNING TITLE I

Here is a delightfully human letter that contains some deserved compliments along with some harsh truths.

Dear Betty:

I really enjoyed my visit to Whiteman School. Let me say that you are not only an excellent Title I teacher but a most persuasive advocate of the Title I program. It does not bother me at all when enthusiastic people make their views known.

It is easy to become defensive, I know, when a specific program is reviewed with such frequency as Title I. At the same time, you must realize that most programs will be examined both carefully and often during this decade. You should see it as a compliment that the program continues to enjoy such support. You can view with considerable pride the fact that it has been scrutinized, scrutinized again, and remains intact.

Frankly, I do not know if we can implement a more cost-effective program and achieve similar results. But you must understand that I do not want to be accused of failing to search for better ways. Oftentimes in that search comes the discovery that we and others are doing an honest, effective job.

Please continue your fine work, and best wishes for a beautiful spring.

PROJECT TO PREPARE TEACHERS FOR MAINSTREAMING

This letter is from a superintendent, expressing his satisfaction with a cooperative program to help classroom teachers handle mainstreaming. Note that he explains the program to some extent (despite the "As you know") because the college president may need to be reminded of what the program is and does.

Dr. Todd Conway
President
Byrnes College
Rutledge, South Carolina 29700

Dear Dr. Conway:

There is a critical need for training regular classroom teachers in the instruction of handicapped children. Most classroom teachers have had little experience or training in dealing with handicapped children.

Project SITE is a way to provide some assistance to the regular class-room teacher. As you know, the project is designed to provide instruction to regular classroom teachers and principals so that they can better instruct handicapped children placed in their classes. It also familiarizes teachers with facts about handicapped children and should eliminate resentment brought about by a fear of not knowing appropriate methods of instruction.

Over a three-year period, Project SITE proposes to provide extensive, vitally needed inservice training in mainstreaming to approximately 480 classroom teachers and principals in approximately 20 Rutledge County Schools. The intended result of the project is better education, management, and understanding for both handicapped and non-handicapped children.

We are excited about incorporating this project into our school system this year and hope that we can continue our cooperative effort with Byrnes for the next two years.

PROCEDURAL SAFEGUARDS, HANDICAPPED STUDENTS

This covering letter is an outstanding example of its kind. Accompanying the brochure, it tells what needs to be done with it and how to go about doing it.

TO: Principals
FROM: Perry Bunnell, Superintendent
SUBJECT: Procedural Safeguards, Handicapped Students

Please read the attached brochure carefully. Federal, state, and local regulations require that parents be fully informed of procedural safeguards available to them throughout the referral, identification, and placement process for handicapped students. Therefore, it is necessary for you to be familiar with these rights when considering possible referral to the Child Study Team.

Review this brochure with all members of your faculty and stress to them the importance of providing parents with the required information. The "informed consent" of parents means not only do they agree that certain procedures be instituted but also that they fully understand their right of involvement in the decision-making process. Basically, they must understand what they are agreeing to. *Understanding* is the key word. The LEA representative, or the person designated by him or her, must take whatever action is necessary to ensure that parents understand their rights.

🕮 A Word on Style 🕮

MAKE EVERY WORD COUNT

Writers on prose style always stress conciseness. Instead of General Bedford Forrest's "Get there fustest with the mostest men," the rhetoricians seem to say, "Get there fastest with the leastest words."

On the face of it, there is nothing wrong with that advice. One of the most prevalent sins in modern letter writing is wordiness, the use of two or more words when one would do. But the obvious solution—cut, cut, cut—may create more problems than it solves.

In writing anything, there is an optimum number of words, not a minimum number. An editorial genius will strike a point somewhere near the ideal figure. An average writer will either overshoot it or undershoot it.

There is no magic formula for concise writing. Some books on writing tell you to write the way you speak. It sounds reasonable, but just try doing it. You may well end up with the most confused prose this side of Tom Carvel.

The best advice is this: Read your own writing. Think about it. Does it make sense to you? Would it makes sense to you if you didn't already know the message? If you have two yeses to these questions, you probably have produced a letter that is as concise as it needs to be.

RECOMMENDATIONS, NOMINATIONS, AND CAREER CHANGES

6

CHAPTER 6

It is always a pleasure to be able to write a letter of recommendation, but it is also a demanding task. This kind of letter is intended to aid someone: to help a student get into college, to help a teacher secure a position or a grant, to help an administrator win a fellowship.

The same is true of nominations. The purpose of the nomination is to help the nominee win: to become Teacher of the Year, to gain an administrative honor, to receive a professional reward.

In order to accomplish these goals, the supporting letters must be impressive—and the letters in this chapter are impressive. Such letters stand out above the other letters being considered.

What is it that makes the letters in this chapter models of their kind? As always, it is a combination of features. But one thing stands out. All of these letters are *specific*. They explain the recommended person's background in thorough detail. They include examples, incidents, and anecdotes. They do more than say in a general way that the recommended person is outstanding—they prove it through factual detail.

RECOMMENDATION OF TEACHER FOR POSITION

 WILLIAMSPORT AREA SCHOOL DISTRICT
Roosevelt Middle School
2800 West Fourth Street
Williamsport, Pennsylvania 17701
(717) 326-3501

Dr. Merrill Baker
Superintendent of Schools
Haycox County School District
McLoughlin Boulevard
Markham, Oregon 97400

June 10, 19xx

Dear Dr. Baker:

Leona Sayre has taught seventh grade English at the Roosevelt Middle School for the past four years. During that time, I have had an opportunity to observe and evaluate her work as well as her potential for growth in her profession.

She has excellent rapport with her students. She shows a sincere interest in them as individuals and is consistently fair in dealing with them. She constantly searches for ways to make her teaching more interesting and more informative. She has great control of her room and has never needed assistance from the office in matters of discipline. Her students like and respect her and are pleased to be in her class.

Leona also relates exceptionally well to her peers, as she is frank and outgoing and exhibits a pleasant and friendly personality. Her appearance is beyond reproach, and her classroom, always brightly decorated, reflects her positive, optimistic attitude about life. I find her very cooperative when assigned special or extra work by her department chairperson. She frequently volunteers to cover another teacher's class when an emergency arises.

Mrs. Sayre is leaving our school this year because her husband is being transferred to your state. If there were any way she could be retained, I would assuredly want to keep her on my staff. I consider her a capable and dedicated English teacher and an asset to my school. I find it difficult to find young teachers with her teaching talent, ambition, and drive, and I recommend her without reservation for the position she is seeking.

Sincerely yours,

Jay F. Livziey

Jay F. Livziey
Principal

RECOMMENDATION OF STUDENT FOR ADMISSION TO COLLEGE

Here is a highly persuasive letter of recommendation. The writer goes into considerable detail about the candidate's achievements and, additionally, shows great personal enthusiasm throughout the letter.

Gentlemen:

It is my sincere pleasure to recommend Virginia Minden for admission to Stanford University. By every standard, Virginia is one of the most outstanding students who ever attended MacKay High School. Her achievements are remarkable. During the summer, she was a delegate to Nevada Girls' State, where she was elected and served as Chief Justice of the Supreme Court. Last year, as a junior, she was awarded second place in the statewide essay contest. Her topic was "Mainstreaming of the Disabled Student." She has been nominated for and participated in the Academy Abroad World Citizens Program and has been recognized in the "Who's Who Among High School Students" program.

Virginia has demonstrated a commitment to the total school program. She has been a member of the National Honor Society for two years, Quill and Scroll for three years, the school newspaper for four years, the tennis team for two years, and the student council for four years. Her eloquence and outstanding writing ability have contributed much to her success as editor of the school newspaper, president of Quill and Scroll, and business and advertising manager of the school newspaper.

Virginia has also been actively involved in community activities. She currently serves as a member of the Advocates for Abused Women, a volunteer for the local radio station, and a swimming instructor for the MacKay Recreation Department.

I recommend Virginia without reservation and consider her to be one of the finest young women in Nevada. If I can be of further assistance to Virginia, please let me know.

RECOMMENDATION FOR ADMISSION TO U.S. MILITARY ACADEMY

This excellent letter of recommendation includes some anecdotes that help illustrate the candidate's fine character, intellect, and personality.

Dear Senator Seaford:

It is my pleasure to recommend Reed W. Harrington as an excellent candidate for the U.S. Military Academy. Reed has been a student at our school for the past three years, during which I have known him personally. I had the privilege to teach him mathematics in his sophomore year.

This young man has many characteristics that make him an outstanding applicant for the U.S. Military Academy. Reed is intelligent and hard-working. Carrying a very rigorous academic schedule, he has earned a 3.9 average (out of 4.0) for three years and ranks fifth in his class of 273 students.

As I mentioned, Reed was in my math class during his sophomore year. This course, in our normal math sequence, is the most difficult one offered to our best juniors. Reed took the course as a sophomore. He struggled somewhat but never gave up. He worked very hard. He put in many hours. Yet he did not let this situation affect his work in other areas. All of us have to face adversity in life. Reed faced this situation squarely, with his best effort. I think he became a more mature person because of it. Reed sets high goals for himself.

He has developed himself physically as well as academically. He brings to the football field the same desire to do his best as he does to his classes. He shows equal persistence and dedication in the weight-lifting program prescribed for him by the coaches. I see him reguarly in the weight room. This setting gives me the opportunity to observe other facets of Reed's personality. He gets along well with his peers. They like him and respect him very much. He is able to joke with them, but, on the other hand, he commands their respect when a serious situation arises.

Reed told me once that his girl friend laughed when her father described him as an athlete. Reed's girl friend thinks he is an intellectual. In fact, he is a well-rounded young man. He excels in some areas, but he is good in almost all areas. His fellow students recognize Reed as someone on whom they can depend. He once remarked to me that, during the school day, students sometimes seek his advice regarding their problems.

To summarize, Reed is intelligent, athletic, hard-working, and friendly. He accepts criticism well and is able to work in a subordinate position. He is also able to command respect and lead when circumstances dictate that he do so. He is a person I trust and admire. He has many talents, which he works hard to develop. We are happy to have him as a member of our school family at Holy Name High School. Fortunate indeed will be the place that he selects for his post-high-school career.

LETTER OF RECOMMENDATION FOR TEACHER'S FILE

Somewhat more general than the preceding two, this letter nonetheless makes a number of important specific points, such as the teacher's volunteering for cafeteria duty and her effective direction of the school's yearbook.

To Whom It May Concern:

I am pleased to write this recommendation to be included as part of Mrs. Joy Latham's file.

Joy has been under my direct supervision for three years. She has taught in this particular building for five years. In my judgment, her intelligence is well above average, and she understands both students and the learning process to a degree that is exceptional even among our best teachers.

She has a thorough knowledge of social studies, which, combined with her excellent verbal facility, enables her to express herself and present topics very well. She has creative imagination that allows her to make classroom work interesting to students. Joy has the physical energy and drive to do a good job, however demanding, in any school setting.

During Joy's tenure here, her moral qualities were above reproach. Her personal characteristics such as patience, consideration, emotional stability, and good judgment were great assets to the school. Moreover, starting here as a first-year teacher, she improved every year.

Each of the five years that Joy worked in this building, she volunteered to supervise in the cafeteria during the students' lunch period. There was never a problem with the operation of our cafeteria when she was supervising, and the rapport she established, and the unofficial counseling she gave, were truly admirable. Joy also was the advisor to the school's yearbook. Under her direction, this publication became what one Board of Education member called "a community masterpiece."

Joy left our school in June, 19xx, to accompany her husband to Europe upon his being named ambassador to Denmark. This teacher will be an asset to any community and any school system. She is eligible for reemployment in the Bellowsville District at any time.

RECOMMENDATION OF TEACHER FOR GRANT

Notice especially the good opening and the good conclusion in this letter. The first paragraph states the exact purpose of the letter. The last paragraph suggests a willingness to do more, if necessary, to support the recommendation.

Dear Ms. Tolland:

This is a letter of recommendation for Mr. Thomas Granbi, who has recently applied for a grant for study and travel in England to be awarded by the English Research Society of the United States.

I have known Mr. Granbi for approximately 12 years, during which time I have served as one of his immediate supervisors. Throughout this period, Mr. Granbi has consistently demonstrated his conscientiousness and genuine commitment to the education of Hale City's youth as well as a concern for professional growth and development.

Through his active participation in education-related organizations (i.e., the Stowe-Hale City Teachers League), Mr. Granbi has shown an earnest desire to improve his skills and increase his knowledge, which has benefited the students within his classroom. I believe that this ability to "transfer" knowledge applies to the possibility of Mr. Granbi's studying and traveling in England. Not only would the opportunity benefit Mr. Granbi personally, it would also result in a new cultural awareness and knowledge on his part that he would fully share with his colleagues and students upon his return to Hale City.

There is no doubt in my mind regarding Mr. Granbi's ability to pursue graduate-level courses. He has clearly shown the initiative, stamina, and intellect necessary to complete a number of educational endeavors, and I am confident he would welcome the challenge you have described at a British university.

In closing, I recommend Thomas Granbi without reservation for consideration for a grant for study and travel in England. I have every expectation that, if selected, Mr. Granbi will prove to be a valuable part of the program and, in turn, an even greater asset to the Hale City school system.

Should you think it necessary or desirable, I would be happy to discuss Mr. Granbi's qualifications with you personally.

RECOMMENDATION OF TEACHER FOR COUNSELOR'S LICENSE

Naturally, the content in a letter of recommendation is closely related to the position or honor being sought. The writer's task in this letter is to show that the candidate should receive a counselor's license. All the statements about the candidate have a bearing on the counselor's job.

Dear Sirs:

I am writing this letter in support of Dolores Guerra's application for a counselor's license. It is a pleasure for me to do so.

Ms. Guerra is beginning her second year with us, having come from an elementary counseling position. She spent five years in elementary counseling after five years of classroom teaching at the elementary and high school levels. These years prepared her well for her assignments at Dobie High

School. Last year she worked with our juniors; this year she will become our permanent sophomore counselor. I am anticipating that she will do an excellent job in this new role.

Ms. Guerra has a good touch with youngsters and communicates well with them. She is sensitive to their needs, and they are aware of this. Faculty response to Ms. Guerra is also very positive. She is excellent at paper work in a position that demands a great deal of it.

I can recommend Ms. Guerra to you without reservation for a counselor's license.

RECOMMENDATION FOR COACHING POSITION

Even though the writer of this letter may be losing a good teacher and coach, he writes persuasively in support of the candidate's application for a college coaching position.

Dear Dr. Kramer:

Mr. Stanley Blaisdell has asked me to write a letter of recommendation in support of his application for a varsity basketball coaching position at Severeid State College. I am happy to do so.

Stan has been on our staff for 13 years with many different teaching and coaching assignments. During this period, I have been principal of the school. Stan has done an excellent job in fulfilling his duties. He has demonstrated consistency and fairness in answering the needs and expectations of his students, his colleagues, and the administration.

He is an effective and efficient communicator. As a coach and teacher, he is dependable and punctual. During the 13 years, I have found him a very positive, honest, and understanding person. He is definitely a good character model for young adults to work with, whether in high school or college.

Without hesitation or reservation, I recommend Stan for your varsity basketball coaching position. If you have further questions, please call me at (701)-234-5678.

RECOMMENDATION FOR PRINCIPALSHIP

The specific details in the second paragraph of this letter, coupled with the writer's obvious admiration for the candidate, result in a strong recommendation.

RE: Craig Newton

Through our association with the Hayes County Public Schools, Craig Newton and I have been acquainted socially and professionally for more than 18 years. He is earnest, resourceful, dynamic, and honest. He is a true leader.

For the past nine years, Mr. Newton has served in a demanding district as the assistant high school principal responsible for curriculum, instruction, guidance, and discipline. He has experienced many successes. He has chaired a complex scheduling and guidance program, evaluated personnel, participated in financial decisions, and written a detailed student code of conduct. In both daily routine and in special creative projects, I have observed his leadership skills, his sense of humor, and his tactful administrative style.

Mr. Newton is a highly supportive administrator. While working with him, I have been continually impressed with his driving commitment to excellence. He is uncompromising in his quest for quality educational opportunities for all young people. He never loses sight of students and their needs.

By asking probing questions, Mr. Newton is able to assess long-term benefits and chart directions for a comprehensive secondary program. He is able to do this, moreover, without preference for one group over another.

Mr. Newton communicates clearly and effectively. He is articulate, tactful, and impressive. As a public speaker, he is at ease with faculty groups, students, and parents. He is informative and keeps faculty members aware of administrative decisions when appropriate. In my judgment, Mr. Newton is a model professional administrator.

There are many proficient and dedicated leaders in education. There are also leaders who, because of their commitment to education and students, must be considered outstanding. Mr. Newton is outstanding.

Mr. Newton has the skill, ability, and experience for a principalship. He has the talent to perform at an exceptionally high level.

If I can be of further assistance, please do not hesitate to contact me.

RECOMMENDATION OF ADMINISTRATOR FOR FELLOWSHIP

This well-written recommendation is specific, detailed, and persuasive.

To Whom It May Concern:

This letter is a recommendation for Dr. Roger Ashford, who, I understand, has recently applied for a Putnam Fellowship at Saybrook University.

I have known Dr. Ashford for about 18 years, during seven of which I have served as one of his immediate administrative supervisors. Dr. Ashford has a varied and extensive background in public education, both as a teacher and as a school administrator. He served as an elementary teacher for nine years, displaying the competence and creativity that have marked his professional life. Following that, he assumed a number of administrative positions within the Hale City Public Schools, including these: Assistant Principal; Principal of Nepaug Elementary School; Director of Elementary Curriculum; and, currently, Director of K–8 Schools.

Throughout his administrative career, Dr. Ashford has established a reputation as an extremely capable, effective school administrator. He has consistently displayed qualities of initiative, conscientiousness, and professionalism. In addition, Dr. Ashford has been recognized as an educational leader who is committed to academic excellence. The various programs he has started or become involved with have greatly improved the effectiveness of instruction in Hale City's schools.

Dr. Ashford has the capacity to work independently. He can be entrusted with difficult, long-term assignments, knowing that they will be completed in a thorough and efficient manner, with minimal guidance or direction needed once the assignments have been made.

I recommend Dr. Roger Ashford without reservation for consideration for a Putnam Fellowship at Saybrook University for the 19xx–19xx school year—and have every expectation that, if accepted, he will prove to be a valuable part of the fellowship program. In turn, his involvement will enable him to continue his professional development, especially in the area of reading instruction.

If you think it necessary or desirable, I would be happy to discuss Dr. Ashford's capabilities and qualifications with you in person.

LETTER SUPPORTING BOARD OF REGENTS CANDIDATE

The details in a letter like this one have to be broadly sketched, because the candidate has done so many different things in education over a 35-year career.

Dear Governor Slocum:

On behalf of Dr. K. Howard Greene, Professor of Education at LaFarge University, I am pleased to offer a personal and professional reference in support of his candidacy to be a member of the Board of Regents for Elementary and Secondary Education.

Dr. Greene has distinguished himself for over 35 years as a strong advocate of public education. In his early training outside the state, he served in the roles of teacher, principal, community developer, and, upon moving to Rhode Island in the late 1950s, he assumed the role of superintendent of the Stuart Public Schools.

Dr. Greene has been active in professional organizations, in community groups such as Rotary, and on scholarship committees. He has served on numerous panels and study boards for the state of Rhode Island.

As a knowledgeable individual, Dr. Greene is aware of the many responsibilities of public education. He knows the realities of establishing priorities in order to use in a prudent way, for the benefit of all our citizens, the limited resources that are appropriated.

I believe that Dr. Greene would provide the requisite experience plus a broad base of knowledge of Rhode Island education, and, therefore, I recommend him for your consideration as a candidate for the Board of Regents for Elementary and Secondary Education.

NOMINATION FOR TEACHER OF THE YEAR

Nominations for Teacher of the Year tend to be somewhat longer letters than other letters of recommendation. A substantial amount of detail is expected. The writer of the following letter supplies that needed detail.

Dear Dr. Kingston:

It is my pleasure to nominate Mrs. Judith Slater as Gorham's candidate for the Teacher of the Year award.

Mrs. Slater has been a valued member of the Gorham High School North faculty for 27 years. Her positive attitude and love of art and children are reflected in the outstanding quality of the program of art instruction that she has maintained at Gorham North.

Her enthusiasm, her innovativeness, and her genuine concern for the arts in education are exemplary. Her flexibility in working with students, teachers, and the public has earned her an enviable reputation as an excellent teacher who truly cares about art and people. Under her leadership as a part-time coordinator, the art program in all the Gorham public schools has benefited. It now includes activities to meet the individual needs of all children.

Mrs. Slater demonstrates the highest level of professional commitment and competency in her work with students and colleagues. To carry out her professional responsibilities, she gives generously of her valuable time, and often her work extends beyond the school day.

Through her enthusiasm, hard work, and careful planning, Gorham students have won many awards in the Hallmark art competition. Her dedication has provided all Gorham students with the opportunity to experience the vitality of artistic expression as it pervades our everyday lives.

This unique melding of personal and professional qualities has enabled Mrs. Slater to lead her colleagues and students into a favorable involvement with artistic expression. It has provided the resources of time and expertise necessary for the success of her program. It has allowed her to share with others her belief in the importance of art and its role in the school curriculum.

What greater tribute to her love and dedication to art can there be than the fact that two of her own three children have been inspired to become practicing artists and teachers?

For all of these reasons, I am pleased to have the support of the Gorham Teachers' Alliance in naming Mrs. Judith Slater as the Gorham School System's nominee for Teacher of the Year.

LETTER SUPPORTING NOMINATION FOR PROFESSIONAL AWARD

This letter is written to the chairwoman of a state science teachers' association in support of a nominee for an award.

Dear Ms. Kerr:

Ms. Carol Cutler has been a teacher at Rawlings Junior High School for the last six years. During that time, she has been instrumental in bringing us to the top of Science Fair Awards in Summerall County. She has also contributed greatly to the articulation of the science curriculum between Rawlings and our senior high school, thereby contributing in some measure to their Science Fair accomplishments, too.

More important than the awards, of course, is her ability to turn students on to science. Her caring attitude and superior knowledge of the subject make her effective with students at all levels of ability. In fact, she is especially diligent with students who have learning disabilities, students who have historically had major difficulties in science.

She is creative and innovative in her approach and has been selected on several occasions to write course guidelines for our county. She sets high standards for herself and her students and then works hard to see that they are met. She is constantly broadening her knowledge, improving her skills, and sharing with her peers what she has learned.

I have never known a finer science teacher. She richly deserves the honor for which she has been nominated.

NOMINATION FOR ASSISTANT ADMINISTRATOR OF THE YEAR

The writer of this letter gives it a note of informality by using the nominee's first name, beginning in the second sentence, after giving her full name twice. Compare the prior letter in which *she* and *her* are used throughout. Both are superior letters, merely different.

Dear Mr. Dunnellon:

Please accept this nomination of Kathleen Tavares for Assistant Administrator of the Year.

Every principal's dream is to have assistants who do not add to the principal's work load, but do in fact reduce it. Kathleen Tavares has answered that dream for me. Kathy never comes with problems without also bringing possible solutions—acceptable, well-thought-out alternatives. In addition, she is always alert. She anticipates and heads off problems.

Kathy has served above and beyond the call of duty this year. The budget crunch of 19xx–19xx left me short a guidance counselor and, most critically, without leadership in that office. Kathy not only filled the breach, but organized and operated the guidance office more effectively than many full-time guidance chairpersons could have done. Along with this, Kathy continued to maintain her excellent performance as dean of girls.

Kathy is great with kids and has earned the respect of our students with her fair, firm, and friendly attitude. Her focus with them has been on behavior modification and growth rather than on punishment.

She has offered counseling services to parents who are having difficulty coping with their adolescents, frequently using her own time for this purpose. Needless to say, our public relations have never been better.

In the three years Kathy has been at Rawlings, she has earned the respect of her peers. I have never heard a complaint from my faculty or staff regarding her office and its functions. She is quick to say "May I help?" when there is a task to be done. She does not check her job specs to see if it is her "duty."

Perhaps I appreciate Kathy more because I had a very rocky beginning as a principal, but I think it is more than that. I really believe that Kathy is a rarity. She gives 100 percent all the time. She richly deserves to be honored as Assistant Administrator of the Year.

LETTER GRANTING PROFESSIONAL LEAVE OF ABSENCE

Here is a brief, straightforward, informative letter that covers all the necessary points.

Dear Mrs. Pendleton:

In response to your request for a year's professional leave of absence, and in accordance with the policy of the Calhoun City Board of Education, you are granted a professional leave for the 19xx–19xx school year.

Please note that this leave is without pay or other benefits, except that you may keep your group medical benefits in effect by paying the total premium. Sick-leave days previously accrued will be preserved but cannot be taken during this leave. They will be available to you upon your return to active status.

Have a good year, one of challenges and excitement. I wish you the very best and look forward to your return to our school system. Please keep in touch with the personnel department regarding your leave and your placement upon your return.

EXTENSION OF PROFESSIONAL LEAVE

The following letter is an answer to a request. Without restating the request, the writer answers it, "Yes, you may . . ." This is a good space-saving device.

Dear Ms. Hanahan:

It was good to receive your letter of March 25 and to know that everything is going well with you and with your studies in France.

Yes, you may apply for an extension of your professional leave with the understanding that it will have to be without compensation. Previously accrued sick leave days will be maintained but cannot be taken during the leave. According to state regulations, no group insurance can be continued during this period. If you wish to keep any of your insurance, you must do so through an individual plan.

Please let me know as soon as possible whether or not you wish to apply for an extension of your professional leave under the conditions stated above.

If you have any questions, I will try to answer them. In the meantime, best wishes as you continue your studies.

APPROVAL OF SABBATICAL LEAVE

In this letter the writer refers the reader to the statement of policy regarding sabbaticals rather than quoting the policy directly.

Dear Mr. Estill:

It pleases me to notify you that the Board of Trustees approved my recommendation to grant you sabbatical leave for the 19xx–19xx school year. I am pleased that our board has seen fit to establish such a program for the benefit of our staff members.

Please review carefully the policy relating to sabbatical leaves so that you are thoroughly familiar with the requirements placed on you while you are away. The personnel department will assist you should you have any questions regarding your benefits while you are on leave.

Let me know if I can be of any assistance as you enter upon this most exciting professional year. Congratulations and best wishes!

MEMO ON REQUESTS FOR CHANGE OF ASSIGNMENT

Here is one district's way of standardizing teachers' requests for changes of assignment.

TO: Rossville Teachers
FROM: Terry Durrell, Superintendent
SUBJECT: Survey to Determine Desire for Change of Assignment

February is the month in which we review our staffing needs for the coming year in order to prepare the tentative budget. It is an appropriate time to survey the teaching staff to see if there are any requests for changes in grade, subject, or building assignments. Although not every request can be granted—since it must be reviewed in terms of our district needs and plans—each request will be considered carefully and given a response.

Request for Change in Grade and/or Subject Assignment
A request for change in grade or subject assignment should be submitted by the teacher to that teacher's present building principal. A teacher whose schedule involves more than one building should submit the request to the home-base principal. This request must be submitted in writing not later than Friday, April 13, 19xx. Please use the form provided by your building principal.

Request for Change in Building Assignment

A request for change in building assignment must be made in writing to either the Director of Elementary Education or the Director of Secondary Education. The deadline is Friday, February 13, 19xx. Please use the form provided below.

(Detach) ────────────────────────────────── (Detach)

Request for Change
in Building Assignment

Name _____ Present Assignment _____

Present Grade/Subject Assignment _____

Desired Building Assignment _____

Reason for Request _____

_____

Date _____ Signature _____

NOTIFICATION TO TEACHER OF TRANSFER

This letter will please some recipients and displease others, a point the writer makes in the fourth paragraph of a well-worded letter that succeeds in being appropriate for both groups.

Dear Mr. Glenshaw:

As you know, we have reviewed assignments in an effort to maintain reasonable staff balance, to ensure a distribution of experience and special competencies needed in the total operation of the district, and, in general, to make certain that the appropriate individual is placed in the proper educational setting. To achieve such goals requires the reassignment of some staff members.

For the school year 19xx–19xx you have been tentatively assigned to teach fifth grade at the Rock Point School.

It is unlikely that this assignment will need to be changed. In the event that an unexpected situation arises and a change becomes necessary, we will notify you at the earliest possible time. During the summer, the building principal will send you additional details about the opening of school.

I am aware that assignments and reassignments please some and displease others. As you know from our earlier discussion on the reason for your transfer, these decisions are not made capriciously or in haste. I hope that the assignment you have received will prove to be a rewarding one.

If you have further questions, I will be happy to discuss them with you.

Best wishes for every success in the coming year.

❧ A Word on Style ❧

EDIT YOUR OWN WRITING

Editing is hard. You know what you intended to say, but the poor, bewildered reader doesn't. The reader has only one way to get your message, and that is from the words you put on paper.

A good writer is sometimes a good editor, but not always. The skills are essentially different. The best way to self-edit is usually not possible for a busy letter writer. The best way is to wait awhile, to put your writing aside and forget about it. When you come back to it, you can see it anew, and you can edit it. You can cut the nonsense and the fuzziness. But a letter writer can seldom wait.

If your secretary is an editor, you are in luck. If not, you will have to cultivate an ability to reread critically, impersonally, instantly. It can be done, but it isn't easy.

❦ A Word on Style ❦

ASK FOR ACTION

Every letter has a point. The reader should get that point as quickly, clearly, and obviously as possible. He or she should not finish the letter thinking, "But what am I supposed to do? What does the writer want? Why was this letter written?"

Some letters, of course, are purely informative. A newsletter fits that description. The writer of a newsletter is not generally asking for any specific action. The reader is not expected to respond in writing. Letters of welcome, appreciation, and sympathy are other kinds that seldom call for a response.

Many of your letters, however, do require the reader to do something—to phone for an appointment, to attend a conference at a specified time and place, to fill out a form, to write a letter in return. With these letters, you should make your purpose absolutely clear. You should ask for action. You should specify what the required action is and when it needs to be taken.

This is common-sense advice, but you have almost surely received letters yourself that failed to heed it, letters that left you wondering what your next move was supposed to be. Don't leave your own readers in the dark. When you expect action, ask for it.

DISCIPLINE, SUSPENSION, AND EXPULSION

7

CHAPTER 7

The letters in this chapter deal with disciplinary matters. They run the gamut from a warning against smoking to a letter imposing permanent expulsion. They are outstanding examples of their kind.

Because of the subject matter, the letters tend to be serious and formal. In most cases their tone is courteous but restrained. All the letters make it clear what action is being taken and why.

It is always important to include everything in a letter that the reader needs to know. It is doubly important when the letters pertain to students' rights. Suspension and expulsion cannot be taken lightly. Parents and students have to be kept thoroughly informed about what they can, should, or must do in regard to these matters.

The following letters achieve that aim. They explain fully and dispassionately the nature of the problem, what is being done about it, and what parents and students are expected to do. Dates, times, places, rules, options and so on, are carefully covered.

ALGONQUIN MIDDLE SCHOOL
AVERILL PARK CENTRAL SCHOOL DISTRICT
BOX 219 R.D. 1
AVERILL PARK, NEW YORK 12018
AREA CODE 518-674-3848

CHESTER A. MEISEL
ASSISTANT PRINCIPAL

JOHN J. THERO
PRINCIPAL

September 30, 19xx

Mr. and Mrs. Hector Sherrill
213 Lagrange Street
Whitman, New York 12100

Dear Mr. and Mrs. Sherrill:

We try to keep the cafeteria at Algonquin Middle School as quiet and orderly as possible for the good of most boys and girls who want a quiet, relaxing lunch. As you will see from the attached report, on October 16, your son James was behaving in a way that created a disturbance in the cafeteria.

This letter is to inform you that James's cafeteria privileges have been suspended for two weeks because of his misbehavior there. During the period of suspension, James may purchase lunch in the cafeteria but will be required to eat in the main office area.

If you think it would be helpful to James, one of you may come to school at his lunch time, in which case he will be allowed to return to the cafeteria to eat under your supervision.

Feel free to discuss this action with me if you have any questions or if you can offer any information concerning James's behavior. Whatever help you can give us by encouraging James to behave properly in school will be appreciated.

Sincerely yours,

John J. Thero

John J. Thero

SUPERINTENDENT'S LETTER TO PARENTS ON DISCIPLINE

This is a strongly worded letter to parents, attempting to enlist their support in helping to maintain standards in the schools.

Dear Parents:

This letter is about discipline and our schools. Discipline is a little like the weather in that everybody talks about it but not many do much about it. In the Pickering School District we are trying to do something about it. We are determined to maintain our high standards of excellence for our students and our schools.

Lately, we have had to exclude a number of students from our schools because of chronic misbehavior involving drinking and drugs. Excluding students from school is very unplesant for us, since we recognize the importance of education in the lives of our students. However, we cannot tolerate chronic misbehavior of the sort that these few students have demonstrated.

We are asking your help as parents to support our schools in trying to teach youngsters that there are consequences for serious misdeeds. In Pickering the consequences will be swift and sure. All students and parents have a copy of the rules, and every student is granted a fair and impartial trial, if involved in a case of serious misconduct, before being excluded from school.

The system is just and fair, we believe, but sometimes the parents of those involved in disciplinary infractions criticize our schools. We feel that such criticism is unwarranted, self-serving, and sometimes actually detrimental to students who must learn to accept responsibility for their actions as young adults.

Please do what you can to be sure your youngsters understand our rules at school. Also, please try to remember that we are attempting to provide a safe and sound educational environment for your child. Such an environment has no place for students who either cannot or will not comply with reasonable rules of order and discipline.

If you agree with us and will sustain our position, we will have taken one more step toward helping students achieve a healthy and happy adult life. If you have any questions about our schools' disciplinary rules and regulations, feel free to contact us at your convenience.

Your help, cooperation, and support of the Pickering School District in these matters of discipline will be greatly appreciated.

NEWSLETTER STATEMENT ON SMOKING

The writing in a newsletter tends to be more informal, more chatty than in a regular letter, and the excerpt below is no exception. Nevertheless, the writer makes his stand on smoking perfectly clear.

Dear Parents:

The 19xx–19xx school year continues to go well. When I say *well*, I am speaking relatively. It does not mean that we have had no problems. Five students have been suspended from school already this year. The most frequent reason for suspension, once again, has been for smoking. Students are never suspended for their first smoking offense. The first time, they and their parents receive notice that suspension for further smoking will occur. If students persist, they are suspended.

We at Fitzgerald Junior High do not object to doing battle with students about smoking. We think there is ample evidence that smoking is hazardous to health and safety. Students who challenge our position, and challenge the wishes of their parents, know the consequences. Perhaps school is the only place that is *un*reasonable about smoking. I prefer to think we are willing to stand behind a principle in which we strongly believe: that Fitzgerald Junior High is not a place where kids learn how to smoke—at least not without considerable risk.

PRINCIPAL'S LETTER ON ILLEGAL DRUGS

In this letter the writer quotes policy from the school handbook. This is an effective technique, showing as it does that the policy was known (or should have been known) to students from the beginning of school.

Dear Parents:

It is always easier to write about pleasant matters than about ones that cause pain, but I feel it is necessary for me to discuss with you certain aspects of our disciplinary policy.

During the past year, seven students have withdrawn from St. Francis because of their involvement with drugs. No one likes asking a student to withdraw from school. But I want you to know that our policy concerning drugs will be strictly enforced. The policy may be found on pages 22 and 23 of your son's handbook. Let me quote the pertinent sections: "Sellers and/or suppliers of drugs: The school will immediately notify parents of the offense and of the resulting expulsion. This may be followed by immediate notification of the proper authorities."

We are all aware of the magnitude of this problem in our society today. It seems that our society is becoming more and more permissive. A person may not conform to an established rule, but in many instances no consequences follow as a result of the violation. That situation cannot be tolerated at St. Francis. As difficult as it is—and it is difficult—our stated policy on drugs will be enforced.

LETTER ABOUT STUDENT'S BEHAVIOR

After reviewing the history of a student's behavior problems, the writer describes the specific incident that led to his exclusion from class.

Dear Mr. and Mrs. Endicott:

Your son John has been excluded from his reading class effective today. As you know, John has been a behavior problem in reading class since the beginning of the year. He has been talkative, disobedient, and disrespectful to Ms. Brewster, the reading teacher. John has been to the office, and I have talked with him and reprimanded him, but his attitude has not been receptive to advice.

In fairness to the many other students in John's class, and in fairness to John himself, it is important that he be obedient, attentive, cooperative, and willing to learn.

Today, after being directed to work quietly while Ms. Brewster worked with other students, John yelled out to another boy across the room. Ms. Brewster felt that John had exceeded his bounds in class and was disrupting the work of other students. She brought him to the office. On the way, John threw his reading folder toward Ms. Brewster.

John may return to reading class only after we have had a meeting with either or both of you and John about his behavior in general and in reading class in particular. Please telephone me for an appointment.

WARNING ON EXCESSIVE ABSENCES

As with most letters involving discipline, this one makes definite, matter-of-fact statements. In such letters there is little attempt—other than "Please" and "Thank you"—to include pleasantries.

Dear Parents:

Your child has missed 20 unexcused days of school this semester, and I am writing you to express my concern. This number of absences greatly reduces the chances of your child's success in school.

Please let me know *within five days of receipt of this letter* whether your child intends to complete the semester or withdraw from school.

Because of the excessive number of absences, your child must bring in a doctor's statement for each day missed in the future. Furthermore, I am asking that you make an appointment immediately with your child's guidance counselor. One of my assistant principals or I will be present at that meeting.

If we cannot resolve this matter satisfactorily, I will ask the prosecuting attorney to begin due process procedures leading to expulsion from Tarkington High School.

Thank you for your prompt attention to this matter.

LETTER CONCERNING TRUANCY

Here the writer begins by citing state law and ends by suggesting that family court will be the only recourse if illegal absences continue.

Dear Mrs. Addison:

New York State law requires that every boy and girl attend school each day that school is in session unless unable to because of illness or some other legitimate reason.

As you know, your son Sidney has been illegally absent from school a number of days recently. Today, according to our attendance person, Mrs. DeGrasse, Sidney was truant again. Mrs. DeGrasse brought him to school at approximately 11:30 a.m.

I have told Sidney—and you should impress this on him, too—that unless he is sick, he must be in school. Otherwise, his absence will be illegal. If he continues to be illegally absent, I will have no recourse but to refer him to Eastman County Family court for violation of the law.

Your assistance in this situation will be appreciated.

LETTER ABOUT STUDENT'S FIGHTING

This brief, pointed note serves as a covering letter for a misconduct explanation form.

Dear Mrs. Platt:

This letter is to inform you that your son Alfred started a fight in school today. See the attached Misconduct Explanation form, which has Alfred's comments. As a result of his misconduct, Alfred is suspended from school for one day: January 27, 19xx.

If we have not talked on the telephone by the time you receive this letter, please call me. We should try to plan together how to have Alfred behave properly in school. I am sure you want him to stay out of trouble in the future as much as we do.

WARNING ON OLDER STUDENT'S TRESPASSING

Note that the writer explains why the student was guilty of trespassing. Without the explanation ("As a high school student, he has no need to be on our grounds") the parent might wonder what the problem was.

Dear Mrs. Garrett:

This is to inform you that your son Frank was on the premises of Harding Junior High School yesterday, September 18, 19xx. As a high school student, he has no need to be on our grounds. All visitors must report to our office to receive permission to be in the building. If your son does not follow this procedure, charges may be filed against him for trespassing.

I would appreciate your attention to this matter and your discussion of it with Frank.

THREE-DAY SUSPENSION FOR ABUSIVE LANGUAGE

This letter, which confirms a telephone call, can be very short. The writer does not have to repeat the specifics discussed on the phone.

Dear Mr. and Mrs. Malone:

In accordance with the required procedures of our school district, this letter is to confirm my telephone conversation with Mrs. Malone concerning Wayne's abusive language to a teacher yesterday. As a result of his misconduct, Wayne is suspended from school for three days: January 19, 20, and 21.

Feel free to contact me in regard to this action if you wish a further explanation or if you can add any information that will help us to understand Wayne's behavior.

FORM LETTER FOR STUDENT'S SUSPENSION

Here is an all-purpose form letter for suspensions.

Dear Parents:

This is to notify you that your child, _____,
has been suspended from Carnegie Junior High School for the following
period of time: _____

The reason for this suspension is _____

_____

On _____[date]_____ at _____[time]_____, we require that
one or both of you accompany your child to school for a short conference
with the principal or assistant principal. This conference is required before
your child can be reinstated.

If you have any questions regarding this matter, please call me at any
time during the school day, 234-5678, ext. 321.

Thank you.

RULES OF IN-SCHOOL SUSPENSION

There are a number of rules for in-school suspension, with which parents and
students must be familiar. These rules are clearly and succinctly stated in this letter to
parents.

Dear Parents:

This is to notify you that _____,
grade _____, is temporarily suspended from regular classes at Benton
High School for the following reasons: _____

_____

Effective _____, he or she will be assigned to Benton's
In-School Suspension (ISS) program in Room 214.

In-school suspension occurs when a student's behavior warrants re-
moval from classes for a period of time, but suspension or expulsion from
school is not recommended. It is an alternative to suspension or expulsion

and is an effort by the administration to help the student. It gives the student another chance.

Your child will remain on in-school suspension until he or she meets the following conditions:

1. Completes all assignments prescribed by his or her teachers
2. Has a conference with his or her counselor
3. Makes a commitment to correct the inappropriate behavior
4. Has a satisfactory conference that includes student, parent, counselor, and administrator to discuss reinstatement to regular classes

Student In-School Suspension Rules

1. Student must report to the vice principal's office by 8:20 a.m.
2. Student must bring to the office all books, notebooks, and other materials needed for assignments. Daily assignments must be completed on time.
3. Student must stay in designated area and not leave unless permission is given. Rest room privileges will be granted only during class time when other students are not in the hall.
4. Student may not visit with other students without permission.
5. Student will eat lunch in suspension area and will not be allowed in the cafeteria.
6. Student will not be allowed to participate in any extracurricular activities during the period of in-school suspension.
7. Student must be out of the building and off the school grounds by 3:30 p.m. each day, unless under the direct supervision of a teacher or an administrator.
8. Student will be expected to participate in group guidance sessions during the period of in-school suspension.

Failure to comply with these rules of ISS will result in suspension from school with no opportunity to make up work. Students who violate ISS for the second time are subject to suspension from school for the rest of the semester.

NOTICE OF ONE-SEMESTER EXPULSION

The serious nature of the penalty in this letter and succeeding ones calls for precise, almost legalistic, wording. The reader has to know exactly what action is being taken and exactly what his or her options are.

Dear Mr. and Mrs. Wesson:

I have been advised that a disciplinary committee has found your son Quincy guilty of violating school board policy in regard to the use of alcoholic beverages on school property. In cases of this kind, school board policy calls for your son's expulsion for the rest of the semester, with loss of credit for the semester, unless there are mitigating circumstances.

School board policy further states that in the event a disciplinary committee reaches a conclusion that results in long-term suspension or expulsion, I am to advise parents in writing that there is a grace period of seven school days in which to appeal the decision.

You have two options. You may ask for a hearing before the full board in which all the facts of the case will be restated. (I have enclosed a sheet that tells you how such a hearing is conducted.) However, if you do not contest the findings of the committee, your other option is to appeal the nature of the penalty. The board will be pleased to grant a hearing on that matter alone.

In the event that you wish either type of hearing mentioned above, you must send me a letter requesting such a hearing within seven school days of the date on this letter.

If you request a hearing, you will be advised of the date and time of the hearing by telephone and letter.

RECOMMENDATION OF PERMANENT EXPULSION

This is the first in a series of letters relating to permanent expulsion.

Dear Mr. and Mrs. Springer:

The hearing officer for Geronimo High School, Mr. Douglas Thatcher, has recommended that your son, Joseph Springer, be expelled from the Wright Public Schools for possession and sale of marijuana, which is a serious violation of school board policies as cited in Mr. Thatcher's letter to you.

Please be advised that the hearing officer's recommendation for expulsion will be conveyed to the Board of Education at the next regular meeting at 8:00 p.m., February 20, in the District Board Room, 4143 Pickering Road. It will be determined at that time whether a formal hearing is necessary and, if it is, whether to hold the hearing in public or private. If a hearing is set, you will be notified of the time and place ten days prior to the actual hearing.

The Board of Education is the only body with power of expulsion from the Wright Public Schools. Expulsion is permanent and terminates any further attendance in any of our schools by your son Joseph.

I regret that this action is necessary, but it appears to be. Please continue to comply with the stipulations contained in the hearing officer's letter to you pursuant to Joseph's suspension from school. We will contact you by letter after the next regular meeting and will give you the proper notice of a hearing in regard to expulsion. In the meantime, suspension continues in effect until further notice.

If you have any questions, please do not hesitate to give me a call.

LETTER ADVISING OF HEARING ON EXPULSION

Besides this letter, the parents previously received a copy of the school board policy on expulsion and, with the letter, a copy of the material relating to the case that will be distributed at the Board of Education hearing.

Dear Mr. and Mrs. Springer:

The Wright Board of Education took under advisement the recommendation that your son, Joseph Springer, be expelled from the Wright Public Schools for possession and distribution of marijuana. The Board has set a public hearing pursuant to this matter for 9:30 p.m. on Tuesday, March 20, 19xx. The hearing will convene following the regular meeting of the Board of Education, which begins at 8:00 p.m. in the District Board Room, 4143 Pickering Road.

The Board of Education is the only body with power of expulsion from the Wright Public Schools. Following the hearing, the Board will determine whether or not to expel Joseph from our schools. Expulsion is permanent and terminates any attendance at any of our schools.

Please be advised that this is an official notice of the hearing to determine whether Joseph will be expelled from the Wright Public Schools. He is entitled to any and all evidence in his case, access to his student school records, and representation by you as his parent, or by legal counsel, or by someone else whom you, the parent, designate *in writing* before the expulsion hearing. If you wish to appear in Joseph's behalf, or to have him represented in accordance with the guidelines stated here, please notify our office not later than 24 hours prior to the hearing.

You have already received a copy of Board Policy GJE, "Suspension and Expulsion of Students." If you have any questions, please contact this office. Enclosed for your reference is a copy of the material that will be distributed to the Board of Education at the time of the hearing.

FORM NOTICE OF HEARING ON EXPULSION

This form accomplishes much the same purpose as the preceding letter but in a more impersonal way.

Student _____

Birth date _____

School _____

Date _____

NOTICE OF HEARING

You have requested and are hereby given notice of an expulsion hearing regarding _____[name of school]_____'s recommended expulsion of your ___[son/daughter]___ from the Rodgers Public Schools. The hearing has been set for ___[date]___, 19xx, at ___[time]___ at _____[place of hearing]_____

_____

As per WAC 180-40-270, you and ___[student's name]___ may inspect, in advance of the hearing, any documentation or exhibits that school authorities from _____[name of school]_____ intend to exhibit at the hearing. The school authority presenting the district's case has the same right to inspect documentation that the family intends to present.

___[name of student]___ may be represented by counsel if you so desire. At the hearing, you and ___[name of student]___ will have the opportunity to present an explanation of the alleged misconduct and to make such showing by way of witnesses and the introduction of documentary and other physical evidence as may be desired. If a student is to testify, written parental consent must be presented at the hearing. Otherwise, the student will not be allowed to testify. You will be allowed to question the school's witnesses.

A tape-recorded record will be made of the hearing by the school district.

If a sanction of expulsion is imposed by this office, you and ___[name of student]___ will have three school business days after the date of the hearing to appeal the decision to the Board of Directors.

If an appeal is not made, the sanction decided upon "shall be imposed as of the calendar day following expiration of the three-school-business-day period." If an appeal is made to the Board of Directors, the imposition of the sanction shall not be imposed until the appeal is decided: "PROVIDED, that an emergency expulsion that is continued pursuant to WAC 180-40-305 need not be either interrupted or stayed if the decision rendered" concludes that "the student continues to pose an immediate and continuing danger. . . ."

RULES FOR CONDUCT OF HEARINGS

Here is a representative set of rules governing the conduct of school board hearings.

RULES FOR CONDUCT OF ANDREWS MUNICIPAL SCHOOL DISTRICT SCHOOL BOARD HEARINGS ON STUDENT DISCIPLINARY MATTERS

1. The school board hearing is an administrative hearing. The only standard for admission of evidence to the hearing panel is relevancy. The hearing procedure is to determine, "Did the student violate the stated policy?"

2. The school board and the superintendent of schools will comprise the hearing committee. A quorum of the board members must be present to constitute a hearing panel. The school board may have its lawyer present, if desired, at any time in the proceedings.

3. The superintendent of schools (the executive officer of the school board) will serve as chairperson of the hearing panel and will be a party to the deliberations of the board in the matter.

4. The chairperson of the hearing panel will state the charges and call witnesses. The chairperson will maintain whatever records of the proceedings are necessary for school board records. The student or his designees may maintain at their own expense whatever records they may need of the hearing.

5. The student charged with a violation of school board policy may be present throughout the hearing, as may be the parents of the student, and, if desired, a lawyer representing the student.

6. Witnesses:
   a. The chairperson of the hearing committee will call witnesses with testimony relevant to the proceedings.
   b. Witnesses will be present in the hearing room only during their testimony.
   c. Prior to testifying, witnesses will affirm that the statements they will make are truthful.
   d. Anyone present at the hearing may question a witness.
   e. A witness may be called to testify any number of times.

7. The deliberations of the hearing committee will be made in executive session. During deliberations, the hearing panel may recall any party to give additional information, if such information is needed to reach a decision.

8. At the conclusion of deliberations, the final vote will be taken in open session.

9. If the finding is that the student has violated school board policy, the board may impose such penalty as is constitutional and is permitted by school board policy.

LETTER OF EXPULSION

This is the last in this series of expulsion letters. It gives the outcome of the hearings and explains once again what expulsion means.

Dear Mr. and Mrs. Springer:

The Wright Board of Education conducted a hearing during its regular meeting on Tuesday, March 20, 19xx, at 9:30 p.m. to decide whether or not Joseph Springer should be expelled from the Wright Public Schools for possession and sale of marijuana.

I regret to inform you that the Board of Education took action to expel Joseph Springer from the Wright Public Schools. Expulsion is permanent and terminates any attendance at any of our schools. You may apply for rescission of expulsion after one year.

Your son Joseph is hereby prohibited from access to any and all school campuses of the Wright Public Schools. His presence on any campus at any time may result in his arrest for trespassing or interfering with the conduct of an educational institution. We regret that this action is necessary, but our school board believes that discipline is essential and that students who willfully disregard the rules and regulations cannot continue in our schools.

If you have any questions about this matter, I hope you will let me know.

TEACHER'S NOTIFICATION OF SUSPENSION

Although this letter is nonjudgmental, it is necessarily rather abbreviated and formal.

Dear Mr. Ulmers:

This is to notify you, in accordance with 19xx South Carolina Code Section 59-25-430, that you are suspended from all duties under your contract with the School District of Rutledge County pending resolution of charges made against you.

A copy of the South Carolina Code Sections on Employment and Dismissal of Teachers is enclosed.

You should notify my office as soon as the charges against you are resolved.

❧ A Word on Style ❧

KEEP IT BRIEF

Naturally, the best letter-writers like to write. That can be both a blessing and a burden. An able, fluent writer—especially when he or she is doing a newsletter—can easily get carried away. If you find that happening, remember: your readers are often as busy as you are. They have their own interests, their own problems. They may be vitally concerned about the schools their children attend, but they will still balk at the prospect of reading a pedagogical *War and Peace*.

Some correspondence, of course, has to be long. No matter how well-written or carefully edited certain letters are, they have to go on for two or more pages. The advice to keep it brief does not apply to these letters. Rather it applies to what word-processing operators call "short and quick documents," to those messages that can and should be succinctly stated.

STAFF EVALUATIONS

8

CHAPTER 8

Although principals sometimes use forms rather than individually prepared letters to rate teachers, there are a number of other kinds of correspondence that deal with staff evaluations. There are memos, guidelines, checklists, self-evaluation questions, and policy statements on the subject. And at the upper levels of administration there are likely to be personally written appraisals.

Putting an evaluation into words is not easy. Even putting the criteria into words can be difficult and time-consuming. That is one of the reasons forms are so widely used. The best forms (or form letters, for that matter) have been carefully worked out to include the desired criteria.

The materials in this chapter do a very good job of pointing out the need for evaluation and listing the characteristics, abilities, and professional achievements that have a bearing on performance.

Even when it makes use of a form, a good evaluation assesses a great many traits. You will notice the precise, specific detail contained in the letters, memos, and forms in this chapter.

City of Augusta
Board of Education

Cony Street Extension - Augusta, Maine 04330
(207) 622-3724

December 30, 19xx

Mr. Byron Patten
Principal
Central School
Curtis, Maine 04300

Dear Mr. Patten:

In accordance with board policy, the following is a mid-year review of your performance from my perspective. It is sent to you in preparation for our conference to be held on January 11 at 3:30 p.m.

I. Schools are purposive; they are established and maintained to achieve certain goals. The outstanding administrator understands the present goals, helps to articulate them, works with dedication toward their achievement, and aids in the development of new goals that are responsive to the general needs and expectations of the larger social order. I observe that you . . .

. . . .
. . . .

(Four more points are covered in detail.)

When we meet on January 11, we will discuss the standards and observations above and may modify them by mutual consent.

Sincerely,

Raymond G. Taylor, Jr.
Superintendent of Schools

The complete text of this letter is on pages 143–145.

PHILOSOPHY OF TEACHER EVALUATION

This memo is an excellent statement of the rationale for teacher evaluations. It reminds teachers of the need for such evaluations and reassures them that the procedure is helpful for everyone.

TO: Staff
FROM: Judy Talbot, Principal
SUBJECT: Teacher Evaluations

Formal teacher evaluations are a necessary part of educational administration. They should be viewed by teachers as a learning experience, as a way for both the teacher and the administrator to grow in understanding and knowledge.

Teacher strengths will be discussed so that they can be capitalized upon and developed further. Teacher weaknesses will be identified so that appropriate methods can be devised to reduce or alleviate them.

Assuming that evaluations are accurate, they will serve to assess strengths and weaknesses of the teacher, the department, and the school, thus providing a direction for staff development and for public relations.

Prior to the evaluation, it is important for the evaluator to indicate the criteria upon which the teacher will be evaluated. The teacher should then be prepared to comment on these criteria as they relate to his or her professional performance.

EVALUATOR'S REQUEST FOR INFORMATION

Here is a memo that involves teachers in the evaluation process by asking them to supply up-to-date information on their professional and personal accomplishments.

TO: Teachers
FROM: Rose Wallace, Assistant Principal
SUBJECT: Completing Summary Evaluations

The Classroom Observation Summary Form is due April 15. The form contains this statement: "The classroom observation is a summary of the teaching situation as seen by the evaluator in the classroom." However, the form also requires a brief narrative statement about (1) the teacher as a professional and (2) the teacher as a person.

Please take a few minutes to jot down some notes that would be helpful to me in completing narrative statements (1) and (2). Here are some items to consider:

Professional
Professional organizations you belong to
Professional journals you subscribe to and read
Professional honors
Additional courses, workshops, conferences, seminars
Visits to other schools
Special projects
School or district committees
Curriculum work
School activities to which you have contributed
Other services rendered to school and students

Personal
Participation in community activities
Clubs or organizations
Sports
Hobbies
Special personal interests

GUIDELINES FOR FORMAL TEACHER EVALUATION

What makes a teacher successful? The following list of traits and abilities is designed to provide guidelines on effective teaching for evaluators to use.

TO: Staff
FROM: Judy Talbot, Principal
SUBJECT: Guidelines for Teacher Evaluations

All of the following characteristics and attributes play a part in successful teaching. Therefore, they are important items in teacher evaluations. The list is long but not exhaustive. It is not necessary for the evaluator to comment on every item in every evaluation.

Personal
Appearance
Sense of humor
Speech—language and tone
Communication skills—verbal and nonverbal
Enthusiasm
Poise and self-confidence
Knowledge of subject matter

Emotional stability—self-discipline, lack of prejudice
Judgment—separating important matters from trivial
Receptiveness to new ideas
Respect for students
Interest in students' welfare, progress, and success
Distractions—mannerisms? air of superiority?

Efficiency
Promptness
Preparedness
Clarity of goals and objectives
Effective use of class time—proper topic emphasis
Relation of presentation to curriculum goals
Cohesiveness of presentation
Accessibility

Creativity
Ability to motivate
Inventiveness
Resourcefulness

General
Classroom maintenance
    Organization and neatness
    Interest centers
    Bulletin boards
Classroom atmosphere
    Students' interest and participation
    Teacher-dominated? student-dominated?
Range of methods, activities, and assignments
Stress on learning rather than grades
Quality of lesson plans
Clarity of goals
Provision for individual differences
Thoroughness of evaluation . . .
    of students
    of goals and objectives
    of plans and methods
    of evaluation techniques
Type, frequency, and quality of tests
Fairness of grading
Maintenance of discipline

TEACHER SELF-EVALUATION QUESTIONS

A valuable way to involve teachers in the evaluation process is through a set of relevant questions. The following memo supplies an excellent model.

TO: Teachers
FROM: Clark Oden, Principal
SUBJECT: Self-Evaluation Questions

The following questions are designed to serve as a guide for your self-evaluation and as a basis for discussion in the conference. In the conference, you will have an opportunity to comment on facts you think are pertinent to your self-evaluation but are not covered by these questions.

Classroom Atmosphere
1. Do I interact with students in a friendly and sympathetic manner?
2. Do I maintain good order without compulsion?
3. In my classroom, do students exhibit an attitude of respect and tolerance for one another?
4. Do I adjust the physical features of the room to provide a healthy and attractive environment?

Classroom Activities
5. Do I set long-range goals and plan carefully the individual units and lessons?
6. Do I use a variety of styles of instruction? (Some familiar styles are question-and-answer, general class discussion, teacher lecture, small group work, seat work, individual work, demonstration, laboratory.)
7. Do I use a variety of materials of instruction?
8. In my classroom, do students actively participate in discussions and activities?
9. In my classroom, do students have opportunities to develop leadership, to practice cooperation, and to share experiences with one another?
10. Do I evaluate learning frequently, using a variety of means?
11. Do I modify my planning as a result of my evaluation of student progress?

Professional Characteristics
12. Do I assume responsibility for the educational success of my students?
13. Do I strive for professional improvement by attending courses and workshops and by personal study?
14. Do I seek and use the assistance and advice of resource persons?
15. Do I work cooperatively within my department and with other members of the staff?
16. Do I exhibit personal qualities that enhance my effectiveness as a teacher?
17. Do I promote and maintain appropriate student behavior throughout the school?
18. Do I complete accurately and on time all necessary records, reports, and other administrative routines?
19. Do I accept extracurricular assignments as part of my overall responsibility, and do I fulfill these assignments conscientiously?

General Assessment

20. What degree of success have I had as a teacher at Peale Senior High School?

21. In what areas of my teaching responsibilities have I shown special competency, achievement, or service?

22. In what areas of my teaching responsibilities do I seek improvement?

23. What specific goals do I have for continued professional improvement?

PROBATIONARY TEACHER EVALUATION

This memo quotes Board of Education policy at length to try to ensure that future evaluations will be timely and correct.

TO: All Principals
FROM: D. M. Marston, Superintendent
SUBJECT: Evaluation of Probationary Teachers

In at least a few cases it appears that not every principal has met all of the Board of Education's requirements in evaluating probationary teachers. It is extremely important that we follow policy closely in this matter. Let me quote the pertinent passages from the guidelines adopted by the Taney County Board of Education in September 19xx:

"At a minimum number of four times a year, probationary teachers shall be observed for a period of time sufficient for an adequate appraisal of the instructional activity. Observations shall be conducted by more than one qualified person as determined by the Superintendent. Within a reasonable period of time subsequent to each such observation, the teacher will be given a written observation report and a post-observation conference."

Please note each requirement in that statement. Each one must be met, as must the following three:

"Probationary teachers shall receive a formal evaluation conference before the end of each semester of each of the two probationary years.

". . . The teacher will sign the evaluation and receive a copy of it. Such signature, however, will not necessarily indicate agreement with the evaluation. The teacher may prepare an addendum to be filed with the evaluation.

"One copy of the written evaluation and any teacher-prepared addenda is to be filed in the personnel office, one copy is to remain in the principal's office, and one copy is to be given to the teacher."

These evaluations are important to both the probationary teacher's career and your own. I know you will exercise care in the future to see that all requirements for prompt and thorough evaluation are met.

TENURED TEACHER EVALUATION

Here is a memo quoting board policy on the evaluation of tenured teachers.

TO: Tenured Teachers
FROM: David Harwood, Principal
SUBJECT: Yearly Teacher Evaluation

A number of questions have been raised recently about procedures relating to formal evaluations. Let me quote from that statement of district policy concerning these yearly evaluations. Note especially the last paragraph, which deals with the teacher's signature and with his or her possible addendum to the evaluation:

"Tenured teachers will receive formal evaluation conferences at least by the end of their fifth year in Taney County and at the minimum rate of one every five years thereafter, and at such other times as are necessary. All observations of a classroom teacher shall be conducted openly.

"Evaluators (principals or supervisors) shall hold a formal evaluation conference with the observed teacher. After the conference, a written statement of evaluation will be prepared and reviewed with the teacher within a reasonable time. Any information presented at the conference that was not previously known to the teacher shall be reviewed by the evaluator and teacher before it may be entered into the written evaluation.

"In the event that the teacher feels his or her evaluation is incomplete or unjust, the teacher may write an addendum, giving his or her point of view. Whether there is an addendum or not, the evaluation is to be signed by the teacher. This signature does not indicate approval. One copy of the evaluation—and addendum, if there is one—shall be placed in the evaluation file in the personnel office; one shall be filed in the principal's office; and one shall be given to the teacher."

If you have any questions about this policy statement, please let me know, and I will do my best to answer them.

REPORT OF OBSERVATION OF TEACHER PERFORMANCE

The accompanying form is an excellent one to use in observing a teacher's performance. It is explicit, concise, easy to work with, and yet comprehensive enough to serve its purpose.

Harford County Public Schools
REPORT OF OBSERVATION OF TEACHER PERFORMANCE

Teacher _____ School _____

Grade(s) _____ Subject _____ Topic/Activity _____

Date of Observation _____ Time of Observation _____ to _____ Date of Conference _____

Factors to be considered in observing teacher performance are described by category. Other items of significance which relate closely to a specific lesson or activity observed should also be used.

	Satisfactory	Causing Concern	Unsatisfactory
1. INSTRUCTIONAL PLANNING This category includes the degree to which instructional planning relates to student needs; reflects the goals, objectives, content, and other aspects of curriculum; causes materials to be utilized appropriately for various age and ability levels; includes a variety of activities which contribute to student achievement; and provides for reinforcement of concepts and evaluation of learning.	☐	☐	☐
2. LESSON IMPLEMENTATION The effective implementation of a lesson includes the sharing of objectives with students, motivation for learning, logical development of the lesson, activities which contribute to the achievement of the objectives, optimum pacing, differentiation of instruction, use of appropriate strategies and techniques, ongoing assessment of pupil progress, and meaningful closure.	☐	☐	☐
3 PUPIL INVOLVEMENT This category includes evidence of time-on-task behavior, the attainment of objectives, significant and meaningful activities, and the maintenance of student interest and participation.	☐	☐	☐
4 MANAGEMENT AND ORGANIZATION Factors to be considered in this category include routine classroom procedures, pupil control and discipline, attention to the health and safety needs of pupils, seating and furniture arrangements, and the use and care of supplies and equipment.	☐	☐	☐
5. PROFESSIONAL CHARACTERISTICS Attributes to be considered include interpersonal relationships with students, communication skills, knowledge of content area, emotional control, response to constructive criticism, appropriate appearance, and the degree to which school policies and procedures are followed.	☐	☐	☐

Specific Concerns, Comments, and Recommendations _____

_____

_____

_____

_____

_____

_____

OVERALL ASSESSMENT FROM OBSERVATION ☐ Satisfactory ☐ Causing Concern ☐ Unsatisfactory

Signed _____ Title _____ Date _____

Signed _____ Title _____ Date _____

Signed _____ Teacher Date _____

(Signature acknowledges receipt of a copy of this form.)

138

TEACHER EVALUATION FORM

The accompanying form is a good example of its type. The reverse side of the form has a Roman numeral V. for Comments and spaces for signatures (and dates) filled in by the principal, supervisor, and teacher.

Harford County Public Schools

TENURED TEACHER EVALUATION

I.   Pertinent Information:

Name of
Teacher _____   School _____   Position _____

Conference Date _____   Total Years of
Teaching Exp. _____   Yrs. of Exp. in
Harford County _____

Conference Participants _____

II.   Overall Assessment:

☐	Performing Satisfactorily	☐	Causing Concern About Performance	☐	Performing Unsatisfactorily

III.   Competencies:

IV.   Recommendations for Professional Growth and Improvement:

V. Comments:

Principal _____ Date _____

Supervisor _____ Date _____

Teacher* _____ Date _____

*Signature indicates copy has been received.

PRINCIPAL'S EVALUATION OF CHAIRPERSON

This letter shows an effective way of combining standard paragraphs with original material. Many form letters do this with single words and phrases, but this letter calls for a number of sentences to be added.

Mr. Dexter Randolph
Chairman, Mathematics Department
Blaine High School

Dear Mr. Randolph:

This letter represents my review of your performance for the school year 19xx–19xx, as required by the City of Maxim Board of Education. It is sent to you in preparation for our conference to be held on May 26 at 3:00 p.m.

I. A department chairperson is both a leader and a valued associate, a person who has the personal and professional respect of the members of his or her department. My observation is that you _____

_____

II. A chairperson has administrative responsibilities involving budgets, reports, requisitions, and other paper work. These responsibilities must be handled fully and on time. My observation is that you _____

_____

III. A chairperson is the school's leading expert on his or her subject matter. Not only other teachers and students but parents and administrators as well look to the chairperson for guidance and direction on that specific subject. My observation is that you _____

_____

IV. A chairperson makes continuing efforts to strengthen the department and to improve his or her own skills and classroom performance. Activities during the school year may mirror these efforts. My observation is that you _____

_____

These are some of the observations I expect to discuss with you when we meet on May 26. I look forward to the discussion and to your own views on the 19xx–19xx school year.

COVERING LETTER FOR EVALUATION OF ASSISTANT PRINCIPAL

A brief explanation of an evaluation checklist, this letter accompanies a completed form like the one that follows it. It also sets the date and time for a performance-appraisal conference.

>Ms. Carrie Van Buren
>Assistant Principal, Administration
>Blaine High School

Dear Carrie:

In preparation for our yearly evaluation conference, I am enclosing a completed evaluation checklist. Each of the 20 items is ranked from a perfect score of 5 down to an unsatisfactory score of 1. This checklist represents my observations of your performance for the school year 19xx–19xx. We will discuss it fully at our conference, which is scheduled for May 29 at 3:00 p.m. This conference will provide you with an excellent opportunity to present your own views on the 19xx–19xx school year and on your performance during it. I am looking forward to having you share your views with me.

CHECKLIST FOR EVALUATING ASSISTANT PRINCIPAL

This checklist will vary somewhat depending on the exact assigned duties of the assistant principal. The following list is for a high school assistant principal for administration.

General Duties

—— 1. Establishes and maintains standards of conduct for students. Monitors student performance to make certain that program standards are maintained.

—— 2. Ensures that assigned facilities are properly maintained, cleaned, and appropriately used. Coordinates the availability of facilities for community use.

—— 3. Oversees the acquisition, maintenance, storage, inventory, distribution, use, protection, and disposal of all school materials and equipment assigned.

—— 4. Develops and administers the budget as assigned.

—— 5. In conjunction with the building principal, enforces contractual provisions and administrative regulations regarding employees' conduct and performance.

—— 6. Provides for emergency and disaster preparedness and, on a daily basis, ensures the safety of students and staff.

—— 7. Evaluates and supervises staff members as directed by the building principal. Assists in teacher evaluations supported by classroom observations and conferences.

—— 8. Determines secondary education staffing needs in relation to building needs, program requirements, and staff preferences and competencies.

—— 9. In conjunction with the building principal, develops secondary education programs to meet identified student needs and district goals and objectives.

—— 10. In conjunction with the secondary education administrator, provides appropriate in-service staff development to build the necessary expertise for accomplishment of goals and objectives.

—— 11. Develops positive school and community relationships through the establishment of school/community organizations or alternative approaches approved by the secondary education administrator.

—— 12. Works with guidance counselors on matters relating to student discipline and adjustment.

Specific Duties, 19xx–19xx School Year

—— 13. Assists the building principal and the English department in revising the English curriculum.

—— 14. Assists the building principal and the Social Studies department in answering their curriculum needs and concerns.

—— 15. Assists the building principal in assessing present and future needs for microcomputers.

—— 16. Visits classrooms on a more regular basis than in 19xx–19xx in order to be in closer contact with teachers and the educational process.

—— 17. Becomes more familiar with all standardized testing programs to further his own education and administrative helpfulness.

—— 18. Implements, evaluates, and improves the planned In-School Suspension Program.

—— 19. Assists the new assistant principal for instruction with guidance and counsel so that he becomes as effective as possible as quickly as possible.

—— 20. Assists the building principal and staff to decrease the drop-out rate at BHS by 5 percent in the 19xx–19xx school year.

EVALUATION OF PRINCIPAL'S PERFORMANCE

Here is the complete text of the chapter-opening letter. Note that it is essentially a form letter to which a substantial amount of text can be added.

Dear Mr. Patten:

In accordance with board policy, the following is a mid-year review of your performance from my perspective. It is sent to you in preparation for our conference to be held on January 11 at 3:30 p.m.

I. Schools are *purposive;* they are established and maintained to achieve certain goals. The outstanding administrator understands the present goals, helps to articulate them, works with dedication toward their achievement, and aids in the development of new goals that are responsive to the general needs and expectations of the larger social order. I observe that you ——

_____

_____

II. Schools are *peopled;* their functions are performed almost solely through human agents. The outstanding administrator amplifies his effort through others. He encourages, understands, supports all persons with whom he interacts, regardless of their organizational relationship to him. I observe that you _____

_____

_____

III. Schools are *structured;* they require organization, rules, and conventions in order to be effective and efficient. The outstanding administrator works within this structure, complying with its rules and honoring its conventions. He constantly reviews the utility of the existing structure and works toward its modification, being loyal to old structures until new ones are formally adopted. I observe that you_____

_____

_____

IV. Schools are *normative;* their existence depends in part upon role-appropriate behavior and a consistent, objective environment. The outstanding administrator is sensitive to the need for appropriate behavior and sound judgment in reacting to the many complex and subtle conditions that arise daily. He develops a personal style that inspires confidence, protects the rights of others to civil treatment, evidencing maturity and clarity in his thinking and actions. I observe that you _____

_____

_____

V. Schools are *sanction-bearing;* authority, respect for authority, and professional trust are necessary ingredients within a sound educational institution in order to assure adherence to its goals and norms. The outstanding administrator is not an unthinking puppet in the hands of his superior, but is loyal, fair, trusting, and supportive. He utilizes established conventions for airing grievances and making suggestions. He is firm with his subordinates, making his will known and calling them into accountability, while simultaneously being open to suggestion and criticism and showing a willingness to review and change his policies when merited. I observe that you _____

_____

_____

When we meet on January 11, we will discuss the standards and observations above and may modify them by mutual consent.

❦ A Word on Style ❦

DOUBLE-CHECK SPELLING

The world is full of strange names. Even some of the not-so-strange names can be hard to spell. There are so many ways to spell a name like *Cheryl O'Neill,* for example, that the mind reels. Still, you may be sure that the person who receives your letter expects his or her name to be spelled correctly. A typist, no matter how capable, will occasionally make errors. It is the person who signs the letter who is, and must be, the last proofreader.

Misspellings within the body of the letter are perhaps less serious—for someone other than you. For a school administrator, they are equally risky. The public expects the correspondence of every school administrator to be letter-perfect. In short, perfect letters, with no misspellings, are important.

❧ A Word on Style ❧

USE ABBREVIATIONS CAREFULLY

Many organizations, departments, agencies, and programs in American education are better known by their abbreviations than by their full names. Close to home for school administrators are the abbreviations AASA, NASSP, NSSEA, and NSPRA. You would not ordinarily use those abbreviations in a letter to a parent or student. If you did, you would almost surely spell them out. You would write American Association of School Administrators, National Association of Secondary School Principals, and so on.

But it is very easy to let familiar abbreviations slip unexplained into letters and memos. Surely, you think, my readers know about PIP's and LEA's and SIS's. Do they? Perhaps. The test is this: If every single reader of what you write is likely to know what your abbreviations (or acronyms) stand for, there is no problem. If a few of them are left in the dark, however—if a few of them sit there, letter or memo in hand, groping for your meaning—then it might have been better to avoid those bunched capitals, or explain them in parentheses, or spell out the whole abbreviated name.

ACCEPTANCES AND APPROVALS

9

CHAPTER 9

This chapter contains letters of acceptance of jobs, honors, resignations, and retirements, as well as letters in a few related categories. Most of them are pleasant and positive, although one, while renewing a teacher's contract, insists that future performance must show improvement.

As a group, these letters have the same virtues as the earlier letters in the book. They begin effectively. They are clear and unambiguous. They are well-organized and well-written. They are concise. They are specific. They show a keen awareness of audience.

In short, they are easy to read and understand. Line by line, the reader knows what is being said. There is evidence that the writers planned them before beginning to write or dictate, and then reread and edited at least one draft.

Another virtue worth mentioning is this: generally speaking, the letters contain fairly short paragraphs. As newspaper editors know, short paragraphs tend to invite readers, while long paragraphs have the opposite effect. The writers of these letters also recognize that fact.

ACCEPTANCE OF TEACHER'S RESIGNATION

Lewistown Public Schools

School District Number One

RONALD B. MATTSON
SUPERINTENDENT

SHARON L. MCNEES
DISTRICT CLERK

LINCOLN SCHOOL BUILDING
215 7TH AVENUE SOUTH
LEWISTOWN, MONTANA
59457

TELEPHONE:
538-8777

October 1, 19xx

Miss Rita Glasgow
44 Moulton Drive
Mansfield, Montana 59400

Dear Miss Glasgow:

At their regular meeting on September 28, 19xx, the School District #1 Trustees voted to accept your resignation as a teacher at Fergus High School, effective December 10, 19xx, because of your poor health.

The Trustees asked me to express their feelings of loss to our school and district. They and I believe that your resignation creates a vacancy that will be extremely difficult to fill.

Your pleasant and positive outlook on life has been a refreshing and motivating influence on our students and faculty for over three decades. Students and former students often mention how much personal benefit they received from your classes and how much they enjoyed them.

Rita, you can and should be proud of your contributions to your students, your fellow teachers, and your community. Thank you for being a part of our faculty and for all that you have given us.

Sincerely,

Ronald B. Mattson

Ronald B. Mattson, Ed.D
Superintendent of Schools

OFFER OF TEACHING POSITION

This letter spells out in detail the terms of the offer, giving special prominence to the proposed salary. All the steps the new teacher must take prior to employment are also included and explained.

Dear Ms. McNary:

It is with great pleasure that I offer you the position on the Grey City Schools staff for which you were interviewed. The term of the contract is December 16, 19xx, through December 22, 19xx.

Your total salary, based on your current academic degree, graduate credit, teaching experience, and special work assignments, is shown below:

M.A. degree	$16,885
Two years' experience	900
	$17,785

Your salary prorated for the remainder of 19xx–19xx will be $8,893.

Your assignment will be ninth grade English teacher, and your immediate supervisor will be Dr. Michael Seligman.

Enclosed are the original and two copies of your contract to teach in the Grey City Schools. Please sign all three copies and return them immediately to me at the above address.

We must also have in our files official transcripts of all your college and university course work. If you have not already sent them, please do so. Also, check your teacher certification through the Teachers Certification Office at 1535 West Jefferson in Phoenix. If your Arizona Teaching Certificate is due to expire on July 2, 19xx, you should begin working toward its renewal immediately. Once you have received your teacher's certificate, be sure to have it registered at the Jacobs County Superintendent's Office, 131 East Cochise Street, Grey City. This is your individual responsibility, and we cannot place you on our payroll until the certificate has been registered.

Our Grey City Schools personnel office must also register a copy of your certificate as well as have verification of previous employment for your personnel file.

You will be eligible for major medical/hospitalization insurance effective January 1, 19xx. You should continue your present insurance plan through that date, if you are enrolled in one. Please remember to sign up in the payroll office for any benefits for which you are eligible. The payroll office would also appreciate your completion of the enclosed forms. The loyalty oath will be notarized when you submit it. All forms should be returned with your signed contract.

If you have any further questions regarding this offer, please feel free to call me at any time. I am looking forward to having you as a member of our Grey City Schools staff.

ACCEPTANCE OF TEACHING POSITION

Acceptances are brief and courteous. Although this is a teacher's letter, one written to accept a principal's position would not be essentially different.

Dear Dr. Bouse:

Thank you very much for your offer of a ninth grade English teaching position at Grey City High School. I accept it with pleasure.

Enclosed are the three signed copies of the contract along with filled-out copies of the forms that you included with them. I will take all the steps that you indicate in your letter of November 24.

I look forward with great anticipation to the challenges of this new position.

ACCEPTANCE OF CANDIDATE FOR PRINCIPAL

Here is a good example of a letter that stresses the word *you*. Everyone likes a letter that speaks directly to the recipient, especialy when the news, as here, is favorable. The use of *you* helps to establish personal contact.

Dear Mr. Hazen:

You will be pleased to learn that at the June 18 meeting of the Kilmer County Board of Education you were approved as the new principal of McClellan Middle School.

Everyone on the board was impressed by your handling of the interview and by your obvious depth and breadth of knowledge and your commitment to public education. It is especially gratifying to be able to choose a candidate who began his career in the Kilmer Schools as a teacher and is now ready to advance to this important administrative position. We are confident you will be as successful as a principal as you have been for the past seven years as a classroom teacher and an assistant principal.

Please make an appointment with my office as soon as possible so that we can take care of the necessary paper work and discuss your new assignment at length.

RENEWAL OF TEACHER'S CONTRACT WITH RESERVATIONS

This letter, too, stresses *you,* but it conveys a message of warning as well as one of good wishes. Note how specific (and imperative) the numbered recommendations are.

Dear Mr. Underhill:

The School Directors of the Dewey Town School District voted to offer you a contract for the 19xx–19xx school year.

At the same time, the administrators and directors expressed concern about certain aspects of your performance that need improvement. Shop housekeeping, tool control and maintenance, and organization of shop procedures are areas that your principal, Mr. Albans, has discussed with you in the past. The reports from Mr. Johnson, the Industrial Arts consultant, and Mr. Cady, the State Fire Marshal, both expressed concern about safety in the shop. Their reports contained the following advice:

1. Clean the shop by removing all unnecessary items that are lying around.
2. Develop and maintain a cleanup procedure for each class.
3. Develop and follow a method of tool control and maintenance.
4. Lock up all tools when the shop is closed.
5. Report safety and fire hazards and remedy them as soon as possible.

We expect improvement in these areas during the rest of this year and next year.

We are not overlooking the many positive things you are doing. You have good class control. Your students, who vary greatly in interests and abilities, receive individual attention and instruction. The projects of your students show workmanship and care.

All in all, many good things are happening in your classes, and we recognize this. However, improved neatness and better organized procedures will help reflect the proper attitude and respect toward good work that are part of your teaching objectives. An example, like a picture, is worth a thousand words.

In summary, you are a valued teacher, but in the future you must show improvement in the areas mentioned in this letter.

ACCEPTANCE OF APPLICANT FOR FOOD SERVICE ATTENDANT

Official notice of a nonprofessional appointment can be quite short.

Dear Mrs. Hibbart:

It is a pleasure to inform you that the Grey City Schools Board of Education at its regular meeting on November 8, 19xx, officially approved your appointment as a Food Service Attendant at North Junior High School.

I look forward to working with you in this new position and wish you every success in the Grey City Schools. If I can be of any assistance, do not hesitate to call me.

Sincerely,

T. R. Gladden
Associate Superintendent
Educational Services

REQUEST FOR ACCEPTANCE OF ATHLETIC ELIGIBILITY CLAIM

This letter is a principal's request to the state interscholastic athletic association to reopen the question of a student's eligibility. The principal makes his points clearly and effectively. The use of numbering helps focus the reader's attention on the major points.

Dear Mr. Washburn:

This letter is written to request that the Board of Control of the Wisconsin Interscholastic Athletic Association reconsider the question of Tony Ingram's eligibility for interscholastic athletics.

As you will recall, during the 19xx–19xx school year, Mr. and Mrs. Merrill Ingram, with our support, petitioned for the eligibility of their son Tony. The petition was denied. However, two changes in circumstances have occurred since then.

1. Tony is enrolled as a full-time student at Ferber High School. Last year that was only a possibility; now it is a reality.

2. The Board of Control has relaxed its position on restricting foreign students to a maximum of four years' eligibility. In a number of cases, it has extended full eligibility to fifth year foreign students. Since Tony spent one of his high school years in England, his situation is similar to that of these foreign students.

Tony, who has a hearing impairment, spent one year in England. He did not meet the educational objectives for graduation, and he has returned to Ferber this year. He is aware that his chances of becoming eligible are remote. My own feeling, though, is that his own changed circumstances plus the new position of the Board of Control have altered the situation.

I respectfully request that Tony Ingram's eligibility status be re-examined at the earliest opportunity. Thank you.

APPROVAL OF AN IDEA

Here the writer strikes just the right note of informality.

Dear Cal:

The more I thought about the idea you presented at our last faculty meeting, the better I liked it. You really have come up with a creative idea for involving parents in our Gifted and Talented Program.

We still have to work out the details of your plan, and to that end I would like to meet with you later in the week to discuss implementing it. Would Thursday at 3:00 p.m. in my office be all right?

Your imagination, so much in evidence as a classroom teacher and basketball coach, will be invaluable in helping us carry out this idea successfully.

Thank you for thinking of it—now let's make it work.

RECEIPT OF A REPORT

Most people, teachers as well as students, like an immediate response to the work they have done. This response can sometimes take the form of a brief acknowledgment, as it does here.

TO: Members of Social Studies Curriculum Committee
FROM: Glen Garfilli, Principal
SUBJECT: Report on Revised Curriculum

Your final report arrived on my desk this morning. At first reading, it appears to be a superbly detailed and highly penetrating examination of the results of our recently revised Social Studies curriculum.

This report will receive my full attention within the next two weeks.

When I have given it the study it deserves, I will let you know my reactions and my thoughts on what steps we might take next. In the meantime, let me congratulate you on completing this demanding task in a thoughtful, thorough, and timely manner. You have shown true professionalism.

ACCEPTANCE OF A GIFT

This is an exceptionally gracious acceptance of a gift. It is a letter that is sure to make the giver proud and happy to have chosen the school as the recipient.

Dear Mrs. Schooley:

What a pleasure and surprise it was to learn that you will be donating the oil portrait of your late father, Mr. Aaron Cooper, to Cooper Junior High School. I cannot think of a nicer gift.

Your father was a truly great teacher and principal in the Paine Township Public Schools. He was an inspiration to everyone who knew him, worked with him, or studied with him. When our new building was built, there was unanimous agreement that it be named for him.

Even so, we have never had a portrait of your father on display. The best we had was a small 5 × 7 black-and-white photograph in a gold frame on my desk. Now we will have the magnificent oil portrait that has hung in your living room for so many years. I am pleased and proud that you would remember us in this way.

I cannot tell you at this time precisely where we will hang the portrait, but I can assure you that we will do everything possible to ensure its visual prominence along with its physical security. When we have received the picture and have had it hung, I will invite you to come to the school for a small ceremony of appreciation.

In the meantime, let me emphasize how delighted the staff and I are with this acquisition. We will continue to do our best to live up to the ideals of you and your father.

Thank you.

ACCEPTANCE OF AN HONOR

A friendly, clever note of acceptance seems apropos in this case. The parenthetical quote adds to the cheerful tone of the letter.

Dear Mr. Norris:

It is probably a cliché to say that my great and unexpected good fortune in being named Elm City's Man of the Year is one of the high points of my life. Still, I want to say it. When I think of the number of outstanding men in this community—men in business, politics, the arts—who might have achieved the honor, I am genuinely overwhelmed.

Yes, I will by all means attend the April 18 banquet and be prepared to say a few words during the awards ceremony. At the moment, words nearly fail me, but I suppose that in the two weeks between now and then I will have at least a partial return of loquacity. ("Getting Tom to talk is easy," said a colleague. "Getting him to stop is what's tough.")

Please accept my personal thanks, and my thanks on behalf of the other educators of Elm City, for this high and unique honor.

ACCEPTANCE OF FOOD SERVICE ATTENDANT'S RESIGNATION

A pleasant, concise letter is appropriate for a resignation of this kind.

Dear Ms. Crozier:

Your resignation has been officially approved by the Grey City Schools Board of Education at its regular meeting on November 7, 19xx.

We appreciate the contribution you have made to the students in the Grey City Schools as a Food Service Attendant at Garcia School.

Thank you for all your efforts. We wish you every success in the future.

Sincerely,

T. R. Gladden
Associate Superintendent
Educational Services

ACCEPTANCE OF REQUEST FOR EARLY RETIREMENT

In this letter, the writer might have gone into greater detail had there not been a retirement banquet scheduled for the near future. As it is, the letter is basically one of official notice.

Dear Mr. Polacca:

You will be pleased to learn that your request for early retirement, effective June 24, 19xx, has been officially approved by the Grey City Schools Board of Education at its regular meeting on March 20, 19xx.

We greatly appreciate the many contributions you have made to the district. Our expressions of gratitude at this time may seem inadequate, but we will show our appreciation more fully and formally at our retirement banquet on May 19, 19xx.

All the best to you. We wish you health and happiness as you prepare for the new and exciting experiences that lie ahead. If we can be of any help in your planning, please let us know.

LETTER ON TEACHER'S RETIREMENT

Here is a letter with a slightly different, and very appealing, opening paragraph. In the third paragraph, the writer mentions a specific accomplishment of the retiree. All in all, this is an excellent retirement letter.

Dear Mrs. Gatlin:

Let me wish you much happiness in your retirement and thank you for the many contributions you have made to Farragut Middle School.

Over the years I have worked with you, it has been an honor and a pleasure to get to know you on both a professional and a personal basis. On both counts, I hold you in high esteem. Indeed, you are not only a caring human being but a professional educator in every sense of the word.

I know the staff and students at Farragut will miss you. You have left behind a fine program, especially the sixth-grade band that you initiated. It will continue to benefit both students and the community in the years to come.

It is my sincere hope that your retirement years will bring you joy and fulfillment. Best wishes, and don't forget to visit us when you have the opportunity.

❧ A Word on Style ❧

PAY ATTENTION TO TRANSITIONS

English teachers call it coherence. It is the "sticking together" of sentences and paragraphs, and it may be the hardest thing for anyone—even the most experienced writers—to do well.

When you start to write a letter or memo, you already know your subject thoroughly. Your reader does not know it half so well. Therefore, you are going to have to join together all the links in the chain, to fill in the gaps, and you are likely to find it difficult.

Most audiences for your letters, as for other kinds of writing, are a mixed group. Some know a great deal about your subject, some know nothing. An informed reader can supply an astonishing number of connections, even in letters that make very few connections on their own. An uninformed reader, of course, is lost.

English teachers will tell you to pay attention to the *however's,* the *therefore's,* the *then's,* and the *next's.* Their advice is good—as far as it goes. The deeper problem is one of clear and sequential thought and logic. The transitional words, important as they are, require a firm grounding in reality. Much the tougher (and much the better) transitions are invisible. They are those that carry the reader from sentence to sentence, from paragraph to paragraph, without the intrusive use of signals.

REJECTIONS AND DISMISSALS

10

CHAPTER 10

The letters in this chapter are excellent examples of difficult-to-write rejections and dismissals. They range from a note rejecting an idea to a letter dismissing, or proposing to dismiss, a nonprofessional employee.

In one sense these letters are negative. They say, "No," or else they take, or propose taking, unpopular actions. Nevertheless, the letters are tactful. Judiciously and courteously written, they are not likely to make their recipients see red.

One reason they work so well is that the writers, particularly of the rejection letters, feel empathy with their readers. Even though the circumstances may be trying, the letter writers try to put themselves in the position of the recipient. They try to take his or her feelings into account. In doing so, they make the rejection less bitter.

Another reason for the success of the letters is that the writers do not just say, "No." They give valid reasons for the rejections. Therefore, while the readers will not be pleased, they will not regard the rejections as arbitrary.

NOTICE OF HAVING HIRED SOMEONE ELSE

NORTH SLOPE BOROUGH SCHOOL DISTRICT

P.O. Box 169 • Barrow, Alaska 99723 • (907) 852-5311

July 2, 19xx

Ms. Ruby Wainwright
160 East 10th Street
Lennon, California 94500

Dear Ms. Wainwright:

This letter is to inform you that I have selected John Burney from San Francisco as the public information officer for our district. This was a difficult task for me because of the large number of exceptionally qualified people who applied. You are well qualified, and I am certain that with your experience and skill level you will continue to be a success in your field.

I want to thank you for the time you took to discuss the position with me and for the interest you have shown in our district. I will attempt to return all the information that you sent me. If I fail to return a particular item that you need, please let me know, and I will do my best to get it back to you.

I sincerely hope you reach the goals you have set for yourself. I hope, too, that someday our paths will cross again.

Sincerely,

Don Renfroe
Superintendent of Schools

161

REJECTION OF OFFER OF SPONSORSHIP

Here is a courteous letter in which the writer points out that what was requested is impossible. Notice that it starts with the always cordial "Thank you."

Mrs. D. Wells Slaton, Chairwoman
Marion Ward Chapter
Daughters of the American Revolution
Dobie, Texas 78400

Dear Mrs. Slaton:

Thank you for your interest in sponsoring an ROTC award in our school this year. We feel that the Daughters of the American Revolution do a tremendous job in upholding the ideals upon which our great nation was founded.

At one time our school had an active ROTC program. However, we no longer have it. Today, the only school in Dobie with an active ROTC program is Rayburn High School.

If we ever have the ROTC program again in our school, we will be happy to ask the Marion Ward Chapter, DAR, to sponsor such an award.

REJECTION OF AN IDEA

Although the reader of this letter will be disappointed, he will probably also be flattered by the detailed, sympathetic content. The writer does not reject the idea out of hand; he explains fully why it cannot be put into effect.

Dear Mr. Nolan:

It is always helpful to receive a staff member's suggestions when they are based on thoughtful analysis and careful research. Your recommendations on how to improve the appearance and acoustics of our school auditorium clearly fit that description. You are to be commended on making an excellent proposal.

Because of budgetary restrictions, however, we will not be able to make the changes you suggest. The cost would be high, as you point out, and the improvements, while real, would not justify spending so great a percentage of our budget. Perhaps the time will come when we can make these changes, but not in the near future.

I wish I could be more positive. You obviously put a great deal of thought, imagination, and effort into your proposal, and I appreciate what you have done. Your idea is sound in principle, but it cannot be implemented. I wish we had a bit more money.

INSUFFICIENCY OF CREDITS FOR GRADUATION

This, in effect, is the rejection of a student's request to receive a high school diploma. The question is sufficiency of credits. The writer reviews the background of the case before concluding that the student must still complete one course.

Dear May:

Thank you for your letter of October 17 concerning the credits allowed for your year of study at the Hughes School.

On the question of whether you now have sufficient credits to graduate from Dobie High School, I have gone over your transcript and evaluated the situation. If I recall our conversation this summer correctly, we were going to see if Hughes granted credit for your incomplete second semester of cosmetology at Dobie.

Since Hughes did not grant credit, and since we can allow credit earned at a private school only for those courses taken through a public school program, you do not have enough credits to graduate. The only thing we can suggest is that you return to Dobie High School the second semester to take cosmetology. If you do this and pass, you will have the credits you need to graduate.

I will hold on to all of your records in case you want to consider enrolling here in January. If you do this, you can enroll for cosmetology only and not attend any other classes.

Please let me hear from you.

NONAVAILABILITY OF APPLIED-FOR POSITION

A superintendent in a district that receives a very large number of unsolicited applications for teaching positions created this letter to answer them. The key sentence is, "Consequently, we consider only those applicants who apply for a listed position."

Dear Ms. Jordan:

Thank you for your letter of April 22 inquiring about teaching positions in the Rankin Public Schools.

Currently there are no openings, nor do we anticipate any, for the 19xx–19xx school year. If a vacancy does occur, it will be listed in all of our in-state teacher placement agencies.

We receive a great many unsolicited applications. Because of the variety of qualifications of the applicants and the variety of qualifications needed for our openings, we have found it difficult to give unsolicited applications proper consideration. Consequently, we consider only those applicants who apply for a listed opening.

I suggest that you watch your teacher placement agency listings, and if you note an opening from our school district, send us a letter of application for that specific opening.

We appreciate your interest in our school district.

RETENTION OF APPLICATION FOR NONAVAILABLE POSITION

This letter implies there is at least a chance that a teaching position will open up in the foreseeable future.

Dear Mr. Montevallo:

Thank you for your interest in obtaining a teaching position in the Andrews Public Schools.

At the moment, there are no appropriate positions open. However, we will give you careful consideration when a vacancy occurs for which you are certified.

Your application will be placed in our active files.

REJECTION OF CANDIDATE FOR POSITION

It is never easy or pleasant to reject a well-qualified candidate, but when teaching positions are at a premium, it has to be done. This letter does it nicely.

Dear Mr. Budd:

When our interviewing was over, and the position for which you applied was to be filled, we found the choice difficult. We interviewed a great many applicants, and all of them had excellent qualifications.

We regret to inform you that another candidate has been chosen for the position. Our decision is likely to be disappointing to you, but in view of the high quality of the candidates, you should not regard it as any reflection on you or your abilities.

Your application will be kept on file through the next school year in case any unexpected openings occur.

Thank you again for your application, your time, and your dedication to the field of education.

RELEASE FROM CONTRACT, WITH PROVISO

In this letter a superintendent cites both policy and law to show that, given the facts in the case, a teacher cannot, strictly speaking, escape her contractual obligations. Nevertheless, she is released with a proviso.

Dear Ms. Heineman:

This is in reply to your letter of August 8, 19xx, regarding a request for release from the contract you signed to teach in the Longstreet County Public Schools during the 19xx–19xx school year.

Please note the following portion of Board Policy #4087:

"After July 15, release from contractual obligations will be approved only for reasons of sickness, change of spouse's residence out of the district, maternity, or family emergencies. No employee will be released until a satisfactory replacement has been secured or the Superintendent of Schools determines that no replacement will be necessary. Generally, employees will not be released after July 15 and/or during the school term to enable the employee other employment."

In addition, I quote South Carolina law on the subject for your information:

"Any teacher who fails to comply with the provisions of his contract without the written consent of the School Board shall be deemed guilty of unprofessional conduct. A breach of contract resulting from the execution of an employment contract with another board within the State without the consent of the board first employing the teacher makes void any subsequent contract with any other school district in South Carolina for the same employment period. Upon the formal complaint of the School Board, substantiated by conclusive evidence, the State Board shall suspend or revoke the teacher's certificate for a period not to exceed one calendar year. State education agencies in other states with reciprocal certification agreements shall be notified of the revocation of the certificate."

The circumstances described in your letter of August 8 were well known to you far in advance of the July 15 deadline. However, I am approving your request for release from contract with the proviso that you are not eligible for reemployment in this school district.

RECOMMENDED TERMINATION OF CAFETERIA WORKER

This is a diplomatic memo on a touchy topic.

TO: Helen Jennings, Cafeteria Supervisor
FROM: Carol Overstreet, Principal
SUBJECT: Wilma Vernon, Cafeteria Worker

This memo is written to request that some consideration be given to terminating cafeteria worker Wilma Vernon.

Wilma has been employed here at Stilwell Junior High School for three years and has been a continual source of disruption and discontent. Several other workers have quit rather than endure her rude and aggressive behavior.

In this school year, she has been the central figure in virtually every unpleasant and disruptive situation. She seems unable to get along with *any* other worker—so it is not a case of bad feelings between her and only one or two others.

The cafeteria is an area critical to the operation of our school, and this constant source of irritation and discontent is detrimental to the service provided to students. I know that many people have tried to counsel Wilma, but to no avail. While I am wholly in favor of helping employees grow and improve in their positions, I think we must identify the time when such counseling has failed and think about other alternatives. It is not fair to other workers, who are trying to run a quality service, to be hampered by a single malcontent.

Do you agree that termination is the appropriate action?

DISMISSAL OF MAINTENANCE WORKER

Signed by the President and the Secretary of the Board of School Directors, this letter conveys specific, exact information. Because of the nature of the letter, its wording is somewhat legalistic.

Dear Mr. Gillett:

You are hereby notified in accordance with section 514 of the Public School Code of 1949, 24 P.S. 5-514, that the District Superintendent has recommended that the Board of School Directors of the Feldon School District dismiss you from employment as a maintenance worker for the district. The Board will hear this recommendation for your dismissal at its regularly scheduled meeting on January 12, 19xx. The Board will decide at that time if you are to be dismissed.

This correspondence will provide you with a detailed, written statement of the charges upon which your proposed dismissal is based.

In determining whether you should be dismissed, the Board will consider whether any or all of the allegations regarding your conduct set forth below are true, and, if true, whether all or part of such conduct constitutes cause for dismissal under the terms of section 514 of the Public School Code of 1949, 24 P.S. 5-514. A copy of the District Superintendent's recommendation is enclosed.

It is specifically charged, and the Board will determine, whether your conduct during the 19xx–19xx school year provides a valid cause for your dismissal for incompetence, neglect of duty, violation of the school laws of this state, and/or other improper conduct.

In particular, the Board will consider these allegations:

1. You were excessively and/or unjustifiably tardy on various dates during July through December 19xx.
2. You were excessively and/or unjustifiably absent on various dates during July through December 19xx.
3. You failed to obey school district policy and procedures by not calling in when you were to be absent or late.
4. You were involved in an assault upon a fellow employee on August 22, 19xx, for which you were suspended for two working days. You were then informed that further violations would result in severe discipline, yet you continued to violate district work rules.
5. You were found sleeping on the job in June and August 19xx.
6. You have otherwise neglected your duty, violated district rules, or demonstrated incompetence as based on the attached documentation, consisting of 19 pages.

Section 514 of the Public School Code of 1949 allows you to demand a hearing before the Board of School Directors prior to the Board's making its decision on your proposed dismissal. Should you choose to exercise this right, you or your representative must request the hearing in writing. This request must be received by the District Superintendent at his office no later than 3:00 p.m. on January 12, 19xx.

Failure to demand a hearing prior to that time will be deemed a waiver of your right to a hearing, and the Board will make its decision at the meeting noted above, based on the evidence presented to it by the administration. If you demand a hearing, you will be advised in writing of the date, time, and place it will be held.

Your suspension without pay is continued pending the Board's decision.

≋ A Word on Style ≋

SIDESTEP GRAMMATICAL PROBLEMS

When a problem in grammar is tricky or obscure—or when the correct choice of a word or phrase sounds wrong—the best solution is often that of the Cowardly Lion. Back off. Get away from it. Instead of puzzling over two poor choices, or taking a hopeful guess, simply forget the sentence as you first drafted it. Rewrite it. That kind of an end run will often take less time than researching Warriner, and it will usually result in a better sentence.

CONGRATULATIONS   **11**

CHAPTER 11

In this chapter the letters are ones of praise. The first of them have to do with students and are written either to students or to their parents. The letters offer congratulations on a straight "A" report card, a project, a science fair achievement, a mathematics contest, and various other accomplishments.

Another group of letters is aimed at teachers, complimenting them for perfect attendance, a first band concert, a Teacher of the Year award. There are also congratulations on a teacher's marriage and the birth of a child.

The final letters in the chapter are written to newly elected, or reelected, school board members and public officials.

All the letters are congratulatory, and, as a consequence, they have obvious similarities. For one thing, nearly all of them use the word "Congratulations" or some form of it. A few of the letters use the word twice. Most of them are relatively short, as good letters of congratulations tend to be.

Indeed, the letter writers themselves merit congratulations for the fine congratulatory letters they have written.

STUDENT'S ELECTION TO NATIONAL HONOR SOCIETY

Department of Public Schools

EAST PROVIDENCE, R.I. 02914

MYRON J. FRANCIS
SUPERINTENDENT
JOAN E. KENT
EXECUTIVE SECRETARY
PETER G. BARILLA
DIRECTOR OF BUSINESS

June 8, 19xx

Mr. Arnold Greene
East Providence Senior High School
East Providence, Rhode Island

Dear Arnold,

On behalf of the East Providence School Committee, the School Department, and the administration and faculty at East Providence Senior High School, I would like to congratulate you on your recent election to the National Honor Society.

This very high honor is indicative of one who has achieved significant success in the field of academics as well as one who personifies the highest standards of service, leadership, and character. You are in every respect a model student and one in whom we have the greatest pride.

We would also like to congratulate your parents, who have contributed so much to what you are and what you have accomplished.

We have the greatest confidence in you and your chances for continued success in your future endeavors, whatever they may be.

Sincerely yours,

M. J. Francis

Myron J. Francis
Superintendent of Schools

CONGRATULATIONS ON STRAIGHT "A" REPORT CARD

The easiest and perhaps the best way to begin a letter of congratulations is the way this writer does, with the word "Congratulations."

Dear Shirley:

Congratulations on your outstanding accomplishment of earning a straight "A" report card for the first marking period. What a wonderful way to begin your three years at Hamilton Middle School!

Knowing that your mark of "A" in every subject did not just happen but required hard work and extra effort on your part, you can be very pleased with your accomplishment. You have once again fulfilled the confidence and pride that your parents have in you.

You have begun the school year exceptionally well. I hope you will maintain your interest in school, persevere in your hard work, and continue to enjoy academic success.

LETTER TO PARENTS PRAISING STUDENT'S PROJECT

This letter would surely be a welcome one for any parents to receive.

Dear Mr. and Mrs. Corum:

This letter is to make you aware of the outstanding job your daughter Roslyn did on a project concerning trees. Roslyn completed the project for science class.

Roslyn's science teacher, Mr. Pulaski, has told me twice how pleased and impressed he was with Roslyn's project and the work that went into preparing her report to the class. I believe Roslyn's work was the highlight of Mr. Pulaski's week.

Mr. Pulaski has congratulated Roslyn on her effort, and I have also expressed my congratulations to her. Because you could not observe Roslyn's presentation, I am writing this letter so that you, too, can have the satisfaction of knowing how well Roslyn performed.

CONGRATULATIONS ON STUDENT COUNCIL CAMPAIGN

The principal of a middle school sent this note to each of the ten candidates in the election.

Dear Catherine:

This note is to let you know how impressed I was with the Student Council campaign today and with how well you handled yourself and spoke to the students in the three assemblies. You were well prepared and very poised.

Good luck to you in the elections. It is unfortunate that every candidate cannot win. Win or lose, however, you have earned the respect and admiration of your teachers and classmates for your outstanding performance today.

PRAISE FOR STUDENT'S SCIENCE FAIR ACCOMPLISHMENT

A letter of congratulations is usually short, but it should specify the accomplishment being honored. The following superintendent's letter is a good example. It starts with "Congratulations," identifies the achievement, points out its importance, and thanks the parents and teacher for their support.

Dear Neal:

Congratulations! Your accomplishment at the 19xx Science Fair was just great. Your "Origin of the 3.28 Micron Line Emission in Planetary Nebula NGC 6369" is an excellent piece of research.

I am especially pleased with your success because it demonstrates the kind of intellectual excellence that is my goal for this district.

Thanks are also due to your parents and to Ms. Tanaka, your science teacher, for their support.

Everyone in the district is proud of you. We wish you good luck in your future academic endeavors.

CONGRATULATIONS ON WINNING STATE MATHEMATICS CONTEST

Generally speaking, the higher the award, the more appropriate it is to send a congratulatory note.

Dear Adam:

You are to be congratulated on your outstanding achievement in the state mathematics contest held recently at Parton-Allman University. This is an achievement for which any student might feel justifiably proud. The fact that you were competing against the best students in the state makes it all the more wonderful.

I want you to know that your teachers and the administration at Franklin Memorial High School are extremely proud of your accomplishment.

It has been a pleasure to have you at FMHS. Let me wish you a very happy spring vacation and continued success in your study of mathematics.

LETTER TO NATIONAL MERIT SCHOLARSHIP SEMIFINALIST

Here is another excellent letter praising a student for a high achievement. Notice the second paragraph, in which, as in a previous letter, the parents are credited, too.

Dear Alex:

Congratulations on your selection as a semifinalist in the 19xx National Merit Scholarship Program. This is an extraordinary honor, and it speaks highly of your academic aptitude and achievement.

Please extend my congratulations to your parents. High achievement is usually the result of many positive factors—initiative, ability, parental influence, and school environment. I firmly believe that the guidance and encouragement of parents is vitally important in promoting academic achievements.

I hope once again to have the chance to hear you perform at concerts and other events during the 19xx–19xx school year.

Best wishes.

CONGRATULATIONS ON SELECTION FOR ADVANCED PLACEMENT

This letter is both congratulatory and informative. It is the student's first notice that she has been chosen for Advanced Placement English.

Dear Florence:

It is my pleasure to tell you the good news that you are one of only 16 eighth graders chosen by the English teachers at Stanwyck Park High School for Grade 9 Advanced Placement English. Congratulations!

You can be very proud of being chosen for the Advanced Placement English class. Your selection reflects the fine work that you, your parents, and your teachers have done over a number of years to develop your writing and speaking skills.

Selection for Advanced Placement was based on the written test you completed in school during December. Actual assignment to your English 9 class will take place when you and your parents meet with Mr. Fancher and Ms. Valcour within the next couple of months to prepare your entire ninth grade schedule of classes.

Best wishes to you in Advanced Placement English.

PRAISE FOR ACHIEVING HIGH ACADEMIC HONORS

Here is a brief note from the superintendent praising a student for her fourth-quarter grades.

Dear Benedicta:

It is my pleasure to congratulate you on receiving high honors for the fourth quarter at Hamlin High School. You will be rewarded throughout life for the extra effort you have put forth to achieve such academic excellence during your high school years.

Have a nice summer!

CONGRATULATIONS ON HIGH SCHOOL GRADUATION

This is a special letter to an outstanding student.

Dear Esther:

Let me congratulate you on the occasion of your graduation from Alcott High School and to commend you most highly for your extraordinary achievements. You have impressed me throughout your four years as a truly outstanding student. You have always been hard-working, well-groomed, extremely well-mannered, most trustworthy, and loyal.

During the past four years, I have watched you grow more poised and confident in your capabilities and have been pleased to see that growth. You have contributed much to your school, and that contribution has helped your own development.

Particularly remarkable have been your accomplishments and many fine contributions in music. You have developed your talent to an extraordinary degree. You have shared your voice with your classmates and the community and, in doing so, have enriched the quality of our school community. I encourage you to nurture and develop your musical abilities further in the years ahead.

I know you will do well at Hawthorne College and will continue to make all of us, including your parents, proud of your accomplishments. More than that, I know you will continue to be the fine young woman you have become.

Best wishes in all the years ahead. May they be happy and fulfilling ones for you.

LETTER CONGRATULATING TEACHER ON ATTENDANCE

Effective letters of congratulations, like all good letters, have strong endings. Note the various endings of the letters in this chapter, including this one: "**Keep up the good work!**"

Dear Mr. Wakefield:

It has been and will continue to be my practice to pass on compliments to personnel in the East Greene Public Schools when I feel they are justified. All too often the only things people hear from administrators are negative ones—and that is wrong!

Recently our Personnel Department made me aware of your fine attendance record for the 19xx–19xx school year. You should be justly proud of having achieved this attendance record. We in the School Department are appreciative of your efforts in achieving the record.

We recognize that illness is many times unavoidable and often not controllable. Nevertheless, we are aware of the fact that there are always borderline days. On those days commitment and personal dedication to duty can and do make the difference in a teacher's attendance. We want you to know that we are aware of your extra effort this past year, and we want to take this means of commending you for it.

Thank you for your conscientiousness, which has contributed in a very real way to the success of the East Greene Public Schools. Keep up the good work!

CONGRATULATIONS TO TEACHER OF THE YEAR

This is a cheerful yet thoughtful letter congratulating the district's Teacher of the Year. The nouns and adjectives are particularly well chosen.

Dear Mrs. Kona:

You are Teacher!

As Pauahi District's Teacher of the Year, you represent the highest ideals of teaching. You richly deserve the recognition and accolades for your excellence, enthusiasm, and concern. You have consistently demonstrated that "high expectations bring high performance."

It makes me very happy that this is part of your philosophy, because through the principals I have been trying to transmit Pauahi District's objective: "Good is not our goal; we strive for excellence."

I know you will ably represent all the good teachers of the Pauahi District in the statewide competition.

Congratulations, and thank you very much for your dedicated and superior teaching.

MEMO PRAISING MUSIC TEACHER FOR CONCERT

Here is a pleasant memo of congratulations. The incident related in it adds a lot to its appeal.

TO: Charlotte Eddy
FROM: G. F. Wilton, Principal
SUBJECT: Band Concert

Last night's band concert was delightful! More parents than ever before stopped me in the hall to congratulate me.

You are the one who deserves the congratulations. The music was exceptionally well received. And when the fire alarm sounded in the middle of your concert, you never missed a beat. Now, that is the sign of a real pro.

Your first band concert at South Hughes High School turned out to be a smashing success! I am looking forward to many more.

Thank you for asking me to introduce the program.

CONGRATULATIONS TO WINNING COACH

Actually, this is a dual-purpose letter. It is a covering letter for a report, and it is also a letter congratulating the head wrestling coach.

Dear Al:

Enclosed is a report I plan to submit to the District Committee on the accomplishments of wrestlers from our district. I would appreciate your looking it over and seeing if I have made any mistakes or overlooked anything. If you find errors or omissions, please give me a call.

I want to congratulate you on another outstanding wrestling season! It is quite an honor to have two state champions, not to mention winning the AA State Team Championship. You have accomplished so much, the praise could go on and on, but you have heard most of it before—from students, from parents, from teachers, and from me.

It is always a pleasure working with you. Thanks to you, District 4 Wrestling is now at an all-time high in interest, attendance, and achievement.

BEST WISHES ON TEACHER'S MARRIAGE

This is a short but excellent note.

Dear Jeannette:

On behalf of the Board of Education and the Fosterville staff, I extend congratulations on your forthcoming marriage and wish you and Howard a bright and happy future. May your lives together as Mr. and Mrs. Vandergrift be rich and full!

CONGRATULATIONS ON BIRTH OF CHILD TO TEACHER

Here is another brief letter that accomplishes its purpose nicely.

Dear Howard and Jeannette:

Congratulations on the birth of your son! Glen William is a lucky little boy to be born into the Vandergrift family. May the years ahead be bright and happy ones for all of you.

On behalf of the Board of Education and all your friends on the Fosterville staff, I extend best wishes to you and to the newest member of your family. What a great way to begin the holidays!

SUPERINTENDENT'S CONGRATULATIONS TO NEW MAYOR

The following letter is an exceptionally gracious one to a newly elected mayor.

Dear Mayor Hughes:

Congratulations to you on your successful bid for the office of Wickersham Borough Mayor.

I must admit that when you announced as a candidate, I thought you had accepted a formidable, if not impossible, task. Your determination and self-confidence became very apparent as the campaign progressed. It became obvious to everyone that you are knowledgeable, articulate, and personable. You have great popular appeal, and the people have responded by placing on you an awesome responsibility.

Recognizing that we must all work together for the benefit of the people we serve, I offer my full support, as well as the talent and resources of my staff, to assist you in any way possible to make your administration a success.

LETTER CONGRATULATING NEW CITY COUNCIL MEMBER

Here is a more pro forma, but still excellent, letter to a recently elected public official.

Dear Dr. Truxton:

Congratulations on your election to the City Council. We in the Grey City Public Schools wish you every success as you assume your new duties.

You are to be commended for your interest in the city and your willingness to give of your time and talent to the community. We offer whatever assistance we can give you in fulfilling your council duties.

Over the years Grey City and the public schools have developed a close and, I believe unique, working relationship. We look forward to a continuation of mutual efforts to improve our community and our educational system.

Best wishes for success in your new position.

CONGRATULATIONS ON ELECTION TO BOARD OF EDUCATION

In addition to being congratulatory, this letter conveys a good deal of specific information. Note that the writer offers his congratulations twice—in the first paragraph and then again at the end. This works well in a relatively long letter.

Dear Dr. Dugas:

Congratulations! We are extremely pleased with your election to the Grey City Board of Education. Your background and experience will contribute significantly to the Grey City Public Schools.

The Board extends an invitation to you to attend all Board meetings, to sit with the Board, and to participate in Board discussions until you officially take office in January 19xx. We will provide you with a complete agenda for each meeting.

Enclosed is a notice of the "ASBA New Board Member Orientation Conference" scheduled for November 14 and 15. I will be attending the conference as a panel member and will be glad to make arrangements for your attendance, if you wish. In addition, I would like to schedule a series of discussions at your convenience to review with you the total district operational procedures.

Again, congratulations, and thank you for assuming this responsibility.

CONGRATULATIONS ON REELECTION TO SCHOOL COMMITTEE

This letter is to a committee member with whom the writer, a superintendent, has worked closely in the past. Perhaps because of that, it is quite detailed and definite about the present situation and what needs to be done in the future.

Dear Mr. Guido:

It is a pleasure for me, on behalf of the professional staff, to extend congratulations upon your reelection to the Williamston School Committee. Your known commitment and service to the Williamston Public Schools has enhanced the educational opportunities for all our students, and I am confident that as we face new challenges in the next two years, the total community will profit from your previous experience.

Williamston is a proud community, and a major source of this pride is the public schools. With the number of candidates seeking positions in city government and membership on the Williamston School Committee, the fact that no significant educational issues relating to philosophy, the direction of our schools, or the delivery of educational services became issues should be considered a vote of confidence in your leadership and a mandate to maintain existing educational priorities and services.

The next two years will be very critical for the Williamston Public Schools as we face major issues of providing adequate school financing, staffing, dealing with declining enrollment, making adequate provision for all handicapped individuals, in addition to maintaining a high level of service to our regular student and adult populations.

Again, I extend my personal congratulations to you and offer, as in the past, any professional assistance that will allow you to be successful as a committee member and will further our mutual desire to meet the needs of the Williamston students and serve the Williamston citizens.

❧ A Word on Style ❧

AIM FOR SHORT PARAGRAPHS

Academic paragraphs are long and thoroughly developed. Because of that, it is hardly surprising that school administrators sometimes write longer paragraphs than their readers would prefer. Too much unrelieved text, without any visual breaks, will bother the average reader. As editors of the tabloids discovered a long time ago, short paragraphs invite readers, long paragraphs do not.

This is not to say that you, as a school administrator, should try to emulate the *National Inquirer*. It is only to suggest that long paragraphs can often be effectively broken into two or more paragraphs, with gains in clarity, visual appeal, and effectiveness.

❧ A Word on Style ❧

CHOOSE THE EXACT WORD

As Mark Twain said, "The difference between the right word and the almost-right word is the difference between lightning and the lightning bug."

The most obvious difference between a good letter-writer and a poor one is the care with which the expert chooses words. Most people know with reasonable accuracy the meanings of the words they use. The difficulty arises because there are so many words in the language—and a lot of them are nearly synonymous. A first-draft writer will get the almost-right word much of the time. A careful writer, a writer who reads and revises, will substitute a better, more exact word.

It seems easy, and in principle it is. But the search for that exact word can sometimes take more time than a busy administrator can spare. Nevertheless, it is fair to say that important letters deserve as much attention as you can give them.

The right word is well worth the search.

APPRECIATION

12

CHAPTER 12

Letters of appreciation may well be the kind most frequently written by school administrators. Most letters of appreciation are not really optional; they have to be written. Unlike some types of communication, where a phone call or a personal conversation may do, an expression of appreciation generally demands a letter.

The thank-you letter—for that is what a letter of appreciation is—may go to a parent, a teacher, a politician, a business executive. It tends to be relatively short, and it usually includes the words "Thank you."

An effective letter of appreciation requires careful word choice. The writer's aim is to flatter the reader, but not in such an excessive, lavish way that he or she is annoyed rather than pleased. A good writer is an honest writer. An honest writer chooses the most appropriate words, not the most phosphorescent or hyperbolic words.

The letters in this chapter are effective letters of appreciation. They exemplify careful word choice. They show how a writer can successfully walk the line between praise and overpraise.

THANKS TO TEACHER FOR COMPUTER CENTER

Carson City High School

1551 Highway 50 East ▢ Carson City, Nevada 89701 ▢ (702) 885-6500

November 16, 19xx

Mr. Willard Johnson
Carson City High School
Carson City, Nevada 89701

Dear Will,

Thank you for all the time and effort you have spent over the past several years to make the Carson City High School Computer Center a reality. I know how much work was necessary to convince people of the actual need and then to test, price, and install specific units that would meet the requirements and goals of the students.

You have brought the computer classes all the way from two Monroe 1666 programmable calculators to the present system of 16 Apple II computers networking with a Corvis Hard-Drive 20 megabyte system. That your program has been well received is shown by the fact that computer mathematics has increased from one class each semester to five classes. In addition, a community college program, in such demand that enrollment is full several months in advance, is utilizing this equipment.

I sincerely value your contributions to the establishment of our Computer Center and appreciate the many extra hours you spent developing the programs from basic BASIC, Applesoft, advanced BASIC, and Pascal to COBOL and FORTRAN.

Sincerely yours,

Dr. Robert Slaby
Principal

THANKS TO STUDENT FOR ENTERING COMPETITION

Most letters of appreciation are sent to adults. This one, however, is addressed to students. The superintendent expresses his thanks for the work done by each contestant in a competition in which there will be only one winner.

Dear Maria:

Your effort and imagination in designing a new logo for the school system are admirable. On behalf of the administration and the Board of Education for the Dempsey Public Schools, I wish to extend a hearty thank you.

Maria, we all enjoyed the presentation of your logo on Thursday afternoon. It is highly welcome to a group of educators to see the talents of our young people displayed in such a professional manner.

As in many competitive events, there will be just one design finally chosen, but I feel you are already a "winner" because you accepted the challenge to participate.

Thanks once more for your time and effort on behalf of the Dempsey Public Schools. I look forward to seeing you again on February 5 at the meeting of the Board of Education.

APPRECIATION FOR SERVING AS STUDENT COUNCIL MEMBER

A letter like this one (indeed, any well-written letter) can be not only an inspiration to students, but a model as well. If students see good letters, they will learn to recognize them—and perhaps to emulate them.

Dear Clayton:

As we close out the 19xx–19xx school year, may I thank you for your services to your classmates and to the school as a member of the Hamilton Middle School Student Council. This year's Student Council was successful because of participation by you and students like you.

Your ability to work as a member of an organization, your well-organized manner, and your concern for making the school a better place were obvious to all who worked with you.

Do not abandon your interest in student government and in your school. We will need your help again next year. Your classmates will benefit from your experience and enthusiasm, and the teachers and I who work with the Student Council will welcome it.

Best wishes for an enjoyable vacation.

LETTER TO TEACHER ON REPLACEMENT AS CHAIRPERSON

In this situation the teacher is neither retiring nor resigning. She is simply stepping down as department chairperson, and the principal wishes to express his appreciation for her past efforts.

Dear Florence:

Florence, it was no easy task for me to think of replacing you as chairperson of the Foreign Language Department. In fact, it was one of the toughest jobs I had to tackle this past year.

You are a tremendously capable person and easy to work with. I could always expect a professional job from you, no matter what the task, and never had to worry about the quality of your decisions.

Thanks for giving your department and me so much of your time over the past seven years. I appreciate it more than I can say.

THANKS TO BUS DRIVER FOR ASSEMBLY PRESENTATION

Very often, as here, a letter of appreciation will start with the words "Thank you." Note that the writer explains why the bus driver's talk went over well.

Dear Alma:

Thank you for participating in our assembly program on bus conduct. Your presence and your comments to the students made the assembly much more worthwhile than if the Assistant Principal or I had attempted the same job, because the students recognized that you are an authority on what really occurs on the buses.

Your comments in the assembly showed that you have a deep understanding of the needs of our students. Everyone who has spoken to me was equally impressed. You let pupils see the feeling that a good bus driver has for her passengers, and the responsibility the driver has to pupils—and that pupils should have to the driver and to each other.

Quite a few students have mentioned to me how much they enjoyed your remarks and learned from them.

A copy of this letter of appreciation will be included in your personnel folder.

LETTER OF THANKS TO SCHOOL SECRETARY

Here is a letter of thanks to a secretary who has made a special contribution to office procedures.

Dear Mary,

Letters are easy to write when the subject is a person such as you. I particularly want to thank you for taking over when you saw a need, using your own initiative in setting up the procedure the personnel office now uses to process health insurance claims and medical benefits for all eligible faculty members.

It is with pleasure that I take this opportunity to write you and thank you for these efforts.

MEMO OF APPRECIATION FOR STAFF WORKSHOP

This memo is friendly and informal, suitable for its purpose. The word processing center is located in the district office of a medium-sized school system.

TO: Elizabeth Proctor, Coordinator of Instruction
FROM: Virginia Carr, Supervisor, Word Processing
SUBJECT: June 9 Letter-Writing Workshop

Betty, you were great yesterday! I've never seen so many women seem so excited about a comma! Thanks to you, district correspondence will look and sound much better from now on, I'm sure.

There have been many positive comments and enthusiastic discussions on letter writing since your presentation. You really generated some activity, and the word processing operators loved you.

Thanks so much for all your help. I know it took a great deal of your personal time, but many people benefited.

(I hope my grammar and punctuation in this memo are "appropriate"!)

LETTER OF THANKS TO PARENTS FOR POSITIVE COMMENTS

A parent has written a letter to the principal, noting her son's progress in school and crediting his teacher for the improvement. This is the principal's response.

Dear Mrs. Spencer:

What a welcome and deeply moving letter you sent me about the progress of your son George. I told Miss Malone that your letter was a wonderful reminder to all of us of the meaning and significance of teaching to the future of each pupil.

Thank you for taking the time to write the letter to us. You can guess that the type of letters and phone calls we usually receive from parents are of a different nature. I have shared your letter with Miss Malone and am making it a part of her permanent record in the Van Buren schools. It is refreshing to receive such a positive letter.

The type of reinforcement you are giving George cannot help but add to his good feeling about himself and to his improvement in school. Let us trust that, with Miss Malone's help and encouragement, George will continue his improvement in school.

LETTER TO TEACHER REGARDING PARENTS' LETTER OF PRAISE

Here is a response to another letter of praise, this one addressed to the superintendent of schools. The superintendent first acknowledged the parents' letter, then sent the following letter to the teacher being praised.

Dear Mr. Seymour:

Enclosed is a letter dated June 19, 19xx that I received from Mr. and Mrs. John Wilton, parents of one of your students at Putnam School.

Letters written in support of a teacher, administrator, or program in the Coltsville Public Schools, unfortunately, are few in number compared to those that express dissatisfaction. It is therefore gratifying to receive a letter stating, "The quality of the Coltsville Public Schools can only be improved by having teachers of the competency and dedication of Mr. Seymour."

As shown by this letter, it is clear that your personal efforts and your professional capabilities as an educator are deeply appreciated. I, too, would like to commend you on your performance. I am confident that the assertions made by the Wiltons are well-founded.

I thought you might enjoy keeping a copy of the Wiltons' letter for your records. A copy will also be kept in your personnel file. Keep up the good work!

THANKS FOR SERVING AS PRESIDENT OF PARENTS' ADVISORY GROUP

This letter is enhanced by the mention of a specific accomplishment.

Dear Mrs. Harrah:

Let me take this opportunity to express my appreciation to you for your two years of outstanding service to Guthrie High School and the community as President of the Parental Advisory Council. I realize that it took a lot of your personal time to accomplish the things we did during the past two years, particularly the Drug Awareness Program for parents.

Although you are no longer serving as president, I hope you will remain active in the Advisory Council. You will find enclosed a Guthrie staff card that will allow you to attend any Guthrie school activity during the 19xx–19xx school year.

THANKS TO INCOMING PRESIDENT OF PARENTS' ORGANIZATION

In this letter the writer mentions some of the shared goals of parents and educators.

Dear Mr. Randall:

On behalf of the Sinclair High School students, faculty, and staff, let me thank you for agreeing to serve as President of the Sinclair Parent Organization for 19xx–19xx. You are to be commended for exercising this kind of commitment to the education of our young people.

I look forward to a sound, cooperative working relationship with the SPO this year. I feel strongly that together we can do much to offset the shrinking educational dollar and improve the somewhat shaky image of public education in Pinckney County.

We at Sinclair recognize that parents are our partners and that our goals are shared ones. Sinclair's tradition of excellence must be maintained. The students require it, and the citizens of the community demand it.

My home telephone number is 987-6543. Should you have a concern, feel free to call me there if you cannot reach me at school.

Best wishes for a successful year as you and your fellow officers lead the Sinclair Parent Organization. The members of the group are fortunate to have your talents at their service.

APPRECIATION TO PARENT FOR BEING BUS TRIP CHAPERON

This is an exceptionally fine letter of appreciation, far more effective than a shorter, more perfunctory one would have been.

Dear Mrs. Oppenheim:

Thank you for your willingness to help make a success of this year's eighth grade trip to West Point. Having been on the trip, you can appreciate that a number of adults were needed to accompany the boys and girls, especially as we traveled around the campus. The trip was possible only because you and other parents and teachers generously gave up a Saturday to serve as chaperons.

The girls and boys experienced a full day of pageantry, history, and the excitement of being enthusiastic spectators at the football game. Some of the students would never have had this opportunity if you and the others were not willing to help. The West Point trip is a morale-builder, too. It gives a boost of enthusiasm to the eighth graders early in the school year, and in that sense the day is important to the success of the entire year—long after the day of the trip.

I hope you enjoyed the day and received a sense of satisfaction from observing the pleasure and the learning that the students derived from it.

Again, and on behalf of the boys and girls, thank you.

COMMENDATION TO PRINCIPAL FOR VISITING CLASSROOMS

Here is a letter that expresses apprecation at the same time it encourages the reader to continue his efforts.

Dear Mr. Gaines:

Approximately a month ago I took the opportunity to commend several principals who had shown exceptional effort in visiting their classrooms.

It has come to my attention that you have joined this growing number of principals who, despite the press of business, manage to visit classrooms regularly and to assess what is taking place. As a result of these visits, you can make adjustments to improve the instruction that occurs in your school.

Recognizing that the principal is the instructional leader of the school, I am convinced that knowing what actually takes place in the classroom is crucial if we in Summerall County are to continue the academic improvement for which we have been nationally recognized.

I congratulate you on placing a high emphasis in this area and for making the extra effort that means so much to the education of our students.

APPRECIATION TO SCHOOL BOARD MEMBER FOR HAVING SERVED

In many cases letters of appreciation go to people who have devoted a considerable amount of their free time to the schools. It makes sense to acknowledge that sacrifice, as the writer of this letter does.

Dear Jack:

Please permit me to express my personal appreciation for your services on the Saguaro School Board.

Your calculated, rational approach to the decision-making process is a valuable trait for a school board member. As a school superintendent, I especially appreciated your ability to provide compromise solutions to a number of difficult board decisions.

I realize how much your limited free time was eroded by serving on the board. Your profession is very demanding. To give so much of your personal time to the district demonstrated your commitment to the importance of education in the Saguaro Public Schools.

Thank you for your concern for quality education, for your concern for my personal well-being, and for being a friend.

THANKS TO MAYOR FOR SUPPORTING SCHOOLS

This letter is a glowing one from a superintendent to a mayor who is leaving office.

Dear Bill:

May your future be as bright as the past four years in Rutledge have been. Your two terms in office have revitalized and enriched Rutledge— both the city and the surrounding area. We are indeed fortunate to have had such an energetic, far-sighted public servant as our mayor.

While it is probably too early for you to think of other opportunities for public service, I do hope that the community will have the benefit of your expert leadership skills in some other capacity before you retire.

I want to thank you for your invaluable assistance to the school district during your term in office, and I wish you and your family health and happiness during the years to come.

May God bless you.

LETTER THANKING LOCAL CELEBRITY FOR TAPING ANNOUNCEMENT

A person who donates his time—and lends his reputation—to the support of an educational cause deserves a letter of thanks. Here is a good one.

Dear Mr. Johnston:

Thank you for taking so much of your valuable time to tape a television and radio public service announcement designed to reduce dropouts. As you know, students who quit school before graduation represent a tragic loss of human resources to the entire community.

Because of the waste of human potential, your help is extremely important during this period in the development of the district and the community. Your athletic and scholastic success has marked you as one of the young leaders in Rutledge and ensures that our youngsters will listen to you and accept your advice when the tapes are played during the 19xx–19xx school year.

Again, we thank you for your generous donation of time and talent, and we hope you have a great season in 19xx.

THANKS TO BUSINESSWOMAN FOR SERVING AS CONTEST JUDGE

This letter is addressed to a company representative who served as a judge in a vocational school competition, thanking her for her help.

Dear Mrs. Dimock:

On behalf of administrators, faculty, advisors, and students, I wish to thank you for your participation as a judge at our Fourth Annual In-house Competition held on Wednesday, December 6, 19xx.

This event provided an invaluable opportunity for students enrolled in trade and industrial education, health occupations, home economics, horticulture, and business education to demonstrate their skill and leadership abilities.

Our vocational students deeply appreciate the interest that people from business and industry show in their future. They appreciate the time and expertise that you personally devoted to judging these competitive events. The day was one of the highlights of this year's educational program.

Once again, my sincere thanks for your help in this significant work.

THANKS TO COMPANY REPRESENTATIVE FOR PRESENTATION

Sometimes a direct, favorable quotation will lend life and interest to a letter of appreciation. The following letter was sent to a regional manager of the telephone company.

Dear Mr. Nichols:

This is to thank you and New York Telephone for providing Ross Fraser's services to Hamilton Middle School.

For a number of years, Ross has presented an outstanding slide show on space exploration that we have included as part of our regular science program in grade 8. For the past four years, he has also given us an interesting look into the future of communications in a program we have included in our grade 7 unit on the future.

Last week, as a seventh-grade science teacher passed me in the corridor after attending Ross's presentation on communications, she said, "He gets better every year." That remark prompted me to write this letter. I want you to know how much we appreciate your making Ross Fraser available to us and how valuable we consider his contributions to be. Ross puts extra life and enrichment into our school program.

LETTER OF APPRECIATION TO FRATERNAL GROUP

In this letter a superintendent thanks a local fraternal organization for its efforts in building a needed facility.

Dear Kevin:

At last our athletic field has a press broadcast booth!

The School District Trustees and school personnel would like to add their appreciation to that expressed by the principal of Russell High School, Mr. Lombard, at the recent presentation of Daly Field's new press broadcast booth. We wish to extend thanks to you and your organization for building this needed facility.

The booth appears to be strong enough to withstand the elements for years to come. Not only that, it is attractive, and it fits perfectly into its environment. It is a valuable addition to Daly Field.

Everyone who uses the booth, not to mention those who benefit from it through more accurate reporting of events on the field, will appreciate your hard work. Our athletic programs and our public relations will profit substantially from its existence.

Your group is to be commended for its interest in and concern for our schools. It seems to me that cooperative, self-sacrificing efforts such as yours, in conjunction with the business community whose members contributed to this project, are especially valuable in that they bring school personnel, members of the community, and businessmen and businesswomen together for a common purpose.

The structure you have built with that cooperation is very impressive.

THANKS TO LOCAL BUSINESS FOR GIFT

Notice that in this letter the writer does more than thank the addressee and his company. He also explains the excellent use to which the gift will be put.

Dear Mr. Ward:

Thank you for your generous gift of white bond paper. The Starr Paper Company has always been a valued supporter of the Rutledge Public Schools, and this gift is further evidence of that support.

The paper will be used in our Drug Abuse Program to distribute information to meetings of the PTA and Citizens Advisory Committee about the harmful use of drugs. Without your contribution, a large part of this important information might not have gotten into the hands of those whose lives may be affected as they decide whether or not to use drugs.

The assistance of citizens like you and companies like Starr Paper have enabled this school district to accomplish far more than it otherwise could have. On behalf of the parents and students in the Rutledge School District, I thank you again.

THANKS FOR DONATION TO VOCATIONAL SCHOOL

This is basically a form letter that graciously invites each donor to visit the school.

Dear Mrs. Gratz:

Let me take this opportunity to thank you for your donation of $500.

It is only through such help and generosity by the community, business, and industry that our school can hope to provide the kind of realistic training needed by students to enable them to obtain jobs upon graduation from high school.

We would like to have you visit the Buchanan Skills Center, not only to see how your donation is being used in the instructional program, but also to observe the many kinds of occupational skills that are offered to our students.

If you will let us know when it is convenient for you to be here, we will be happy to arrange a tour of the building.

Once again, thank you for your contribution.

APPRECIATION TO COMPANY FOR HELPING OUT IN CRISIS

Whenever a company donates money, goods, or services, it deserves a letter of appreciation. Here is an instance where a company seems to have been particularly responsive.

Mr. Paul Benson, Manager
Wendy McKing's Hamburger Restaurant
333 Cochise Canyon Road
Wright, Arizona 86500

Dear Mr. Benson:

On behalf of the Wright School District, I want to express my appreciation to you for your assistance during the recent crisis in which Udall School students and the surrounding community were evacuated.

Everyone I have talked to appreciated the prompt way in which you provided food and beverages to dislocated students and residents. It is very pleasing to see the Wendy McKing's Corporation take such an active and public-spirited role at a time of crisis.

Your kind help during this difficult time will be long remembered.

SYMPATHY

13

CHAPTER 13

Letters of sympathy are often painful to write. The circumstances themselves are unpleasant, often tragic, and even the best letter writer knows that soothing words will do little to ease the pain or materially lessen the grief. Nevertheless, these letters must be written.

When a student, or a teacher, or a staff member dies, what can anyone really say? Essentially, all one can say is, "I'm sorry"—and it needs to be said in the most careful, sensitive way possible.

A letter of sympathy does not ordinarily have to be very long. If indeed it is true that words are small comfort, there is no reason to go on and on about the sadness of the occasion. The reader is only too aware of that sadness already.

The critical element in a letter of sympathy, aside from brevity in most cases, is tone. The letter must "sound" right. Much ink has been spilled about tone in written expression, but tone remains an elusive concept. There is no formula for testing it. Yet when a letter has the appropriate tone, readers, even unsophisticated readers, sense it.

The letters in this chapter have that tone.

SYMPATHY LETTER ON DEATH OF A STUDENT

C. MEADE BEERS, Ed.D.
District Superintendent

JOSEPH FARESE, Ed.D.
Assistant District Superintendent

ROBERT R. KLING
Business Administrator

P E N N S B U R Y   S C H O O L   D I S T R I C T

Yardley Avenue   Post Office Box 338
Fallsington, Pennsylvania 19054
Telephone (215) 295-4131

October 22, 19xx

Mr. and Mrs. Scott Vroman
1467 Marshall Avenue
Anderson, Pennsylvania 19100

Dear Mr. and Mrs. Vroman:

    All of us in Pennsbury are shocked and deeply saddened by the tragic death of your son Glenn. Words are totally inadequate to express our feelings, but please know that our thoughts and prayers are with you.

    On behalf of the Board of Education and your friends on the Pennsbury staff, I extend our sincerest sympathy, trusting that remembrance by so many friends will bring you comfort.

Sincerely,

C. Meade Beers

C. Meade Beers, Ed.D
District Superintendent

LETTER TO STUDENTS ON DEATH OF THEIR FATHER

This is a heartfelt and moving letter from a superintendent to two students whose father, a school administrator, has died.

Dear Russell and Marian:

Like many others, I am very saddened at the loss of your father and want you to know that I share your sense of grief.

You must be able to take some consolation in the knowledge that your father is now at peace with God. I hope you will be able to find even greater solace in pleasant memories of your father as a fine and understanding man.

As unfair as this premature passing of your father may seem to you, you must accept it as God's will. You know that your father loved you very deeply, wanted you to do well, wanted you to be challenged and productive in your life's work, and, most of all, wanted you to be happy. He would expect you to recover from this setback, redouble your efforts in school, achieve those goals you set for yourselves, and find the self-realization that comes from living productive, good, and wholesome lives.

It goes without saying that you will have to take on a greater share of family responsibilities. I know that you will be up to these added tasks. I know, also, that you will be helpful, considerate, kind, and thoughtful toward your mother and a tremendous source of strength and comfort to her in the years ahead. I am confident that you are prepared to do what you must do in these respects.

You are a fine family, and you should be able to find many ways to help and support one another.

In closing, let me extend to each of you a standing invitation to come to me for counsel or assistance in any way during the weeks, months, and years ahead. If either of you ever wishes to discuss any matter with me, please feel free to telephone me, either at home or at my office. I want to help you in any way I can.

PRINCIPAL'S SYMPATHY LETTER ON DEATH OF A STUDENT

No letter is harder to write than a sympathy letter under these circumstances. The death is tragic, and there is very little consolation a principal can offer the parents. A brief letter, such as this one, is appropriate.

Dear Mr. and Mrs. Denton:

There are no words that can adequately express our sorrow for the loss of your son Daniel. It is hard for all of us, staff and students, to realize that Farber High School no longer has the pleasant, smiling, caring, conscientious, freckled young man we knew and liked. His tragic death has had a profound impact on everyone who knew him.

Please accept our deepest sympathy in this time of sadness.

LETTER OF SYMPATHY ON DEATH OF A TEACHER

Circumstances dictate to some extent what is appropriate in a letter of sympathy. A premature death is always hard to deal with, but the writer of the following letter handles it well. The letter is to the teacher's widow.

Dear Mrs. Byram:

All of us at Halsey High School were deeply saddened by the news of Blair's passing. His presence will be sorely missed. He was liked and respected by all those who knew him, and the students who had him in class have been profoundly touched by this tragedy.

You can take some solace in the good and lasting work that Blair did in his too-brief lifetime. The results of his outstanding teaching and his beneficial influence on students will live on. His students, in a very real sense, are monuments to Blair's life and dreams.

You have our heartfelt sympathy during this difficult time.

CONDOLENCES ON DEATH OF A TEACHER'S SPOUSE

This is a superintendent's letter to a teacher in the district.

Dear Jeff,

We were saddened to learn of the untimely death of your wife Mildred. We know that the anguish you and your children are suffering is very personal, but we want you to know that we are thinking of you at this time.

On behalf of the Board of Education and all your friends throughout the district, I wish to express our deepest sympathy to you and your family. Those of us who knew Mildred realize what a wonderful person she was and know how greatly she will be missed.

CONDOLENCES ON DEATH OF A TEACHER'S PARENT

Like most of the letters in this chapter, this one is brief but excellent. It says everything that needs to be said.

Dear Alison:

How saddened all of us at Stewart Junior High School were to learn of the tragic death of your mother. Although there is little anyone can do to lessen your grief, we want you to know that you are very much in our thoughts and prayers.

You will undoubtedly hear from many of your fellow teachers individually, but, in addition, and on behalf of everyone here at Stewart, let me extend our deepest sympathy. If there is any way we can be of service, please let us know.

SYMPATHY LETTER ON DEATH OF AN ADMINISTRATOR

This letter is considerably more personal and detailed than many letters of sympathy, since the writer and the deceased and his widow were friends.

Dear Dorothy,

The news that George died over the weekend saddened me more than I can say. George was a man so filled with life, so joyful. He was such a fine person and so brilliant a school administrator that I truly never expect to see his like again. You have my profound sympathy in this tragic hour.

Dorothy, there is so much to remember. George and I were friends at the time you and he met and married. We began our careers together at the old Kilmer School, where George was one of the finest, most dedicated teachers I ever met. Students adored him. His rise in school administration—and it was a rapid rise—surprised no one. He deserved every promotion and every honor.

It was a privilege to have known, worked with, and fished with your husband. I will never forget that day when he pulled a seven-pound pickerel from Lake Nariticong and shouted, "This is the proudest moment of my life." In truth, George had many proud moments. Much as he loved fishing, I would say that his life was more importantly a testament to the work he did. The number of students, teachers, and other administrators he influenced is legion.

You must always remember George as he was, Dorothy, however sorrowful or even bitter you may feel at the moment. If ever there was a life fully lived, one filled with lasting achievement, it was George's.

My heart goes out to you in this time of mourning. You know better than I, better than any of his army of friends and admirers, how irreparably great is the loss.

GET-WELL NOTE TO HOSPITALIZED TEACHER

This is a more cheerful letter than the preceding ones, although the situation itself is serious. The administrator who wrote it struck just the right note.

Dear Chet,

As you might well guess, all of us here are deeply concerned about your hospitalization and your impending surgery. What we want most is for you to follow your doctor's orders and do whatever is necessary to regain your health. That includes forgetting about the work and problems at Penn Arthur High School and concentrating on a full and speedy recovery.

On behalf of everyone here, I extend our best wishes for your complete recovery. We need you, Chet! In the meantime, if there is anything I can do for you, please let me know.

LETTER TO SPOUSE OF HOSPITALIZED TEACHER

Here is a letter of both sympathy and encouragement to the wife of a teacher who has been hospitalized.

Dear Sharon:

Everyone at Kirkland Middle School is concerned about Dale's need to be hospitalized. Please let him know that our best wishes are with him—and with you—and that we all hope he has a full recovery soon. Don't let him worry about the work at Kirkland. His health is what is important, and he should concentrate on nothing else right now.

All of us are praying for Dale's speedy recovery. We look forward to his return when he has regained his health. If there is something we can do to help, just let us know.

❥ A Word on Style ❥

AVOID EDUCATIONAL JARGON

You will notice that educational jargon is all but absent from the letters in this book. The best letters from school administrators, even those to knowledgeable colleagues, show a clear awareness of the fact that readers generally appreciate nontechnical language.

Think about it. How comfortable are you when reading a legal brief, a physician's report, an accountant's statement? Are you restive? Uneasy? Less than thrilled? Probably you are. So are most people outside the profession—and many of them in it—when they read the jargon of modern American education. Avoid it.

REPRIMANDS AND COMPLAINTS

14

CHAPTER 14

Fortunately, reprimands and complaints have to be written less often than letters of congratulations or appreciation. But they do have to be written. A student's behavior problem, a teacher's habitual lateness, a secretary's inadequate performance—these and other circumstances can require a letter of reprimand.

As for complaints, the possibilities are endless. However, the formula for complaint letters is rather simple: State the complaint, explain the background details, and ask for redress, all without becoming shrill or threatening.

The last part of that formula—"without becoming shrill or threatening"—applies to all the letters in this chapter. Both reprimands and complaints, by their very nature, have to be firm and direct. No purpose is served by beating around the bush when a person is being charged with incompetence or unprofessional conduct. On the other hand, even less is gained by the letter writer's displaying anger, dislike, or vindictiveness.

The ideal is the kind of equilibrium, firmness without rancor, that the letters in this chapter display.

LETTER TO PRINCIPAL ON LACK OF COMMUNICATION

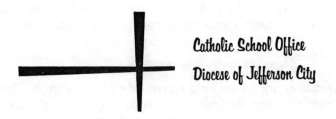

Catholic School Office
Diocese of Jefferson City

June 3, 19xx

Mr. Marvin Barnett
Principal
St. John's School
Pershing, Missouri 65100

Dear Marvin,

It has come to the attention of our office that there seems to be a lack of communication between teachers on your staff and parents of their students.

I am sure you know that good schools require ongoing and quality communication. Communication is the key to developing a partnership between educators and parents in working for the best interests of children. Such communication has been the strength of the Catholic School System.

May I suggest that a weekly appraisal report be sent home in order to keep parents informed. Parents do want to be informed. It is only when they are not informed that problems arise.

Excellence will be achieved if your school has a direct line of communication with parents. Therefore, I am strongly recommending that in formulating your school's goals, communication with parents be a priority. The strength of your school will be built upon your ability to communicate to parents in a positive way.

God's richest blessings be yours.

Sincerely,

Therese

Therese M. Fenney
Assistant Superintendent

PRINCIPAL'S LETTER ON ASSEMBLY INCIDENT

In this letter the principal goes beyond condemning the actions of a few students in order to explain the purpose of assemblies. He also quotes the Board of Education's policy statement concerning conduct at assemblies.

Dear Students:

Assemblies are an important part of your education. They are not merely entertainment designed to provide a break in the day. Nor are they—except for pep rallies—occasions for students to let off steam, become vocal critics, or otherwise express contempt or hostility toward those on stage. A few students apparently forgot that fact yesterday afternoon.

This letter is directed at the small group of students at our Amateur Day assembly program who seemed to think they were watching something like the old *Gong Show* on television. It should hardly be necessary to remind them—but obviously it is—that many of our young men and women at Van Buren High School are uneasy enough about performing before an audience of six hundred students without being subject to such indignities as pennies thrown at them on the stage by those sitting in the front rows.

Let me quote from the Board of Education's policy statement on school assemblies: "No student shall be made to feel slighted, embarrassed, or outcast because of the content of any assembly." It was not the content of Amateur Day that made two or three of our most talented students feel "slighted, embarrassed, or outcast" yesterday, but rather the poor manners of a few members of the audience.

We expect no repetition of this kind of incident. If there is any, not only will future Amateur Days be in jeopardy, but I will seriously consider canceling all assemblies for the rest of the school year.

LETTER TO PARENTS ON STUDENT'S BEHAVIOR

This letter gets straight to the point about a touchy matter and requests that action be taken.

Dear Mr. and Mrs. Thaxton:

While the school does not want to interfere in students' personal lives, when their personal conduct becomes offensive to other students and faculty, the school must step in.

The personal behavior of your son Henry with Charlotte Keene involves the public display of overt affection in a way that can only be described as embarrassing. This type of conduct is best reserved for personal, intimate, and private moments and not for the halls and grounds of a public high school.

We think that you, as parents, should know about this behavior. We trust that we have your support in this matter, and we hope you will take steps to see that corrective measures are taken.

NOTICE THAT STUDENT IS NOT PARTICIPATING IN GYM

Here is a brief letter from a principal informing a parent of her son's problem in gym class. The letter leaves the way open for an explanation, if there is one.

Dear Mrs. Chapin:

This letter is to inform you that your son Wayne is not participating regularly in gym class because he does not have a gym suit.

Physical Education is an important part of the school program, and Wayne must participate unless excused for a medical reason. In order to participate, Wayne must have a gym suit for every class.

May I suggest that you contact Wayne's physical education teacher, Mr. Vincent Barnes, if you wish further details or if you can offer some information that will help to explain this situation.

PRINCIPAL'S LETTER ON TEACHER'S TARDINESS

A no-nonsense letter on a continuing problem, this is a good model of the kind of documentation needed when face-to-face meetings have failed to bring results.

Dear Mr. Arnett:

With regret, I am writing this letter as another means of bringing your attention to what has become a serious problem of tardiness. Since our March 19xx conference, in which this matter was discussed, I have seen little or no improvement in your promptness. Your persistent disregard of the contract requirements for on-time attendance has made it necessay for me to include a copy of this letter in your permanent personnel records.

Please make arrangements to ensure that your arrival each day will meet the mandated schedule. Failure to correct the problem of tardiness at this point could well lead to disciplinary action. Your immediate, positive attention is needed.

WARNING TO TEACHER ON MISSING SCHEDULED CONFERENCES

Here is another strongly worded letter to a teacher concerning his failure to meet professional obligations.

Dear Mr. Thomas:

This letter is written as an official means of expressing my disappointment at your recurring failure to attend scheduled parent conferences. I attempted to reach you at 555-0123 on May 8, 19xx, to remind you of your 7:30 appointment the next day. There was no answer, and you arrived on May 9, 19xx, at 8:00 a.m.

My disappointment increased when I learned that you have missed still another parent conference, one scheduled for May 12, 19xx, at 7:30 a.m.

Your responsibility as a professional educator is clear. You must attend such conferences. Excuses will not do. It is my full intent to initiate disciplinary action upon any future failure to carry out your duties.

MEMO CONCERNING TEACHER'S DETERIORATING PERFORMANCE

Specific details are advisable in nearly every kind of correspondence, and they are especially important in a complaint or reprimand. The following memo contains many specific details.

TO: Amelia Osteen
FROM: Helen Sears, Principal
SUBJECT: Classroom Performance

It has become necessary for me to apprise you of some concerns I have regarding your performance in the latter part of the 19xx–19xx school year and to suggest ways in which I hope you can become more successful in the coming school year.

Shortly after your March 15 evaluation, there was a marked change in the following areas:

1. Lack of attention to personal appearance and dress, so much so that both your peers and students felt compelled to comment

2. Tendency to leave your classroom unattended, something that occurred many times in the last three months

3. Failure to respond to notes to come to the dean's office or my office (I sent you two such notes in the last week of school but have not seen you yet.)

4. Lack of effective preparation of materials on a timely basis, possibly resulting in your using students' assistance inappropriately

5. Failure to follow guidelines regarding students who did not pass MLST, resulting in some students being unaware that summer school was necessary

We have already discussed the possible reasons for the large number of failures on MLST in your classes. I am counting on you to work more closely with your department chairman in the future to alleviate that problem.

You have many good qualities, and if you are planning on a lifetime career of teaching, you need to build on them. I know that your personal life has been upset by divorce and its attendant difficulties this year, but although I can understand and sympathize, I cannot overlook your poor performance in the latter part of the year. I would like to see you recapture some of that bright and enthusiastic manner that so impressed me when I first interviewed you two years ago.

Frankly, if evaluations had been done on May 15 instead of March 15, I am not sure yours would have been satisfactory.

I am ready to assist you in whatever way possible, but I think the real need probably is for self-motivation, application of effort, and attention to detail. I hope your summer work and vacation will allow time for some rejuvenation of spirit and dedication.

REPRIMAND TO TEACHER FOR NEGLECT OF DUTY

The writer of this letter is supplying written confirmation of a verbal reprimand, with a copy of the letter to go into the teacher's personnel folder.

Dear Mr. Lacey:

This letter summarizes our conference of Monday, January 7, 19xx, concerning an incident that occurred in your classroom on January 3, 19xx.

It was determined that a fight involving two students with weapons occurred in your class during third period on January 3. It was further determined that you were not in the classroom at the time. Your absence from class ignored both professional practices and personal responsibilities, and it has therefore become necessary for me to take the following administrative position.

My conclusion is that your absence from class was improper and neglectful. You will be held personally liable for the injuries sustained and the damage caused by the students involved. As a result of this incident, you are hereby reprimanded for neglect of duty.

I am encouraged to know that you plan to correct the mistake of leaving class, and I trust you will call on me for assistance in providing alternatives if and when emergencies arise in the future.

REPRIMAND TO TEACHER FOR VERBAL CONFRONTATION

In this case the teacher's actions in the classroom were appropriate, but his subsequent outburst to a parent was not. The letter, written by his principal, tells the story.

Dear Mr. Newby:

Now that I have completed a thorough investigation of the events of October 10, involving ninth-grade student Jay Beggs, let me state my conclusions.

It seems to me that you exercised your authority reasonably in directing Jay Beggs not to get involved in a potential problem with two other students. You also acted responsibly in asking Jay to leave the classroom after he implied that he would not obey your instructions.

Had the incident ended there, no problem would exist. Unfortunately, when Jay's father, Byron Beggs, phoned you to ask for an explanation, you used the sort of language and displayed the kind of verbal immaturity for which we routinely reprove students. I should hardly need to tell you that negative, inflammatory statements directed at parents are not acceptable to me personally, nor are they in keeping with district policy.

As a result of this unprofessional verbal confrontation with Mr. Beggs, I feel obliged to reprimand you formally and to direct that a copy of this letter be filed with your permanent records.

Any repetition of this kind of behavior will not be in your professional best interests. In the future, please work with me in finding acceptable solutions in dealing with students who pose problems to you in class. Beyond that, please respond to parents' questions—even when they seem intemperate or argumentative—in a way that will reflect credit on the school and the district.

MEMO ON TEACHER'S NEED FOR IMPROVEMENT

This memo not only explains at some length what is wrong with the teacher's performance but also gives workable suggestions on how she might improve.

TO: Mary Jane Hildreth
FROM: Helen Sears, Principal
SUBJECT: Need for Improvement

As you know, I have serious concerns about your teaching effectiveness and, indeed, about your professional future unless improvements are made in the following areas.

Concern #1: Your teaching methods lack variety. Although Ms. Eddy and I have both talked with you on several occasions about teaching techniques, you have shown no inclination to improve. Students are asked almost daily to copy work from the overhead projector. Use of such equipment is often worthwhile but should not be your only recourse. Boredom is not conducive to learning. I have heard many complaints from students and parents regarding the lack of challenge in your classroom.

Suggestion: I recommend that you immediately initiate different techniques, including but not limited to (1) student discussion groups, (2) learning stations where small groups participate in a variety of learning experiences, (3) laboratory activities.

Concern #2: Students and parents feel that they are not adequately informed as to their status in your class. When we discussed this matter, you admitted that you often did not return papers or tests and sometimes did not inform students of their grades.

Suggestion: Begin having students keep a record of all grades they earn in your class. They should, of course, be told the weight of each grade so that they can average their grades at any time to determine where they stand.

Concern #3: You do not skillfully initiate and guide classroom discussion in such a way as to motivate student learning. In fact, you appear to be afraid of open discussion with your students and thus pass up many opportunities for stimulating give-and-take in the classroom. You refer students to "the book" rather than leading them to think about problems constructively.

Suggestion: Try using panels or small groups to permit students to explore problems. Even if you are not comfortable in being the center of attention, you may be able to moderate discussions effectively.

Concern #4: For some time, you have had difficulty in being prompt and accurate in regard to reports and other areas of responsibility; i.e., (1) by failing to read the newsletter and to check your box before school, (2) by failing to relieve the ISSP teacher on assigned days, (3) by making multiple errors in homeroom attendance reports, (4) by failing to turn in class-load sheets on time, (5) by failing to submit grades accurately or on time. While anyone might have these things happen occasionally, you have had them occur frequently.

Suggestion: Begin immediately to note all due dates, check all paper work, and exhibit a more positive attitude toward the routine responsibilities of teaching.

Concern #5: Despite our discussions, you have not assumed a share in the total school program. I do not see you participating in any extracurricular activities or even attending athletic contests or other school-sponsored events. I think this lack of participation contributes to your inability to establish rapport with your students.

Suggestion: Start now to participate actively in such activities.

It is evident that improvement in your teaching performance has not yet occurred. Improvement is needed. It is needed now, and it is needed desperately.

LETTER COMPLAINING OF SUBSTITUTE TEACHER'S BEHAVIOR

Addressed to the district office, the following letter explains in detail why the principal who wrote it does not want a particular substitute teacher again.

Dear Mr. Christie:

You asked that I elaborate on the situation I described to you on the phone this morning, and I am happy to do so.

Mr. Lyman Perkins, a substitute teacher, took over Ms. Foraker's mathematics classes at Tallchief High School on Friday, September 29, while Ms. Foraker attended a regional convention. He was here only one day, but in that time he demonstrated a particularly unorthodox and questionable approach to teaching.

According to statements made by a number of students, Mr. Perkins made casual and evidently untrue references to his relationships with various female students. He put his arms around some of them, proclaiming them to be his "girl friends." He also raised the subject of incest and asked students about their experiences along that line.

Although I have not talked with Mr. Perkins about these allegations, I have interviewed several students about the events in their mathematics class on September 29. Each student shared with me in private conference a number of observations that support the statements made above.

I have no idea what Mr. Perkins meant to accomplish by his behavior, or whether he considered it to be aggressive and manipulative. Whatever the explanation, I think it is fair to say that his teaching methods are not compatible with community norms and expectations.

As I said on the phone this morning, I request that Mr. Perkins not be assigned again to Tallchief High School in any capacity.

COMPLAINT ABOUT SECRETARY'S PERFORMANCE

In this letter the writer, a principal, is expressing dissatisfaction with the work of a secretary in the guidance office.

Dear Ms. Shattuck:

One of your main responsibilities is preparing and mailing the "unsatisfactory notices" at the end of each marking period. I was not satisfied with the manner in which you handled the task recently.

As I mentioned to you yesterday, the unsatisfactory-notice assignment has traditionally taken three or four days. It has always been done by one person, the guidance office secretary. You required nearly two weeks to prepare and mail the notices, which is far too long.

Your lack of organization appears to be a factor affecting your efficiency. May I suggest that you consider taking a refresher course or trying some other method of remediation. Somehow you will have to learn to work faster.

I am willing to assist you in this matter. Please realize that your effectiveness is a crucial factor in the overall effectiveness of our guidance office.

WARNING AGAINST TRESPASSING AND USING SCHOOL PROPERTY

This letter is both a complaint and a warning. It is direct and forceful, wasting no words.

Dear Mr. Pomeroy:

It has come to may attention that on Thursday, July 15, 19xx, you were in the building and used school board property. You are now under personal notice: <u>Under no circumstances should you at any time use Hayes Junior High School property for personal reasons.</u>

As you are aware from the several signs posted throughout the building, all visitors must report to the central office before proceeding to a task within the building. You are not entitled to an exemption from this clearly posted regulation.

Any further use of this facility without my express permission will be considered an act of trespassing and will be reported to the local police.

PROTEST OF PENALTY FEE CHARGED BY STATE ASSOCIATION

Here is a model letter of complaint that could apply to many situations. The writer states his complaint and then explains why he believes it is justified.

Dear Ms. Ackley:

This morning you informed Mrs. Rudd, our vocal music instructor, that our school will be charged a penalty fee for late registration for the All-State Audition. I am quite upset about this news.

Last week, on Tuesday, September 12, 19xx, Mrs. Rudd and I filled out the form for the All-State Audition and made out a warrant for the check in the amount of $48. The check was put in the mail on the 14th, so why it was not postmarked until the 16th is beyond me.

We expected a postmark no later than that required—the 15th—and we think our actions justified that belief. I also feel that since we agreed to host the small school solo and ensemble contest in April, you might have considered that fact before imposing the penalty.

Like you, I believe that dates have to be adhered to, but it seems to me that in this case the one-day-late postmark could easily have been overlooked.

ANSWERING CONCERNS AND CRITICISM

15

CHAPTER 15

It is important to be able to answer criticism and to allay concerns, because whatever course of action one pursues, there are sure to be critics. These critics may be parents, community groups, or newspaper editors. Within the school, they may be teachers or students.

Answering criticism can be a delicate matter, even when there is no real foundation for the critic's concern or complaint. One's first impulse may be to counter the criticsm directly—to show why the critic is wrong. But to rush in too hastily can increase the problem rather than solve it.

The aim of answering criticism is to neutralize the complaint, to mollify the critic, not to win a verbal victory. Because of this, the key to effectiveness is tact. The successful writer attempts to answer all concerns and criticism rationally, thoughtfully, and fully.

Each letter in this chapter illustrates how to write a tactful letter in response to criticism or concerns. In some instances, there appears to have been a basis for concern; in others, the critic seems off base. Whatever the case, the administrator takes an open and tactful approach.

ANSWERING CONCERN ABOUT DISCRIMINATION

GEORGE R. ARIYOSHI
GOVERNOR

DR. DONNIS H. THOMPSON
Superintendent

DR. KIYOTO MIZUBA
District Superintendent

STATE OF HAWAII
DEPARTMENT OF EDUCATION
OFFICE OF THE DISTRICT SUPERINTENDENT
HAWAII SCHOOLS
75 AUPUNI STREET
P.O. BOX 4160
HILO, HAWAII 96720-0621

March 20, 19xx

Mrs. Beverly Colfax
6304 Whitman Drive
Paulsen, Washington 98300

Dear Mrs. Colfax:

Welcome to Hilo and the Hawaii District Schools.

Let me try to answer your questions. Discrimination is a relative thing. Most Caucasian children do not experience discrimination from their classmates. A few do but mainly because they themselves do not get along well with other children. In recent years, the number of Caucasian children has increased to the point where they are no longer looked upon as different. Further, we are such a melting pot that we have come to accept differences. Principals and teachers will not tolerate discrimination and teach toward the acceptance of all cultures and races.

Yes, there are several private schools in Hilo, but I do not recommend your sending your children to them unless you hold some strong personal reasons. I have enclosed a list of private schools and have checked those in Hilo.

Also, I have enclosed a brochure for your guidance. I'm sure your children will enjoy school in Hilo.

Sincerely,

K Mizuba

Kiyoto Mizuba, Ph.D.
District Superintendent

CLARIFICATION OF DAMAGING OUT-OF-SCHOOL INCIDENT

This letter attempts to put in perspective the events that occurred when an out-of-school party got out of hand. In explaining what happened, the writer makes no excuses for the students who were involved but does try to defend the reputation of the school.

Dear Parents and Students:

There are a number of things that need to be said about the party at Morgan Creek Park on Thursday, May 26. First, I want you to know of the deep concern we at Rowlands High School and everyone associated with the Rowlands Metropolitan School District feel. It was shocking to read of the events that occurred at what was called the "Rowlands Senior Skip Day Party."

You should be aware of the following facts:

1. The "Skip Day" was not a school function. No approval or sanction was provided by Rowlands. Rather, this type of activity was actively discouraged. My letter in early May to the parents of all seniors made this clear.

2. "Skip Day" on May 26 did not result in any class or school time being missed. Exams were scheduled for the morning hours, and students attended and took those exams. Some students and many nonstudents then attended the party at Morgan Creek in the afternoon.

3. None of the four adults placed under arrest has attended Rowlands High School during the past year. The one juvenile issued a citation is a Rowlands student.

4. The fight apparently involved several nonstudents and several Rowlands students.

5. There had been no lack of student activities during the 19xx–19xx school year. The Rowlands Student Council Social Committee, in conjunction with other organizations, sponsored 18 dances and parties throughout the year. At none of them was alcohol consumption permitted.

6. Scheduled end-of-year activities included a Senior Breakfast on May 25 to honor seniors and staff members, a Senior Banquet on May 25 honoring seniors and parents, Senior Dress-Up Day on May 27, Senior Honors Convocation on May 27, End-of-Year Dance on May 28 to honor graduates, Commencement Ceremony on June 5, and Parents' Senior Party on June 7.

7. It is clear that many school-planned and sponsored activities were available to students. It is also clear that this party was not exclusively a "senior" party inasmuch as many underclass students and nonstudents at-

tended and disrupted the proceedings. And it is abundantly clear that great damage has been done to Rowlands' reputation as a result of the fight, police action, and subsequent publicity.

The Rowlands community has always had great pride in its high school, insisting that it maintain strong academic achievement within a structured, well-disciplined school atmosphere. Everyone on the staff is most disappointed that this incident occurred, and we ask that you as students and parents help to assure us that we will never have a recurrence. We will do what we can at Rowlands—and we need the support of all of you—to make sure the Rowlands name and reputation are not tarnished in this way again.

Thank you.

ANSWER TO PARENTS' DEMAND THAT CHILD CHOOSE COURSES

The writer of this letter is an administrator in a parochial school system. She tactfully overrules the parents of a girl who they believe should be allowed to decide herself what courses she will take.

Dear Mr. and Mrs. La Motte:

One of the most difficult things to do in life is to make choices. Children learn to make choices by watching adults. It is a very important part of their learning experience.

I can understand your desire to allow Elizabeth to make her own choices. However, Elizabeth is only eleven years old. She may not always have the information or experience needed to make wise choices. Sometimes we can help our children by limiting choices. At the same time, we can teach them to see the effects that result from their choices.

In this situation, I must uphold the school's decision. Elizabeth will, with proper guidance, learn to make mature decisions. Until then, I believe the school has a right to limit choices in the best interests of its students.

While we tend to emphasize what subjects students are taking, we must also pay attention to what they deeply care about, their attitude toward life, their zest for living.

If I can be of further service, please feel free to contact me.

REASON FOR EXCLUSION FROM NATIONAL HONOR SOCIETY

Here is a response to a parent who believes his son should have been elected to the National Honor Society. The writer of this letter explains the nature of the selection process, an explanation that in itself provides the answer.

Dear Mr. Stannard:

Thank you for your letter of March 20 in which you ask why your son Harvey was not voted into the National Honor Society.

The charter for the National Honor Society at Fisher High School is granted by the National Association, and its guidelines are followed in the selection process, except that in our school, because of its small size, the entire faculty votes rather than a special committee. The balloting is written and secret. All academically eligible candidates are considered.

If a student fails to receive a majority vote, he or she can be reconsidered, and, in fact, your son Harvey was voted on twice. I cannot give you a specific reason why a majority of teachers voted not to recommend him. Each teacher must make an individual judgment, and I believe that professional teachers attempt to be fair and objective.

Your assumption that Harvey's character was the overriding factor may or may not be true. Since evaluating character requires judgments about a person's reputation, moral strength, patterns of behavior, and personality, we must rely on the maturity and fairness of the teachers who make the assessment.

I would say that any type of assessment of one person by others may be unfair or erroneous. By the same token, it may have enough elements of truth to be justified.

EXPLANATION OF CHILD'S OMISSION FROM BANQUET LIST

A parent is unhappy because her daughter, a Merit Roll student (third in a three-level honors system), cannot attend the annual Awards Banquet. This is the principal's reasoned and persuasive reply.

Dear Mrs. Ruggles:

Thank you for expressing your concern about our Conway Junior High School Awards Banquet, 19xx–19xx. Your letter points up a dilemma that always faces a school's administration when some students are included in an activity and others are not.

In the past, Merit Roll students have not been included in the banquet plans. The decision was made this year to continue that practice.

We are proud of all our students. We are especially pleased with the academically talented youngsters—Les Excellents, Honor Roll, and Merit Roll students. I wish it were possible to invite those on the Merit Roll to the banquet. However, because of their large numbers, our limited banquet space, and the escalating costs, we are not able to include these students.

Caroline is a bright and talented young woman. Her participation in honors classes is commendable and meets her need for competitive academic challenges. It is unfortunate that Caroline cannot participate in the banquet. However, I hope you will understand that she does not qualify this year because she does not meet the standards for the Honor Roll.

If you have any further questions, I will be pleased to try to answer them.

ANSWER TO PARENT'S PROTEST AGAINST PADDLING

This long and detailed letter is necessary in view of the seriousness of the parent's complaint.

Dear Mrs. Dinsmore:

Thank you for your letter expressing concern about your son Earl and his recent problem.

I have discussed the matter with Mr. Trilby and submit the following for your consideration:

1. The written notice that you inquired about is a copy of the referral. In this instance, both boys were sent to the dean with a single referral, and the second boy received the copy. (My teachers have been reminded to make out one referral per student.)

2. Corporal punishment has been approved by the courts as a reasonable action and does not require prior permission from the parent. However, we will always honor a parent's request not to use corporal punishment if the parent has informed us of his or her objection. I regret that your objection came after the fact.

3. Dean Trilby says that he asked the boys if they had done what Ms. Griffin stated on the referral. Both answered, "Yes," and he saw no need to pursue it further. Please encourage Earl in a situation like this to continue the discussion if he feels there are extenuating circumstances. Also, should he feel unjustly accused or judged, he may ask to see me or another administrator for a hearing.

4. The dean's clerk, Ms. Meigs, has her desk right outside the open door where Mr. Trilby administers paddlings. She can see or hear all proceedings without causing any additional embarrassment to the students

involved by being in the same room. Many youngsters do shed a few tears, and boys, in particular, do not want to be observed in that situation.

5. Earl was given the alternative of detentions but opted for paddling, apparently because of your difficulty in picking him up. Please be assured that when there is a problem in this respect, we are always happy to find other options—e.g., morning detentions, use of the activity bus home. We do require the parent to call, however, because every child (as you might suppose) would have us believe there is an insurmountable problem connected with every option.

6. The difference between paddling in school and at home is that in school the person offended (the teacher) is not the person who paddles. Therefore, the paddling is not the venting of anger but simply a reminder to the child that rules are meant to be obeyed.

One of the real difficulties in administering discipline today is that there are so few options available. We try not to assign writing essays because (a) writing is part of our instructional program, not a punishment, and (b) assigned homework, which we have difficulty in getting children to do, should take precedence over busywork. Grounds cleanup, another possibility, would mean lost class time. Detention is effective because it takes away children's "free" time. Paddling *may* be effective because it is an immediate response to an unsatisfactory action. Suspension of any kind is always a last resort.

Rest assured that Earl's file for this year will reflect your objection to corporal punishment. It will be necessary for you to renew it each year.

It is not my intent for any child ever to be mistreated at Rawlings Junior High School. I would like to have every child feel that this is a pleasant place to be, yet one in which rules are to be respected and obeyed.

The obvious lesson that I hope Earl learns is that the dean deals only with those sent to him for disciplinary action. Good behavior in the classroom will keep him out of the dean's office.

I appreciate your concern and urge you, in the future, to reach me by phone as quickly as possible for the resolution of any problems that may arise.

A copy of this letter is being sent to each of those persons designated to receive a carbon copy of your letter.

RESPONSE TO PARENT'S COMPLAINT ABOUT FAILING GRADE

In this well-reasoned memo, the issue is whether a music teacher should have given a student a failing grade for not bringing his band uniform to school on the day of an important performance.

TO: Joshua Stuart, Assistant Superintendent
FROM: Esther Bell, Principal, Rawlings Junior High School
SUBJECT: Failing Grade in Band, Ben Foley

In my opinion, Mr. Foley has clouded the issue somewhat in his recent letter regarding his son.

The basic question is whether band students can be held responsible for appearing in scheduled performances. The band program is a performance-oriented course, and certainly those who elect the course expect to perform. Both Dr. Orlando and I believe that the performances are, in effect, "exams" for band students. If there is no penalty for the student who fails to keep his or her commitment to the group, I believe we are condoning the abdication of responsibility.

If it is determined that group performances cannot be required—and cannot be considered in determining grades—then the entire band curriculum should be rewritten or perhaps removed from the school program. Without group performances, the program would amount to little more than private music lessons.

When I talked to Ben, who is a fine boy and a good student, he said he had "forgotten" his uniform on the performance day, even though the band concert had been announced in class several times as well as on the public address system. Dr. Orlando had stressed all year the attendance requirement for performances.

It seems to me that the whole issue to be dealt with is whether a band student can be held responsible for—and be graded on—scheduled performances such as this one. We think the nature of the band program in this county makes it both desirable and necessary.

REPLY TO NEWSPAPER EDITORIAL

Since a newspaper editorial can strongly influence public opinion for or against a school budget, it may be necessary to reply to it, especially if, as in this case, the editorial writer is not on firm ground.

Dear Editor:

Permit me to respond briefly to your editorial entitled "A 1.84-Mil City Tax Hike" in the March 18 issue of the Coltsville *Herald*. This editorial unwittingly perpetuates a myth about the percentage of the city budget allocated to education. After a specific reference to the amount requested, your editorial states that "this amount represents about one third of all city spending." Unfortunately, that statement makes an apples-to-oranges comparison that is as unfair as it may be hard to explain.

Only through an understanding of the complexities of the Coltsville city budget can an accurate percentage be estimated. One difficulty is that the Department of Education remains the only department to reflect fringe benefits and debt service in its budget. All other city departments have fringe benefits and debt service included in separate accounts. This badly skews any direct comparison.

Another difficulty is that all monies for negotiated contracts involving the Department of Education are included in the education budget, while many other city departments have their contract negotiations shown in a separate account. If all Department of Education negotiated salary increases were included in that separate account, comparisons would become more meaningful.

The city does not incur any pension costs for certified Department of Education personnel, while it incurs substantial pension costs for employees of other departments. Yet these pension costs do not show up in those other departments' budgets, but rather in another separate account.

If the real costs of running every department were budgeted in a parallel manner to those in the Department of Education budget, the true percentage of each department's share could easily be determined. But that is not the case. The result is that the press and public tend to perceive the Department of Education as having an insatiable appetite for city funds.

Clearly, this works to the disadvantage of the Department of Education and, by extension, to the school children of Coltsville. Our department is now preparing a brochure that will show the actual percentage spent on education more accurately than your editorial does. We are hoping that this brochure will be believed.

DEFENSE OF CONTROVERSIAL SCHOOL PROGRAM

Any special program may draw the wrath of some members of the community. When, as here, the program is inherently controversial, the outcry may be loud enough to require careful handling.

TO: School Directors and Superintendent
FROM: Rupert V. Barton, Principal, Dewey High School
SUBJECT: Program on Communal Life

"They need to learn to live with other human beings"—Quote from Dewey High School Philosophy, adopted 1967

About a week ago, Mrs. Wolcott, our home economics teacher, asked me if she could get in touch with the Search for Alternatives group in Fisk

Corners to furnish resource people to talk about communal life. She mentioned that her class was studying the family in tribal systems here and abroad. After brief consideration, I told her to go ahead, with the stipulation that I would sit in on the sessions and would allow no indoctrination or political discussion.

The two people from the commune came last Friday and met twice with students. Mr. Fletcher and Mrs. Wolcott attended the first session. Mr. Fletcher and I were at the second one. At no time, so far as I am aware, did the Search for Alternatives people meet any students without a teacher present.

I will not go into specific details of the session that I attended, but it was very low key, and no attempt was made to sell this kind of life. I have talked to students who took part in each of the sessions. The common reaction was that the lifestyle described to them represents a national problem, not a solution. No one expressed a desire to emulate these people.

This memo is for your personal information. I know you are receiving flak on the program.

ANSWER TO COMMUNITY GROUP'S CONCERN OVER STAFFING

This letter is addressed to a woman who represents a community council concerned about high school staff cuts. The writer, a district superintendent, attempts to reassure her.

Dear Mrs. Wang:

Thank you for expressing your concern about staffing at Liluokalani High School. At the present time there are twelve teachers on the master schedule at Liluokalani. I would like to be able to promise you that those twelve positions will remain, but I cannot do so. Of course, I will do everything I can to protect the twelve positions. Perhaps your council will wish to seek continued legislative support for the kind of guarantee that I cannot give.

Even if your fears are realized and a position is cut, I believe that Liluokalani can continue to offer a basic high school curriculum. The decreased staffing would still compare favorably with that at Kaahumanu High School, which, like Liluokalani, has had decreasing enrollment.

Perhaps classes would be slightly larger with eleven teachers than they have been with twelve. However, there seems to be a misunderstanding about class size and school learning. Whether classes have twelve or thirty students, achievement is not affected. That has been proven in many studies of the effects of class size on students' learning. Far more important than class size are the quality of instruction, the amount of studying done by students, and the involvement of parents with their children's schoolwork.

Thank you for your council's involvement. Please continue to communicate with me when the district office may be of help. If necessary, we can jointly push for legislative support.

Best wishes for a good school year.

RESPONSE TO CONCERN OVER POSSIBLE REASSIGNMENT OF STUDENTS

Reassignment of students to other schools can be a necessity fraught with peril. In this instance the students are not being reassigned, but the writer, a superintendent, nonetheless gives a thorough explanation of how assignments are made. Notice that he leaves open the possibility of future reassignments.

Dear Mr. Hampton:

This letter is in response to your letter of March 28, 19xx, concerning assignment of students from the Port Hutton area.

By board policy the area assistant superintendents have the responsibility of recommending student assignments each year. The area outlined on the map enclosed with your letter will not be affected by proposed changes in the assignments for the 19xx–19xx school year. I am told that at no time did the area superintendents give serious consideration to assigning students in your area to Eastside High School.

Assignments are reviewed annually and changes made in accordance with prevailing conditions. Therefore, I cannot project what future changes might be made in student assignments. Our current practice is to assign students to the closest school, assuming that other requirements are satisfied.

We use computer studies to generate a variety of options for assigning students to schools. Each option depends on the constraints fed into the computer. However, if a particular option is considered by our board, data provided by the computer are used only as a guide in determining actual student assignments. Area assistant superintendents still do the actual proposing of assignment changes, taking many factors into consideration. We always try to make changes that will result in the least amount of disruption to well-defined neighborhoods.

Since demographic changes are occurring constantly, it is impossible to give you absolute assurance that your community or any other community will not be affected in the future by changes in assignments.

Please know that we care very much about your children and will always consider their best interests before making any recommendation.

ANSWER TO CRITICISM OF STUDENT CODE OF CONDUCT

A number of parents, angry at the penalties imposed on their children, have tried to persuade the Board of Education to weaken the Student Code of Conduct. This letter, addressed to the board's chairman, makes a strong case for not changing the code.

Dear Mr. Santos:

The Secondary Principals Association of Plant County takes exception to the criticism recently made by a group of parents against the Student Code of Conduct. We believe the code has been of significant importance in the improvement of the system over the past five years and that weakening the code could only adversely affect our continued growth and progress.

We agree that the code should be reviewed annually for appropriate revision, but we believe that such review should take place during the summer months. The code must be administered equitably. To revise it during the school year would create severe public relations problems and invite legal action because of the inequity of punishment in similar cases.

Class III offenses are those identified as being against civil law and warranting police action if they occur off school grounds. All schools ensure that students and parents are familiar with the code and the consequences of violation, including Class III violations. Any student who flouts the code, regardless of previous performance, has made a studied and deliberate decision to do so, with full awareness of the possible outcome.

There is sufficient flexibility in the Class I and II offenses to give students credit for past good behavior. Class III offenses are such that they warrant sterner measures, regardless of the offender's previous record. All of us have had students for whom we really did not want to recommend expulsion, but the strength and effectiveness of the Class III code has been that all students have been dealt with equally.

To change the code would be to return to the time when the wealth, position, or persistence of the parent determined the penalty assessed. It would lead to the kind of inequities from school to school that in the past gave credence to charges of bias and prejudice.

Please do not allow the loud protests of a few parents whose children have erred to drown out the voices of the majority of parents whose children respect the code and those of the school officials who administer it. It was, after all, the protection of the majority's rights that led to the code. They still deserve that protection.

EXPLANATION TO CRITIC OF CLINICAL INSTRUCTION

Innovations are sure to be upsetting to someone, and it may be necessary to answer the critic with a letter. Here the innovation is clinical instruction, and the critic is a special reading teacher at the elementary level.

Dear Mrs. Drennan:

Let me try to answer your questions about clinical instruction as it was explained recently in a staff development seminar. Sometimes it is difficult to see major differences between old and new theories. Perhaps clinical instruction is not so much a new theory anyway as it is an improved method—a way of setting standards for observing and understanding effective teaching techniques.

You are quite right in saying that every teacher should be aware of the need to analyze what is to be taught and to know at what point the student is ready to learn. That means thorough planning, well-thought-out instruction, and careful evaluation of results. I believe that clinical instruction, by helping both the teacher and observer know for sure that each of these steps is taking place, and in the proper order, may be one good way to improve our day-to-day teaching.

My experience in working with clinical instruction has shown that, far from making the teacher less independent or less professional, it enhances the teacher's individuality and creativity and allows a great deal of personal decision making. It helps educators understand that while learning is our concern, instruction is what we control. Therefore, we should focus on and be accountable for our instructional decisions and successes.

It is my belief that, in the past, observers or evaluators did not always know when instruction really was taking place. Clinical instruction is an attempt to improve upon that situation, to increase the observer's ability to judge instructional effectiveness and to give assistance for improving the teaching process. We hope that our administrative and teaching staff will give this approach a thoughtful trial, seeing if the method proves beneficial in our continuing search to improve instruction. That, of course, is the goal of all of us.

If you wish further information on clinical instruction, you may wish to talk with either Edith Ward or Juanita Valdez.

RESPONSE TO COMPLAINT ABOUT STAFF MEMBER

The complaint this letter answers was evidently made by a number of parents at a particular school, but it is being relayed to the superintendent by a watchdog community group.

Dear Mrs. Orcutt:

This is in response to your letter of June 12, 19xx, in which you voice the complaint of certain parents of children in the Higher Quest Program, relating to a staff member at the Tyrell School. You make the following statement: "It has come to our attention that there is a staff person currently at the Tyrell School who has publicly taken a position in opposition to the Higher Quest Program."

You can be assured that I am committed to having a staff at each school that is dedicated to the program there. Naturally, I would hope that all staff members at the Tyrell School support the goals and purposes of the Higher Quest Program. However, I find it difficult to go much beyond that statement in view of the following considerations:

1. Your letter does not specify the staff member with whom the Tyrell School parents are concerned.

2. It is the responsibility of members of the administrative and supervisory staff to bring to the attention of the Personnel Office and the Superintendent any problems or concerns relating to staff members. These must be presented in writing, using appropriate evaluation documents, and must be specific in nature. The documents must provide necessary supportive information.

3. The Board of Education has a legal responsibility to comply with the provisions of all negotiated contractual agreements, including those relating to the transfer or termination of a staff member.

4. All staff members have a right to be informed of any complaint that is being submitted regarding their performance.

It is reasonable to expect that if a problem does exist relative to a staff member at the Tyrell School, the administrators there will present to the district office an appropriate written, documented report.

I share the concern you have expressed, and I hope you can understand and appreciate the position I must take in regard to it. Also, please note that I am bringing your letter to the attention of the appropriate members of the administrative and supervisory staff.

Thank you for your continued interest in the Higher Quest Program and the Coltsville Public School System.

Sincerely yours,

Principal, The Tyrell School

❧ A Word on Style ❧

"PLEASE DO NOT HESITATE TO . . ."

Some books on letter writing have long lists of overworked phrases to avoid. The only trouble is that most of us have long since left off starting letters, "Responding to yours of the 18th instant," or ending them, "I remain, therefore, your obedient servant."

Nevertheless, there are a few phrases of more recent vintage that tend to be overworked. One of them is "Please do not hesitate to [write, phone, call, contact me, let me know, or whatever]." Actually, this is a very comfortable phrase. It serves its purpose. It neatly straddles the line between being formal and being helpful. And nobody seems to object strongly to it. It is seldom encountered in usage books of no-no's.

A number of letters in this book use the phrase. The reason is that many excellent letter writers include it in their last or next-to-last sentences. Because of that, alas, the phrase is fast becoming a cliché. If you want your letters to sound somewhat more original and personal, you may hesitate to end them with, "Please do not hesitate to . . ." There are many alternatives, as the letters in this book illustrate.

SPECIAL DAYS AND SPECIAL EVENTS

16

CHAPTER 16

The letters in this chapter all deal with special days or special events. Some of them are invitations. Some are greetings. Some are simply informative letters or memos explaining an event.

Since the purposes of the letters vary, so do the letter-writing approaches used. Invitation letters contain all the information needed—the who, what, when, where, and why. Greetings are more akin to letters of appreciation, but with a special slant because of the time of year.

The informative letters and memos serve a number of purposes. A few simply make the reader aware of a special day or an event: a festival, a convention, a field trip. Others request or require specific action: early dismissal, out-of-school rehearsals.

Whatever its purpose or type, each letter or memo in this chapter is clear and courteous. The reader never has to puzzle out what the writer is saying. Beyond that, the reader is always made to feel that the writer has taken the reader's feelings, wishes, and circumstances into account.

Calcasieu Parish Schools

BILLY J. MOSES
Superintendent

April 13, 19xx

TO: High School Social Studies Teachers
FROM: Deirdre R. Foreman, Social Studies Supervisor
SUBJECT: Contraband Days Festival, April 27-May 9

For the past 25 years, Contraband Days Festival has taken place during the last of April and early May in Lake Charles. The event has evolved into one of the major festivals of Louisiana.

Enclosed is some information on the origin and history of the festival. As we discuss events happening on the international, national, and state level in our classes, we should also include events occurring locally.

If you have any questions on this material, please feel free to call me.

Deirdre R. Foreman

TEA AND COFFEE HOUR FOR STUDENT TEACHERS

Like all good invitations, this one addressed to next-semester student teachers contains the necessary specifics. Notice that it sets a cut-off date for the return of the acceptance form.

Dear Ms. Fremont:

You are cordially invited to attend a special tea and coffee hour on Wednesday, June 8, at 9:00 a.m. in the Sherman Junior High School cafeteria.

As principal of Sherman Junior High School, I would like to share with you some of the significant opportunities for growth and professional development you will find available as a student teacher at S.J.H.S. In addition, our school will present several exciting student-oriented programs that we think potential student teachers will find useful.

We are always pleased to have energetic, creative, dedicated student teachers at Sherman Junior High School, and we are looking forward to the 19xx–19xx school year with great enthusiasm.

If you would like to attend our tea and coffee hours, please complete and return the attached form by June 2.

PRESCHEDULED ELEMENTARY FIELD TRIPS

This memo lists the field trips that have been approved and scheduled for each grade in a large city school system.

TO: Elementary Principals
FROM: Loretta Crowell, Director, Elementary Education
SUBJECT: Elementary Field Trips

As in past years, a number of field trips have been prescheduled for elementary teachers. Bus transportation will be provided for these prescheduled trips, which for 19xx–19xx are as follows:

Grade 1   Burwell Farm
Grade 2   Public Library (Teacher to schedule visit and then request a bus through the Department of Instruction)
Grade 3   Lloyd City Tour
Grade 4   Exeter Art Museum
Grade 5   Purdum Forest
Grade 6   Table Rock Planetarium

Private transportation may be used for two other trips approved for each grade level, as listed in the Elementary Field Trips booklet, if drivers are responsible and insured.

Pupils or teachers should *not* pay fees for admission to the places listed below. Such admissions will be paid by the Lloyd City Public Schools.

Burwell Farm
Purdum Forest
Table Rock Planetarium
Eli Spalding Zoo
General Wymore's House
Museum of the Great Plains

Guidelines

1. Each group of children must be supervised by qualified adults, at least one of whom must be among the certificated personnel of the Lloyd City Public Schools.

2. Each child participating in the field trip must go and return with the group.

3. Each child must have the written approval of his or her parent for each trip.

Further information can be found in the Elementary Field Trips booklet.

EARLY DISMISSAL FOR TEACHER WORKSHOP

Although a teachers' workshop is not a special day in the sense that a field trip is, still it requires arrangements to be made, in this case early dismissal. Recognizing that early dismissal will inconvenience some parents, the writer takes pains to explain the nature and value of the workshop.

Dear Parents:

On Monday, October 3, the administrators and staff in each of our district schools will participate in a two-hour workshop on standarized testing. They will examine and analyze the results of the testing conducted last fall. The workshop will familiarize them with how groups of students, as well as individuals, have performed. It will enable them to plan strategies to overcome weaknesses and improve performance. This use of test results to improve instruction has always been one of our objectives, but it has not received the attention it deserves.

Therefore, we are creating an opportunity to concentrate our efforts on test results and focus our attention on what to do about them. This workshop will require an early dismissal on October 3. So please make a note on your calendar: *Students will be dismissed one hour early on Monday, October 3.* This hour plus an extra hour that staff will remain that day will provide a two-hour workshop that should result in improved instruction at all grade levels.

We trust you will recognize that the inconvenience of an early dismissal is far offset by the benefits for students that we believe can result from a workshop on testing.

Thank you for your understanding and cooperation.

NATIONAL AND STATE PROFESSIONAL MEETINGS

The intent of this memo is to interest teachers in their national and state professional organizations. It is not a hard-sell memo, but it is persuasive.

TO: Secondary Social Studies Teachers
FROM: Elizabeth Reeves, Social Studies Supervisor
SUBJECT: Professional Organizations

The National Council for the Social Studies 61st Annual Meeting will be held in Detroit, Michigan, November 21–24, 19xx. The theme of this year's conference, "Renaissance for the Social Studies," will be explored in over 120 sessions and workshops. An exhibit will display the most up-to-date social studies textbooks, instructional materials, and services now available. Many tours, social functions, and other activities have been planned to take advantage of all that Detroit has to offer.

I have included with this memo a message from Theodore Kaltsounis, NCSS President; a pre-registration form; an NCSS membership application; and a housing reservation form for your use if you plan to attend.

The annual state conference of the Louisiana Council for Social Studies has just concluded. It was held at the Sheraton Chateau Charles on October 10, and plans are already being made for next year's conference to be held in Baton Rouge. If you would like to join LCSS, send the enclosed form with a check for $5.00 to me, Elizabeth Reeves, Dufour Parish School Board.

If you have any questions, please do not hesitate to call. I appreciate your interest.

GUIDELINES FOR CHRISTMAS PROGRAMS

This set of guidelines comes from a medium-sized Western city. It reflects the superintendent's desire to permit students and staff to celebrate the holiday season in a way that will not exclude or offend non-Christians.

TO: All Administrators
FROM: Superintendent of Schools
SUBJECT: Guidelines for Christmas Programs

It is important to preserve the spirit of good will that is characteristic of religious holidays. Therefore, whenever special holiday programs are planned, administrators should make every effort to see that these programs, in content and presentation, show respect for the religious sensibilities of all students and members of the staff.

During this holiday season, school administrators must be highly sensitive to their obligations to protect the religious feelings of students of every faith. To that end, the following guidelines should be observed:

1. Administrators should participate in the planning of holiday programs and should be continually aware of their development.

2. The planning of holiday programs should take into consideration the diverse religious faiths represented in the community, student body, and faculty.

3. Pupils and staff members whose personal convictions prohibit them from participating in a holiday program should be excused without penalty.

4. Sectarian pictures, music, and tableaux in classroom and assembly halls should be avoided.

5. Time spent in the preparation and presentation of any holiday program should be educationally justifiable.

If questions arise concerning these guidelines, they are to be referred to the Superintendent of Schools.

SCHEDULE FOR CHRISTMAS CHORUS PERFORMANCES

This letter is addressed to a vice president of a local bank. It confirms a schedule for school chorus performances that was previously agreed upon.

Dear Mr. Collins:

Thank you for your support and enthusiasm for another year of Christmas Lobby Sings in the Second National Bank of Russell Falls. This letter indicates the schedule and directors for this coming Christmas season.

Monday, Dec. 20	Noon to 12:30 p.m. Daly Junior High School Rita Browning, Director
	12:30 to 1:00 p.m. Marcus James Junior High School Lee Thurlow, Director
Tuesday, Dec. 21	Noon to 12:30 p.m. Huntley Junior High School Geraldine Hammond, Director
	12:30 to 1:00 p.m. Parker Junior High School Winifred Blakeslee, Director
Wednesday, Dec. 22	Noon to 12:30 p.m. Russell Falls High School Choir Roy Jordan, Director

I will arrange for an appropriate number of risers and will ask the directors to bring one music stand. Thank you for arranging for the piano.

All of us appreciate your help and encouragement. We are looking forward with great anticipation to this opportunity.

SEASON'S GREETINGS

Here is a good nonsectarian message for the holiday season, one that stresses the joy of life and the purposefulness of education.

Dear Staff:

It is with great joy that I send you season's greetings. This has been a very special year.

Let me say what a privilege it has been to work with all of you. I am grateful for your help and your patience. The experience of working with outstanding educators and dedicated service personnel is always refreshing and stimulating, and never more so than this year.

We should be thankful that we have been permitted to be of service to others. We have helped students learn how to learn—and learn how to live. The glory of education is the opportunity it gives us to work with and help other people.

This is the time of year for rejoicing and for rededication. A quote from Thomas Drier says it well: "If we are ever to enjoy life, now is the time—not tomorrow or next year. The best preparation for a better life next year is a full, complete, harmonious, joyous life this year."

Now is the time to reflect on our blessings and to recharge our spirits.

Happy holidays!

CHRISTMAS GREETINGS FROM LUTHERAN SCHOOL PRINCIPAL

While the previous letter was nonsectarian, this one is understandably and strongly Christian. Like the other one, it stresses the values and idealism of teaching.

Christmas Blessings:

Christmas is a time when I think of the special people in my life, of my family, friends, and co-workers with whom I share Christian ministry.

To you, I want to say thank you for your loving and dedicated approach to young people. Without this, Lutheran High would not be the special place it is. We experience many joys in our teaching, but we also know sorrow and frustration as we become involved in the lives of our students. This happens because we care. We share their joys and excitements, but we also experience the uncertainty, the confusion, and the hurts that are so often a part of their lives.

Christmas again confronts us with the reality that Jesus left His place in heaven to become our brother and to share His life with us. Christmas reminds us that Jesus is always at our side with His love, His forgiveness, and His power as we carry out our Christian ministry at Lutheran High.

I thank God for Christmas. I thank God for each of you, because in your giving of yourselves for young people, you are, as Luther said, "Little Christs," through whom others experience the love of Jesus.

May these holidays also be a time of recreation and relaxation with family and friends, so important as we prepare to face the challenges and opportunities that come again in January.

Meanwhile, let us pray for the young people each day, in particular for those we know who have not found Christ's place in their lives.

My wife Laurel, my daughter Roslyn, and I wish you every blessing of the season.

CLASSROOM VISITS DURING AMERICAN EDUCATION WEEK

In this letter a middle school principal invites all parents to sit in on classes during a regular school day. The reverse side of the letter suggests specific days for each homeroom in order to try to distribute visits throughout the week.

Dear Parents:

The faculty and I invite you to accompany your daughter or son to classes during a regular school day as your way of celebrating American Education Week, November 15–20, 19xx. It is our hope that a day in school will further your appreciation of the middle school educational program and provide encouragement for the schoolwork being done by your child. Even if you cannot spend a full day with us, we believe that any part of the day you are here will be interesting for you and supportive of your son or daughter.

A suggested day for your visit is shown on the reverse side of this invitation. If you cannot visit according to the schedule, however, please come when your schedule permits.

We look forward to seeing you in class next week.

CAREER DAY

Although a career day is intended primarily for students, there is likely to be a great deal of parental interest in it. In this letter the principal invites those parents who want to come, requesting that they make prior arrangements.

Dear Parents:

On Wednesday, May 2, 19xx, we will hold our annual career day at Kilmer High School. We are expecting more than thirty speakers from business and the professions to be here to explain to interested students the nature and requirements of their occupations. We have found this to be an invaluable way of helping students make informed choices about the careers they wish to pursue.

In the past, a number of parents have asked if they can attend career day. The answer is yes. If you wish to come to school that day, please call 654-3210 before April 28 so that we will be expecting you.

OPEN HOUSE AT SKILLS CENTER

Here is another invitation, this one to an open house at a vocational high school.

Dear Friend:

On Wednesday, November 15, the Cosby Skills Center will hold its Ninth Annual Open House from 9 a.m. to 10:30 a.m. and from 6:45 p.m. to 8:45 p.m.

The Cosby Skills Center offers training in seven career clusters that provide skill development for fifty different occupational areas. Students progress at their own rate of speed through an individualized, competency-based instructional program.

I hope you can find the time in your busy schedule to be with us for this open house.

FOREIGN LANGUAGE NIGHT

The following letter is both an invitation and a request, since parents who attend the Foreign Language Night activities are expected to bring an appropriate foreign dish.

Dear Parents:

As the parent or parents of a student taking a foreign language course, you are cordially invited to attend our Foreign Language Night on Tuesday, April 17, at 8:00 p.m. in the Paine High School cafeteria.

This event begins with an international dinner and concludes with a program presented by our German, French, Italian, and Spanish classes.

First, about the dinner: Parents who attend the evening's activities are expected to bring one foreign dish, ready to be served. Ideally, the parents of French students will bring a French dish, parents of a Spanish student an Hispanic dish, and so on. That ensures a good selection of each of the four kinds of foods. However, do not feel bound by this request. If your child is studying Spanish, for example, and you wish to bring a German, French, or Italian dish, that will be fine.

Long tables will be set up on each of the four sides of the cafeteria. They will be appropriately labeled by nationality, so you will know where to place your dish. Please put it there as soon as you arrive, and then take a seat. We will appreciate it if you try to arrive as close to 8:00 p.m. as possible. Mrs. Rumson, Chairwoman of our Foreign Languages Department, will say a few words before the dinner begins.

After the dinner, we will proceed to the auditorium where our foreign language teachers and students will present the evening's program. In the past, these Foreign Language Night programs have been exceptionally well-received, and I am sure this year's will be no exception.

We look forward to seeing you on April 17. It is sure to be an evening you will enjoy and remember.

GRANDPARENTS' DAY

Here is an invitation to a special day put on by a Lutheran school. The principal needs to know how many grandparents will be attending; consequently, he includes a reply form at the bottom of the invitation.

Dear Grandparents:

The students, faculty, and board of Trinity Lutheran School, 1771 Borah Drive, request the honor of your presence at our first "Grandparents' Day" to be held May 14, 19xx, beginning at 9:45 a.m.

Please complete and return the reservation form below or else call the school office (234-5678) regarding your participation in this special day. Reservations should be made prior to Monday, May 5.

<u>Schedule of Activities</u>

9:45–10:00	Registration
10:00–10:15	Welcome by Mr. Oakley, Principal
10:15–10:45	Visits to classrooms by grandparents
10:45–11:30	Chapel service with students and grandparents
11:45	Lunch. Those who wish to stay and eat lunch with their grandchildren may do so. The cost is $2.00 for each adult.

—— Yes. (I, we) will be attending Grandparents' Day
—— No. (I, we) will not be attending Grandparents' Day
If eating lunch ($2.00 fee per adult), please check here. ——
Amount enclosed. ——

Your name(s) _____

Address _____ Phone No._____

Name(s) of your grandchild(ren) attending Trinity Lutheran School

_____

REHEARSALS FOR STRING-O-RAMA

This letter from a music supervisor explains the rationale of the String-O-Rama program and tries, very skillfully, to enlist the support of parents.

Dear Parents:

We are pleased to announce plans for the 19xx String-O-Rama, a concert that will include string players in grades 4 through 12 from throughout Russell Falls.

Most students seldom have a chance to play in a full orchestra before they enter junior high school, unless they happen to be selected for the Elementary All-City Orchestra.

Several years ago a committee of music teachers, principals, and classroom teachers began searching for ways in which more elementary students might be given the chance to play in a balanced orchestra. The concept of the String-O-Rama developed from the committee's work. It has been a notable success.

Most of the practice for String-O-Rama occurs during your child's normal instrumental instructional period in the school. However, if the total experience is to be meaningful, we feel that three full-orchestra rehearsals of one hour each are also desirable. A schedule for these rehearsals is given on the back of this sheet. The five elementary instrumental music teachers will organize and conduct the rehearsals.

Although planning by the music staff and school principals has been in progress for months, the success of this project and the benefit to your child depend very much on your cooperation as a parent. The full-orchestra rehearsals must be held at times other than the regular school day, because we are borrowing larger facilities to accommodate the concert. We are asking you to bring your child to each of the rehearsals, or to arrange to have students brought by neighbors whose children may be involved. These large-group rehearsals are as vital a part of your child's music education as performing in the concert.

Rehearsals will start and end on time. The concert will be approximately one hour long. You are encouraged to attend both the rehearsals and the concert, and to bring family and friends.

This is a fine opportunity for your child and your family to realize the thrill of an orchestral performance and to inspire the community with a musical celebration. We think you will want to be part of this exciting experience!

INVITATION TO BAND CONCERT

Parents have already been invited to these four regional concerts. This letter from a music supervisor is individually addressed to each Board of Education member, inviting him or her to attend one of the concerts.

Dear Mr. Lombard:

The elementary instrumental music department is conducting what are called Elementary Regional Band Concerts with approximately 900 students on the evening of Monday, April 7, at 7:15 p.m. at each of the four junior high schools.

There are bands of two different ability levels at each of the junior high schools. This ensures that every child who participates in the instrumental music program will have an experience appropriate to his or her present state of preparation. Although concert participation is optional for these young people, our rehearsals indicate a high degree of interest.

We would like to invite you to attend one of these concerts if your schedule permits. Given the number of elementary youngsters involved, I anticipate fairly large audiences.

PUBLIC RELATIONS AND THE MEDIA

17

CHAPTER 17

It is vital for the public to view the schools favorably, and one way to achieve that goal is through public relations. The public needs to be informed, not just through media-initiated stories but through stories that educators themselves want told.

Public relations is a very broad topic. Every letter makes some sort of impression on the reader, and in that sense every letter is an instrument of public relations. However, the wider audience provided by the media—the press, radio, television—is the usual target of most public relations efforts.

The letters and memos in this chapter have various audiences and purposes, but the desired end result of all of them is that the public will know more about the local schools and will view the schools more favorably.

School and district newsletters and periodicals are an important part of public relations. Their use has been touched upon throughout this book, and consequently, except for a newsletter article specifically on public relations, this chapter deals with media other than the schools' own publications.

REQUEST TO REPRINT ARTICLE

Office of Communications

726-3267

November 3, 19xx

Ms. Pauline Rhiner
Managing Editor
PTA Today
700 North Rush Street
Chicago, Illinois 60611

Dear Ms. Rhiner

Your November issue of PTA Today contains an article about tuition tax credits that is very well done. Many of our PTA people locally have remarked about it and have referred to the article in discussions about this timely subject.

Would you allow me to reprint your article in the January issue of the Springfield Schools Report? This publication is a district quarterly that goes to school district residents in Springfield, Oregon, and has a circulation of 20,000.

Thank you for considering this request. Rest assured that the material will be credited to you and properly acknowledged.

Sincerely,

Stephen M. Barrett

Stephen M. Barrett
Asst. to the Superintendent

MEMO TO ADMINISTRATORS ON PUBLIC RELATIONS

The intent of this memo is to remind principals and other administrators to keep public relations in mind when innovative programs are started, honors are won, awards are presented—in short, when anything positive, out-of-the-ordinary, and newsworthy occurs in their schools.

> TO: Administrative Staff
> FROM: Maurice Pitman, Superintendent
> SUBJECT: Public Relations

> Our schools are an important part of community life, and as such they deserve a certain amount of media attention. To help ensure that we receive a favorable press, I would like to ask each of you to keep in mind this need to inform the public about what our schools are doing.

> Naturally, the day-to-day activities in the schools, no matter how excellent, do not constitute news. What the media are looking for is the extraordinary event or development. This might be an unusual and successful new course. It might be a student who has distinguished himself or herself to the extent of being newsworthy. It might be the presence of a celebrity in the school, as, for instance, when Judy Blume recently spoke to the students at Crane Middle School.

> When you do prepare press releases, please forward them to the district office for dissemination. Make sure that you check all facts, dates, and names very carefully before submitting a release. Misspelled names, which are among the most common of errors, can be an embarrassment if they are not caught.

> We are all proud of our schools. We know they are doing a good job and that exciting things happen in them. It is up to all of us to let the public know this, too.

ADVICE TO TEACHERS ON PUBLIC RELATIONS

Although this memo is aimed at music teachers, it offers guidelines that are applicable to most other teachers who are concerned with public relations.

> TO: All Music Staff
> FROM: Emory Belmont, Music Supervisor
> SUBJECT: Publicity

> We welcome good publicity about our citywide music activities, and we have been fortunate in the past in making them known to the community. Here are a few things to keep in mind about obtaining publicity.

1. Generally, the Gazette will not publicize a strictly elementary or junior high event that is confined to a single school. Limited space may be given to a senior high event.

2. Events tied to a broader purpose or theme may be considered for publicity. Some imagination may help.

3. We are not always going to get equal billing on the same kind of events, nor will we necessarily get ample billing on some events. Much has to do with the flow of other news.

4. Please advise this office in advance if you intend to seek publicity for one of your programs. Then keep us informed as the publicity develops.

5. Since this office has certain priorities for publicity that help us present a comprehensive and balanced interpretation of what we are doing, we need exact, continuing information on any programs that may impact on the press and other media.

PRESS RELEASE TO LOCAL NEWSPAPERS

A press release is written in the form of an article for publication. It may be cut or edited by the newspaper staff, but frequently it will be printed without change. Press releases are usually headed "Press Release" or "For Immediate Release."

For Immediate Release

Beverly Delanco, an English teacher at Caulfield High Shcool, has written a new children's biography of Walt Whitman. Recently published by Robinson-Boles, Inc., it is entitled Walt Whitman: He Heard America Singing.

A prepublication reviewer in Publishers World wrote that the book "shows young readers the human side of Walt Whitman. Writing in language appropriate for youngsters in their early teens, Miss Delanco creates an exciting story out of the life of one of America's greatest poets. Highly recommended."

The author, a native of Newark, has taught English at Caulfield High School for the past eleven years. Prior to that, she taught English for nine years at Bennett Junior High School in Lake Warwick. Her first book, a children's biography of Stephen Crane, was published four years ago and won a number of regional writers' awards. She has also written several articles for professional journals on the teaching of English.

The biography of Walt Whitman "took longer than I had expected," Miss Delanco noted. "So much has been written and published about Walt

Whitman for adults." She added, "I should point out, however, that contrary to what many people think, a biography for young people is not just a simplified version of an adult biography. It is a brand new book."

LETTER TO NEWSPAPER SOLICITING COVERAGE

This letter provides the kind of information a newspaper editor needs to decide whether the event described is indeed important enough to warrant sending a reporter.

Dear Mr. Husted:

An assembly program we have scheduled at Kilmer High School for 9:00 a.m. next Tuesday may be an event the Star-Journal would like to cover.

The reason I say this is that the speaker will be Monty Idell, Kilmer's most famous recent graduate, last year's Superbowl star, and the man who has led the Philadelphia Eagles to three straight NFL championships.

When we at the high school learned that Monty would be spending a few days with his family on Sparta Avenue, we asked him if he would be able to return to Kilmer and say a few words to our students. He agreed to come on Tuesday morning.

Given the national publicity he has received, I wanted you to know that he will be visiting his high school alma mater where, twelve years ago, he broke virtually every football record in the Highview Conference. His visit may be worth covering.

FOLLOW-UP LETTER ON MEDIA COVERAGE

This letter is, in itself, an admirable example of public relations, yet its direct purpose is to thank a television station for its coverage of a school event.

Dear Mr. Jewett:

Let me take this opportunity to thank you for complying with my request—on such short notice—to cover the ceremony held yesterday afternoon in Merrill Park, at which time 500 students were honored for their academic achievements during the past school year. The television coverage of this function provided the public with a positive image of our school system and was, in effect, a tribute to those students who were being recognized for their scholastic excellence during the 19xx–19xx school year.

The importance of favorable news coverage cannot be over-emphasized. Our society is, unfortunately, too frequently confronted with unpleasant situations, which often receive extensive coverage from the media. I strongly believe, however, that news coverage should not be limited to unfavorable or negative situations. As a community, we need constant reassurance that the majority of people and, in particular, the students within our school system, are good citizens and are genuinely concerned with the betterment of their community. The coverage of the honors assembly at Merrill Park exemplifies such favorable news reporting.

On behalf of the Elgart Public Schools and, in particular, those students who have displayed initiative and genuine concern for their education, I would like to express my appreciation to the WXYZ news team, who effectively portrayed the honors assembly and, thus, a positive aspect of our school system.

I look forward to a continued, cooperative working relationship with the WXYZ news team.

NEWSLETTER ARTICLE ON PUBLIC RELATIONS

Here is an exceptionally informative article on what one school system has done to involve the whole community in its activities.

Bismarck—
"Keep in Touch" (KIT) Focuses on Ideas,
Projects to Involve Parents with Schools

Keeping in touch is a most important task for vigilant and concerned school districts. The Bismarck School District encourages imaginative and resourceful actions by staff to enhance school-community relations.

The latest success story involves the Bismarck Public School personnel's play, Little Casino. Written by a local teacher, the play netted $10,000 for the United Fund Campaign in October. Teachers, administrators, maintenance personnel, and delivery boys spent weeks rehearsing and preparing for the production. The overwhelming success played to sold-out houses three nights.

On tap for American Education Week are free mini-courses for the public. Teachers throughout the system are preparing evening topics such as "Winter Storage for Lawnmowers," "Swedish Embroidery," "Hands-on Clay," "Travel Tips for Europe and Mexico," "Reading the Label," and "Holiday Parties from Around the World." One of the elementary schools is sponsoring "Hi, Neighbor," especially intended for people in the area who have no children in school.

Another contact is with senior citizens. For a number of years Golden Age Passes have been free for the asking. They admit our senior citizens to local sports contests, musical programs, and other events.

Guest speakers from a large roster of doctors, lawyers, firemen, policemen, clergymen, politicians, and businessmen accept invitations to speak to classes throughout the Bismarck Public School System. Some make several repeat appearances through the years. Students are also taken on field trips to hospitals, architectural firms, banks, and business places in the community.

Bismarck High School recently celebrated its 100th birthday with a week-long celebration. The public, including many BHS graduates, attended programs, enjoyed fellowship with students and teachers over coffee, and were able to purchase a history of BHS researched and produced by journalism students. This book included a list of every graduate from the first class to the date of publication.

The parents of Bismarck High students have established a Booster Club which provides refreshments to members and to all participants in evening athletic events. BHS supports this strong, active group wholeheartedly and provides use of the cafeteria when needed.

To encourage participation of parents and the public, student achievement awards assemblies are held at BHS periodically during the year.

When Bismarck High School began the process of renovation, an advisory committee of nine community members was established. Last year this group met several times to suggest ideas regarding structural changes. Some members of this group made trips to other schools in cities that have recently constructed new buildings or renovated old ones.

To get parents involved and to make them aware of the needs of BHS, a group of eight to ten parents is invited to spend a couple of hours in the building. This is done on a weekly basis, and for some parents, it is the first visit to the place where their high schoolers spend three years of their lives. In addition to having the opportunity to express ideas about the renovation, the parents see the school "at work."

Keep in touch!

Emeroy Swanson
Principal, Bismarck High School

LETTER TO BOARD OF EDUCATION CANDIDATE

In a sense, every school administrator's letter that attempts to win support for the school system is a public relations letter. The following letter is the result of a newspaper article announcing a candidacy for a position on the Board of Education.

> Dear Mrs. Hyder:
>
> We were pleased to read about your candidacy for the Saguaro Board of Education. You are to be commended for your desire to serve the community as a school board member.
>
> During the course of the campaign, many questions will be raised and concerns expressed. We will be happy to provide you with general information, to answer your specific questions, or to discuss school district operations with you. Please do not hesitate to call upon us.
>
> Our compliments on your personal commitment to the young people of this school district.

OPEN INVITATION TO BOARD MEMBERS

This letter from a principal to each member of the Board of Education is a fine example of public relations in action.

> Dear Dr. Ridgeway:
>
> Much of what occurs during a school year is influenced by prior actions of the Board of Education. Because it seems only fair that you get a chance to view some of the end results of your work as a Board member in regard to staffing, school procedures, and supplies, the faculty and I would be pleased to have you spend some time at Hamilton Middle School as an observer during this school year. Feel free to visit for part of a day, for a full day, or for part or all of a number of days. No advance notice is needed. Come unannounced.
>
> The faculty and I look forward to seeing you.

LETTER TO EDITOR SEEKING COMMUNITY UNDERSTANDING

It may sometimes be necessary to respond to a widespread misconception about a school or school system. Here the writer is explaining how a great many students can legitimately be away from the school grounds during school hours.

<u>Letter to the Editor</u>
<u>Reasons for Student Mobility</u>

The more than 12,000 high school students in the Harte Public Schools are a very mobile group. Many people have the idea that students attending a high school stay put all day within the building or on the grounds. That belief causes much concern when people observe our students in other places.

The question is asked, "Why are so many students out of class, out on the street, getting on buses, wandering about, and so on?" The answer is that most of these students are attending school and are doing what they are supposed to do.

Regional Occupations Centers are located all over the city, and students often attend classes at schools other than their own. They come and go all day.

Many schools do not have athletic facilities, and students must leave the campus on foot or by bus to attend classes or games.

Some schools do not have the facilities to feed their students. Consequently, students must leave campus at lunch time in order to eat.

Early Classes, called "A" Periods, are held before school in the morning. Other students may thus appear to be coming late, while A Period students may seem to be hanging around when in fact they are waiting for Period I to begin. The A Period students usually leave early, having completed their day.

Some high schools hold classes away from the main campus. Many students attend adult school or college classes as well as their regular high school campus classes.

In short, most of our students are responsible, hard-working, reliable young adults, busily attending to their educational needs all over the city. They should not be confused with the much smaller number of truant or problem young people who may be seen under similar circumstances.

BUDGET AND FINANCIAL MATTERS

18

CHAPTER 18

In this chapter the letters deal with money. There are letters on budgeting, on financial statements, on special funds, on scholarships, on phone bills, on private schools' and nonresident students' tuition, and more. The letters are addressed to parents, accountants, architects, other school administrators. There is even one addressed to a student.

Financial matters can be tricky to explain in writing, but the school administrators represented in this chapter do it admirably. The letters are clear, explicit, and detailed enough to make their points unmistakably. A few are somewhat legalistic because of the nature of their content.

Legal language, despite the ridicule it is sometimes subjected to, is precise language. The wrong word, a missing word, or the legendary misplaced comma can be fatal in a legal document. It can cost the client money—a lot of money. Small wonder, then, that when school administrators write about money matters, they tend to exercise special care, to make sure that their facts and figures are correct.

All good letters contain precise language, but the ones in this chapter are especially noteworthy in that respect.

Lubbock High School

2004 Nineteenth Street
LUBBOCK, TEXAS 79401

OFFICE OF
Knox Williams
Principal

"Sportsmanship, Then Victory"

PHONE
765-8821
Ext. 61

February 3, 19xx

Ms. Mary Ann Sutton
Director, LEARN
Educational Talent Search
P.O. Box 558
Lubbock, Texas 79408

Dear Ms. Sutton:

It causes me a great deal of concern to hear that there is even a possibility that the LEARN Educational Talent Search will not be funded after this year.

Lubbock High School uses the services of LEARN and depends upon the help offered to our students. LEARN has benefited our students for several years with the services offered them in exploring the possibilities of attending college.

The counselors at Lubbock High also depend upon, and use, the services of LEARN on a regular basis. I feel that the program increases their effectiveness.

I would strongly urge the Department of Education to fund this excellent program that offers so many benefits to the students of our community.

Sincerely,

Knox Williams
Principal

EXPLANATION OF SCHOOL BUDGETING PROBLEMS

This letter from a superintendent is written in response to a student's request for information about the problems that arise in budgeting for the public schools. The explanation is clear and exceptionally detailed.

Dear Miss Hunt:

May I compliment your school on requiring senior English students to write the kind of essay you have described. The ability to express yourself in writing is very important. Your school and your teacher are providing you with an excellent opportunity to develop your skills in a meaningful way.

Let me try to answer your questions concerning our budgeting procedures and difficulties.

The process of budgeting for Arizona schools has been established by laws passed by the Arizona Legislature and through procedures determined by the Arizona Department of Education and the Arizona Auditor General. These procedures are contained in a document called the Uniform System of Financial Records. I have attached, for your information, a copy of the budget forms used by all Arizona school districts.

There are many problems related to budgeting for the public schools. I will outline a few of the difficulties schools face because of limited revenue, or dollars. All schools in the district are permitted to spend a specified amount of money each year. That amount is determined by a formula based on the average number of students in attendance.

For example, to determine the allowable expenditure limit for 19xx–19xx, a district will multiply what is called the Average Daily Membership (for the first 120 days of the current school year) by a specific amount of money (called the Base Support Level). The dollar value of the Base Support Level is permitted, by law, to increase no more than 7 percent a year.

This means that a school district budget can increase by only 7 percent a year if the number of students remains constant. The problems associated with this limited yearly increase are significant:

1. For a number of years, the yearly inflation rate has far exceeded 7 percent, and school districts have not had enough money to give employees salary increases to keep up with inflation.

2. If the number of students declines, a school district receives an increase of less than 7 percent, but expenses do not decline correspondingly.

3. With higher costs and limited dollars, districts find they must cut costs to balance the budget each year. They reduce costs (a) by eliminating certain programs, or courses, and by reducing other costs, or (b) by reducing the number of teachers, administrators, custodians, and secretaries.

Many of the costs of operating the school district are beyond the control of the schools. Utilities are a good example. The rates for natural gas, electricity, and water are controlled by the Arizona Corporation Commission. Those rates must be paid regardless of how much they increase. Often the rates increase faster than schools can reduce the amount of gas, electricity, or water they use. This means that a district must take money from the instruction of students to pay the increasing utility bills.

The cost of transporting students to and from school each day has been an ever increasing cost. Once again, that cost is allowed by law to increase no more than 7 percent a year. School districts must either reduce the amount of transportation or divert money from other programs to pay for the increase.

This year the federal government has reduced the amount of money given to school districts for special educational programs and for support of school cafeteria programs. This reduction has caused schools to cut many programs and to raise the price of cafeteria meals.

Let me give a few examples from the Saguaro district to help you get a better idea of how large some of our costs are.

1. A 10 percent salary increase for Saguaro school employees will cost an additional $1,300,000 a year.

2. For every 1-cent-per-gallon increase in the price of gasoline, our transportation costs increase $1,000 a year.

3. During the 19xx–19xx school year, our utilities will cost approximately $700,000. If utility rates go up only 10 percent next year, we will have to spend $70,000 more.

The only way a school district can increase spending by more than the 7 percent each year is by a vote of the citizens of the school district. This is called an Override Election. The effects of an override election last for three years. After that, the district must hold another election or else cut its budget back to the amount it would normally have been.

There are many other problems involved in school district budgeting, but I hope I have given you information that will help you write your essay. If I can be of further help, please let me know.

LETTER TO PARENTS ON TAX LEVY

The public needs to have a thorough understanding of the effects of a property tax increase and the reasons behind it. In this letter a superintendent explains precisely what is being asked of taxpayers and why.

Parents of District 92 Students:

As you know, the school district will be asking voters to approve a $12,340,752 tax levy on September 14, 19xx. The levy will provide about half the necessary income for the district to continue to provide quality educational services for the 9,500 school children in the Markham Public Schools.

We hope you will take a minute to look at the enclosed fact sheet and discuss it with your family and friends. It answers the questions that are asked most frequently about this levy.

The 19xx–19xx tax levy, if approved, will increase the tax rate on homestead property from last year's figure of $11.06 per $1,000 of true cash value to $11.55 per $1,000 of true cash value of your home. This represents an increase of 6.2 percent in the tax rate. On a $50,000 home, the new rate will increase taxes by $2.05 per month.

This new rate is required by an increase in bond debt payments for the construction of a new elementary school in west Markham and additions to Pauling and McLoughlin High Schools. These projects were approved by voters in 19xx, and work has started on them.

We are anticipating a significant decrease in revenues other than the tax levy. The school district's budget will be lower as the result of a loss in state and federal revenues. Current estimates indicate that the loss due to reductions in federal revenue sharing will be a minimum of $220,000 and a maximum of $430,000. Further reductions may be required to offset the loss of state revenues.

At this time, the budget review committee and the Board of Education have not determined where specific cuts will be made in the District 92 budget. Such a determination will be made after the state has notified the district of the specific amount of lost revenue.

If you need more information, or if you would like to have a school district representative discuss facts concerning the budget with you or a group of your friends, please call 789-6543 to arrange a meeting.

SUPERINTENDENT'S LETTER SUPPORTING FINANCIAL STATEMENTS

The following letter is addressed to an accounting firm. It states, essentially, that the financial statements of the school district are accurate insofar as the superintendent knows.

Gentlemen:

I have read the letter of representation dated August 25, 19xx, addressed to you from Henry Fowler, Herbert Carlisle, and Andrew Kershaw in connection with your examination of the financial statements of the Rutledge School District as of June 30, 19xx, and for the year then ended. I recognize that obtaining representation from management concerning the information contained in that letter is an important procedure in enabling you to form an opinion on the financial statements. I recognize that the members of management of the Rutledge School District are responsible for the fair presentation in the combined financial statements of financial position, results of operations, and changes in financial position, in conformity with generally accepted accounting principles applied on a basis consistent with that of the preceding year. In connection therewith, I make the following representations, which are true to the best of my knowledge and belief.

I have no reason to believe that the information contained in the letter referred to above is incorrect.

No events or transactions have occurred since June 30, 19xx, or are pending or in prospect, which would have a material effect upon the financial statements at that date. In addition, I know of no event since June 30, 19xx, which, although not affecting such financial statements, has caused any material change, adverse or otherwise, in the financial position or results of operations of the Rutledge School District.

MEMO DEALING WITH SELECTION OF ARCHITECT

This memo invites local architects to apply for an assignment involving major renovation of a high school. It spells out the guidelines carefully.

TO: Architects of Fort Owens Area
FROM: Frederick Danforth, Superintendent
SUBJECT: Renovation of Fort Owens High School

The Fort Owens School District has scheduled the resurfacing of the high school roof for June 19xx. Since this 42,188-square-foot resurfacing plan calls for extensive renovation, the school district will be screening applications for the selection of an architect. We expect to make our choice by October 1, 19xx. Candidates should send a letter of application, a resume, and credentials to me at the address shown above.

In selecting the architect for this project, the following criteria will be considered:

1. Experience in school construction

2. Evidence of relevant experience in special situations, such as designing facilities for the handicapped

3. Creative design ability

4. Technical knowledge to control the design so that the best results are obtained for the least amount of money

5. Executive and business ability to oversee the proper performance of contracts

6. Proven ability in all major phases of planning and construction: predesign planning, schematic design, design development, bidding, construction

7. Ability and temperament to work cooperatively with others

8. Willingness to consult with district and school staff on educational specifications

9. Experience of architectural staff on projects of the scope of this one

10. Reasonableness of fee. Because of economic conditions, the Board of Education will give particularly careful consideration to each candidate's fee schedule for this project.

The architect will be selected by the Board of Education on the basis of the above criteria and will be employed under a contract that meets the current standards of the American Institute of Architects.

Applications for this project will be received until the closing date of August 31, 19xx. Interested candidates are encouraged to tour the high school plant. Please call the Administration Center for an appointment.

THANK-YOU LETTER FOR MAKING FUNDS AVAILABLE

Here is a letter thanking a superintendent for permitting funds to be used for a special conference. As always, the writer's use of direct quotations is effective.

Dear Dr. Makika:

Your unfreezing of $1,700 to enable us to stage a language arts conference, "A Celebration of Language and Learning," really supported our efforts. Thank you very much for your help.

More than 200 teachers and principals participated. All the people I talked to were enthusiastic about the results. We even managed to do a little PR by welcoming 12 private school teachers to the conference.

Comments such as the following show the enthusiasm the teachers felt about the conference:

"Please have another celebration."

"This is the kind of workshop that would be meaningful for Teachers' Institute Day."

"Make it an annual event to rejuvenate our teaching and teachers."

"Perhaps a conference like this should be planned before every school year so that teachers can help suggest topics."

We all feel good about the excitement that was generated and about the raised expectations of the participants. I am sure that better teaching and better student performance in the language arts will result.

Everyone who was involved appreciates your efforts in releasing the funds even during this period of severe financial constraints.

PRINCIPAL'S RECOMMENDATIONS ON SCHOLARSHIP FUND

This letter is to the president of a parents' group that is trying to decide how to award a scholarship or scholarships to deserving students at an all-girls' high school.

Dear Mrs. Barclay:

As you continue to discuss the issue of establishing a Parent Organization scholarship fund for Carroll High students, allow me to make a number of recommendations.

In my judgment, a single Carroll Parent Organization Scholarship should be awarded each year, with either a fixed dollar figure or a fixed financial range. Specific, simple criteria should be established by the parents for the awarding of the scholarship; e.g., financial need, a certain grade point average, service to the school.

These criteria should be put in writing for the school's Scholarship Committee records, including the understanding that while the Scholarship Committee will select the student recipient, the Parent Organization will receive a follow-up report as to the reasons for her selection and her specific plans for college. Procedures should be put in place to have the scholarship winner report her college progress to the parents the following year.

Establishing this kind of scholarship would serve several purposes. First, it would allow parents to continue their public support of Carroll students' preparation for college. Second, it would involve the Parent Organization more directly in the awarding of scholarships. And third, it would permit the majority of funds raised by the Parent Organization to be channeled back to the school for the benefit of the entire student body.

We continue to be grateful for the support, financial and moral, that we receive from Carroll parents.

TAX EFFECTS OF PRIVATE SCHOOL DONATIONS

Although the deductions and credits in this letter are based on what is allowable on Idaho's Income Tax Return, Form 40, similar tax breaks are allowed in a number of other states.

Dear Friends of Trinity Lutheran School:

If new religious education materials could be purchased for 50 children at a total cost of $8.50, our sharing of God's Word would be great, considering that a full year's instruction would cost only 17¢ per student. If you could give Trinity Lutheran School four new desks and chairs for a total of $11.00, no doubt you would feel your money was well spent. If an old and torn carpet in the library could be replaced for $29.00, it would be a God-pleasing management of money.

It sounds too good to be true—but it is true.

Mr. Joseph Riggins, a certified public accountant with Hayden Riggins Associates, has investigated the 19xx Idaho tax credit laws and has prepared the enclosed information for us. In short, and to take a single example, it works like this:

Mr. & Mrs. Friend of T.L.S. contribute $200

As contributors they can deduct 38.5 percent of this amount
    based on their salary of $20,000 .... (deduction) ...... $ 71

Filing a joint return, they can claim a 50 percent tax credit as
    contributors to an approved Idaho educational institution
    (credit) $100

The net cost to Mr. & Mrs. Friend of T.L.S. by their donation of
    $200 is .... $ 29

This information applies to contributions made since January 1, 19xx, and will apply until December 31, 19xx. These deductions and credits were confirmed in the recently released instruction booklet for the 19xx Idaho Income Tax, Form 40.

We ask you at this time to consider making a contribution to Trinity Lutheran School in view of the low net cost to you and the tremendous benefit you can give God's children by supporting Christian education.

EXPLANATION OF LONG-DISTANCE PHONE BILLS

A sudden increase in long-distance phone calls from a high school prompted questions about them from the district office. Here is the principal's reply.

TO: Waldo Snyder, Assistant Superintendent
FROM: Howard McCrory, Principal
SUBJECT: Long-Distance Phone Bills

After our talk yesterday, I went over the phone bills for the period between September 21 and October 21, which I agree are unusually high. Most of the bills were incurred in connection with these four activities at the high school:

1. The greatest number of calls originated from the Music Department and concerned our new band uniforms. We have had a continuing problem in reaching agreement with the Tahoe Mills Company of Oakland, California. These calls were necessary to bring us closer to a satisfactory settlement. Once the problem is resolved, as we expect it to be this month, the calls to Oakland will cease.

2. A number of phone calls were made in regard to our band's participation in the Rose Bowl Parade. These calls were necessary in order to finalize travel plans and to discuss organizational matters. Some further calls will be needed, but Mr. DeWitt has indicated that in the future he will charge such calls to the Band Boosters' phone.

3. Our school is serving as host for the Region AAAA East Girls Volleyball Tournament, and a few phone calls have been made in this connection. All of Mr. Waldron's calls, which totaled $23.64, will be reimbursed by Region AAAA East.

4. Our school is also serving as host for the Region Choir All-State Tryouts. The phone calls for this event have not been expensive, but all costs for them will be reimbursed by the Region Choir Clinic Association.

Our staff may have made a few person-to-person calls when station-to-station ones would have served as well. Perhaps you can give us some guidance on this subject.

I hope this memo will help to clarify the matter of the high school's large phone bill for the month in question. We do have a great many activities and programs that require long-distance phone calls, but we also realize the importance of keeping these calls to a minimum. We pledge our continued support in achieving this goal.

If I can be of further assistance, please let me know.

LETTER ON TUITION ARREARS AT PRIVATE SCHOOL

This is a courteous form letter advising parents that tuition is overdue and explaining what will happen if it is not paid within a specified time.

Dear Mr. and Mrs. Doty:

This letter is in regard to the tuition arrears on your account. We wish to bring this to your attention and, at the same time, to refer to the policies that have been adopted by the Board of Directors of the school. These policies are necessary in order for us to operate on a sound financial basis while continuing to serve students.

The board's policy is as follows: "For students to continue their studies in school, and to take final examinations and receive report cards or have records transmitted, regular payments must be made. Where accounts are in arrears for more than 60 days, the board may require withdrawal unless satisfactory arrangements are made."

Please note that unless such arrangements are made,

1. Students cannot take semester exams, and therefore credit cannot be given.

2. Report cards and transcripts may not be issued.

3. Withdrawal may be required after 60 days of arrears.

Your account shows the arrears indicated below. We are anxious to work with you in handling this matter since we want to continue to serve your family, but you must make arrangements for a satisfactory settlement. Our bookkeeper can be reached at 678-9012 from 8:30 a.m. to 12:30 p.m. Monday through Friday. Thank you.

Student _____

Date _____

Total Arrears $ _____

Length of Arrears _____

LETTER ON NONRESIDENT TUITION ARREARS

Here is a form letter that accompanies a copy of the school board's policy statement about tuition for out-of-district students. Since it is basically a covering letter, it is quite short.

Dear Mr. and Mrs. Ripley:

Our records show that at the close of business on February 28 your tuition account was one of several in arrears. Payment is due on the first day of each month and must be paid no later than the 10th, as required by school board policy.

At the regular board meeting on February 24 the school board reviewed these accounts. I was instructed to advise all persons whose accounts are not current.

In the event you may not be aware of school board policy in this matter, I am enclosing a copy of the policy statement regarding out-of-district tuition payments so that there will be no misunderstandings. Please note the action that may be taken on delinquent accounts.

Your prompt payment will be appreciated.

POLICY STATEMENT ON NONRESIDENT STUDENT TUITION

This is the statement of policy accompanying the preceding letter.

Issue Date: 7/15/xx

PAYMENT OF NONRESIDENT STUDENT TUITION

Tuition is to be paid in advance. Prior to enrolling a student or students for the year, the parent or guardian will notify the school principal in writing as to whether the tuition will be paid a year in advance, a semester in advance, or a month in advance. The terms of each of these plans are as follows:

1. Yearly payment plan. Prior to enrollment for the 19xx–19xx school year, payment may be made in full for the school year. The cost will be $300 per student in grades 1 through 9, $350 per student in grades 9 through 12, and $160 per vocational student.

2. Semester payment plan. Prior to enrollment for each semester of the 19xx–19xx school year, payment may be made in full for the semester. The cost will be $150 per student in grades 1 through 9, $175 per student in grades 9 through 12, and $80 per vocational student.

3. Monthly payment plan. Nine equal payments shall be made, with the first payment ($33.34 grades 1–9; $38.89 grades 9–12; $17.78 vocational) required on enrollment day and the remaining eight payments to be made on the first day of each calendar month beginning with the month of October and ending with the month of May.

If at any time payments become ten days late, then the School Board shall have the option of requiring the nonresident student to return to his or her home school of record outside the Mobley Municipal Separate School District.

Any change in tuition status or withdrawal from classes in the Mobley Municipal Separate School District will justify a partial refund based on a daily cost rate if an advance payment has been made.

LETTER REQUIRING TUITION PAYMENT

The purpose of this letter is to ensure that tuition will be paid on a problematic account. The letter calls for the payment of overdue tuition plus at least a semester's advance payment.

Dear Mr. and Mrs. Ackerman:

Our school records indicate that your still owe $66.68 in overdue tuition for the 19xx–19xx school year. This letter is to inform you that all past monies due for tuition must be paid before your child can enroll in a Mobley school this fall.

Because you are in arrears for a previous school year, the policy set by our school board also requires that you pay tuition for at least a semester in advance for the upcoming school year. That payment is due when tuition students register later this month.

We appreciate your understanding and cooperation in this matter.

❧ A Word on Style ❧

EMPHASIZE THE WORD <u>YOU</u>

The word *you* is a pleasant one to most of us. Like flattery, it is often effective even when its intent is obvious. Advertisers know this and use it. They concentrate on *you* in their copy, and they do it because it works. Effective school administrators often use the same technique.

Look at some of the recent letters you have written. Are they more formal than they need to be? Do they use the word *I* more often than necessary? Do they express thoughts in a roundabout way? If they show any of these symptoms, you may find that using the word *you* provides a partial cure. If nothing else, it forces you to pay closer attention to the needs and attitudes of your readers.

❧ A Word on Style ❧

DO NOT OVERUSE <u>I</u>

When you write, you have a natural tendency to use the word *I*. You have to refer to yourself some way, and neither the imperial *we* nor the Nixonian third person is ordinarily a good choice. Is there really anything wrong with *I?* No—not if it is used in moderation.

The problem with *I* arises when it is overused. If every paragraph in a five-paragraph letter begins with *I*, for instance, the reader is likely to be put off, consciously or unconsciously. On the other hand, if only one of the paragraphs—preferably not the first one—begins with *I*, no reasonable reader should object.

END OF SCHOOL YEAR   **19**

CHAPTER 19

Some kind of farewell is traditional at the end of the school year. It may take the form of a letter or memo of appreciation for a job well done. Or it may be a brief review of the year's achievements or difficulties or both. In some cases, its emphasis may be on next year's challenges rather than on this year's accomplishments.

Generally speaking, the letter will be positive in outlook, although circumstances may not always be favorable. That is the case with a number of letters in this chapter. They are written in the face of budget cuts, unfavorable election results, attempts to lower academic standards, unfriendly newspaper editorials—discouraging signs and perhaps unjustified provocations.

Yet the letters and memos are good-humored and optimistic. They emphasize what is right about the schools, the students, and the staff. They tell what kinds of improvements have been made. They set the record straight and lift the spirit of those who read them.

That is what the writers of the letters in this chapter set out to do.

LETTER OF APPRECIATION TO TEACHERS AFTER CUTBACK

Dear Staff:

As the 19xx-19xx academic year draws to a close, I want to express to all of you my deepest appreciation for your support and a most earnest commendation for a job well done.

With 30 percent cutbacks in the custodial/clerical staff, 10 percent cuts in the professional staff, and cuts ranging upward to 100 percent in supplies and equipment, you have more than survived. This staff has overcome!

You have done a superb job under trying and difficult circumstances during this first year of proposition 2½. Your ingenuity and creativity in coping with the hardships caused by deep budget cuts have helped our students to have an excellent school year. You cushioned the blows for them, shielded them from the problems, and made sure they had a good, productive, and happy school experience.

From the moment I came to Wayland in 1971, I believed that the real strength of the Wayland Public Schools was in its exceptionally able and talented staff. That belief is now a conviction. I hoped you would come through this year, and you came through in a way that exceeded my highest expectations.

Things look good for next year—not perfect, but good. I think we can prevail. I believe that the people of this town will support a quality educational system.

Good luck and best wishes for a great summer. I wish I were able to find the right words to thank you for your extraordinary performance and support this year.

Sincerely,

William G. Zimmerman, Jr.

William G. Zimmerman, Jr.
Superintendent of Schools

Wayland
public schools

ENCOURAGEMENT TO TEACHERS IN FINAL DAYS OF SCHOOL

This is a motivational message from a principal's newsletter to his staff. It calls upon teachers to avoid a letdown in the last few days of the school year.

The End as the Beginning

As we close the circle of an experience, a unit of knowledge, or a work of art, the result should be an organic whole. One should be unable to determine where that experience begins or ends. The blend should be complete.

The challenge of these final days of the school year can be likened to the circle. There are no instructional days that one can label as being unimportant or expendable. Last days are as important as first days. The waning days of the semester can and do have an enormous impact upon a student's impression of a course and teacher.

The efforts and achievements of an entire term can be dissipated in the final days of a term if those days are devoted to idleness or frivolity. What may have been carefully constructed and developed can collapse if the same effort that went into the early part of the year is not invested in its last days.

Our capacity to meet the challenges of June is there. The proof of that capacity was very much in evidence to me as I walked around the building yesterday and found meaningful instruction going on in virtually every room each period. You are to be commended, for, as you know, this is the time of year when schools are traditionally on their ears. (You may substitute another part of the anatomy if you wish.)

Keep up the fine work. With commitment and resolve, we can continue to make the end as exciting as the beginning. Teaching and learning can complete the circle begun in September, creating an organic whole.

LETTER TO EDITOR UPHOLDING STANDARDS FOR GRADUATION

In this letter a principal takes a strong stand on graduation requirements. He insists that the minimum standards for high school graduation be maintained and implies that he will deny petitions to waive the requirements.

Letter to the Editor:

Every year, during the last weeks before graduation, there are a number of students who finally get the message that they will not graduate because they have not taken the responsibility to do the work that is required. They try petitioning for a waiver of required courses not completed or units not earned. A high school principal has the power to waive some of the requirements if the requests are valid. If the petition is disapproved, many students try to find someone to blame other than themselves.

The people of Harte City through their School Board have set minimum standards for graduation. These allow for a student to flunk six courses in grades 10 through 12. Most of the students petitioning have already flunked these six courses and have failed to complete at least one more. Their record does not meet the minimum standards set by the board.

It is time to give real worth and dignity to the high school diploma and to those who have taken the responsibility of earning it. The young men and women who walk across the stage at graduation have earned the right to do so. Otherwise, the diploma is a worthless piece of paper. I intend to see that a graduation diploma from Redford High School is a thing of dignity and worth, signifying the completion of valid educational tasks. I will resist all pressures to give it away unearned.

To quote Reverend Jesse L. Jackson: "The full responsibility for learning cannot be transferred from the student to the teacher. Students must stop blaming others and their environment for failing to learn."

PLACEMENT AGREEMENT FORM

While no parent likes to have his or her child held back, it may be necessary. The accompanying placement agreement form, although not a personal letter, conveys an impression of thoughtfulness and concern.

OMAHA PUBLIC SCHOOLS
PLACEMENT AGREEMENT

Dear _____ ,

    As you are aware, children grow and progress at different rates. They are promoted on the basis of their learning progress and achievement. Some children need more time than others to make satisfactory academic achievement.

    The educational progress of your child is important to us. When a child has not mastered required skills, we recommend that s/he continue at the present grade level for the next school year. Therefore, we recommend that _____ be placed in Grade _____ for the _____ school year.   *(Child's Name)*

    This placement recommendation represents our professional judgment and should give your child a chance for success and progress in later years.

_____	_____
(Teacher's Signature)	*(Date)*
_____	_____
(Principal's Signature)	*(Date)*

_____ I agree that my child's educational needs can best be met by being placed in Grade _____ for the _____ school year.

_____ I disagree with the school staff's recommendation and want my child placed in Grade _____ for the _____ school year.

_____	_____
(Parent Signature)	*(Date)*

Comments: _____

_____

_____

END-OF-YEAR OBSERVATIONS

This letter, like some of the other end-of-year messages, alludes to ongoing financial difficulties. The writer, a superintendent, notes that these problems face educational institutions at all levels.

Dear Colleagues:

We are rapidly approaching the end of what has proven to be another busy and, I believe, successful school year. I wish to thank all of you for your efforts and contributions during the past year.

The importance of the Board of Education elections scheduled for this November should not be minimized. The quality and dedication of the board will to a large measure shape the quality of the school system and the educational climate in which we work. In my judgment, we need candidates who are intelligent, rational, open-minded, strongly committed to the improvement of public education, able to make difficult decisions, willing to study issues carefully, and ready to devote the time needed to fulfill the obligations of the office. Many of you know people who, if elected, will enable us to continue to make improvements in the school systems in order to serve our students even better than we have. For obvious reasons, you can be more direct than I in encouraging high quality candidates to run for office.

The months ahead may be very difficult financially. Reduced federal and state revenues will place a heavy burden on local property taxes and will probably lead to a reduction in the services and programs we can offer. The educational community—elementary, secondary, and university—will not escape the sting of reduced revenues. We must therefore unite with our colleagues in other school districts and those in the New Hampshire University System to ensure that public education receives an equitable share of tax revenues. Forcing the University System to raise tuition sharply and/or to select an even higher proportion of its student body from out-of-state is not in the best interest of New Hampshire residents. An accessible, quality public educational system, grade one through graduate school, must be one of our highest priorities in this state. Approximately 125 Nashua High graduates annually enroll within the state University System—Durham, Keene, Plymouth—and we must be concerned about the costs and opportunities they face as they leave Nashua Senior High School.

Despite these problems, I feel that as a school system we have made considerable progress during recent years. I consider myself fortunate to have the privilege of serving as your superintendent. I strongly believe that as we take a comprehensive view of our school system—the quality of staff; student achievement scores; quality and scope of our educational programs; services offered; success with extracurricular activities; and quality of school facilities, to name just a few—we can see that the Nashua School District does not have to take second place to any school district in the state of New Hampshire. Indeed, admittedly with perhaps some degree of bias, I am of the opinion that the Nashua School District is among the best in New England.

Again, thank you for your efforts during the present academic year. We look forward to 19xx–19xx. Best wishes for a relaxing summer reprieve or, at least, for an enjoyable change of pace.

BEST WISHES DESPITE FUTURE UNCERTAINTIES

This letter begins on a somewhat tentative note, yet what it says is undoubtedly on everyone's mind and cannot be ignored. After that, the writer, a superintendent, reassures his readers that, despite the lost election and recent editorials, they are doing a solid, professional job.

Dear Colleagues:

As we close this academic year, I fear some of us may have mixed feelings about the success of 19xx–19xx. Certainly, the loss of the Override Election, coupled with recent newspaper editorials, could leave us with a great deal of uncertainty about what the future holds.

Please permit me this opportunity to express my personal appreciation for the efforts you have made over the past months. We have continued to put emphasis on the quality of academic programs available to Saguaro students. We have demonstrated again this year that Saguaro students are learning well, and they rank high on all measures of academic achievement. Under your direction, many of our students have represented Saguaro in an outstanding manner throughout the state.

I believe we have achieved significant improvement in staff and administrative relationships this year. Our relations with the board are notably better. The tremendous effort devoted to improved relationships should benefit all for many years to come.

Have a pleasant and safe summer. I look forward to seeing you next fall.

END-OF-YEAR MEMO NOTING PROGRESS

This is basically a friendly note that reviews the gains made during the school year and offers continuing assistance to the teachers addressed.

TO: All Secondary Social Studies Teachers
FROM: Angie L. Buhler, Social Studies Supervisor
SUBJECT: Close of School Year

We are near the end of the school session and the close of another year of working together. A great deal of progress has occurred this year. We now have curriculum guides in a number of areas; supplies and materials are in greater abundance than they were a year ago; and new textbooks are in almost all classes.

As we work together, I know we will accomplish a great deal more. I want you to know how much I enjoyed working with each of you and how much I appreciate your good work.

I will probably be in your school again before the end of the session. If not, I hope you have a safe and enjoyable summer. If you need any assistance, please do not hesitate to call me. My office number is 234-5678, and my home number is 654-3210.

LETTER TO ROTARY MEMBERS ON YEAR'S ACHIEVEMENTS

It is pleasant to be able to end the school year on a strongly positive note, and this letter does. The superintendent informs Rotary Club members of the district's clear, documented academic improvement.

Dear Herb:

The Rutledge School District has just completed its best year ever! For the first time, student test scores across the board exceed both state and national averages. Ten years ago our students were averaging two full grades behind national averages and even trailed state averages. The present results are based on national tests given to all students in this state and throughout the country.

I know that you too will be elated over this most significant improvement. It has taken several years of effort, with all of us working together to strengthen our instructional program, to bring us to this point of achievement. This could not have been done without the help and encouragement of citizens such as you. Thank you very much for being a friend and for believing in what we are trying to do for young people.

May God bless you and your family.

PLANNING FOR NEXT YEAR

This end-of-year memo emphasizes the future. Although the writer comments favorably on achievements of the preceding year, his main focus is on further improvements.

TO: Principals and District Staff
FROM: George Kahana, District Superintendent
SUBJECT: Next Year

It is not too early to begin planning for next year. Analyze your successes and failures and try to determine what needs to be done to consolidate gains and to improve weaknesses.

To pursue our goal of excellence in the district, we will continue to emphasize these areas:

1. High achievement in basic skills

2. Excellent school climate, including attendance, discipline, and beautification

3. Instructional leadership

4. Parent involvement

5. Staff development

Thank you for your achievements this past year. Students benefited greatly from your efforts. The quality of instruction in this district has never been higher, and yet there is always room for improvement.

Have a restful and enjoyable summer. I look forward eagerly to your return in the fall.

ABBREVIATIONS OF STATES, TERRITORIES, AND POSSESSIONS OF THE UNITED STATES

Alabama	AL	Missouri	MO
Alaska	AK	Montana	MT
Arizona	AZ	Nebraska	NE
Arkansas	AR	Nevada	NV
California	CA	New Hampshire	NH
Canal Zone	CZ	New Jersey	NJ
Colorado	CO	New Mexico	NM
Connecticut	CT	New York	NY
Delaware	DE	North Carolina	NC
District of	DC	North Dakota	ND
Columbia		Ohio	OH
Florida	FL	Oklahoma	OK
Georgia	GA	Oregon	OR
Guam	GU	Pennsylvania	PA
Hawaii	HI	Puerto Rico	PR
Idaho	ID	Rhode Island	RI
Illinois	IL	South Carolina	SC
Indiana	IN	South Dakota	SD
Iowa	IA	Tennessee	TN
Kansas	KS	Texas	TX
Kentucky	KY	Utah	UT
Louisiana	LA	Vermont	VT
Maine	ME	Virgin Islands	VI
Maryland	MD	Virginia	VA
Massachusetts	MA	Washington	WA
Michigan	MI	West Virginia	WV
Minnesota	MN	Wisconsin	WI
Mississippi	MS	Wyoming	WY

FORMS OF ADDRESS IN LETTERS

<u>United States Officials</u>

President	The President The White House Washington, DC 20500 ------ Dear Mr. President:
Vice President	The Vice President United States Senate Washington, DC 20510 ------ Dear Mr. Vice President:
Cabinet Members	The Hon. Eli Jones Secretary of State Washington, DC 20510 ------ Dear Mr. Jones: *or* Dear Secretary Jones:
U.S. Senator	The Hon. Shana Smith United States Senate Washington, DC 20510 ------ Dear Senator Smith: *or* Dear Senator:
U.S. Representative	The Hon. Matthew Green House of Representatives Washington, DC 20515 ------ Dear Mr. Green: *or* Dear Rep. Green: *or* Dear Congressman:

Member of Agency,
   Bureau, or Commission
	The Hon. Alan White
	Chairman, Federal Communications
	   Commission
	Washington, DC 20554
	------ 	
	Dear Mr. Chairman: *or*
	Dear Mr. White:

Governor of a State	The Hon. Carole Price Governor State of New Hampshire Concord, NH 03301 ------ Dear Governor Price: *or* Madam: ·································
Judge	The Hon. Gary Fields Associate Justice of the Supreme Court of the United States United States Supreme Court Washington, DC 20543 ------ Dear Sir: *or* Dear Mr. Justice: *or* Dear Judge Fields: ·····································

Members of the Clergy

Pope	His Holiness, the Pope State of Vatican City Italy ------ Your Holiness: *or* Most Holy Father: ·································
Cardinal	His Eminence John Cardinal O'Shea ------ Your Eminence: ·································
Archbishop or Bishop	The Most Rev. George Miller Archbishop of Chicago ------ Your Excellency: ·································
Priest or Minister	The Rev. Francis Marin ------ Dear Rev. Marin: ·································
Rabbi	Rabbi Isaac Rudder ------ Dear Rabbi Rudder: ·································

Members of the Military

Commissioned Officer	Lt. Gen. Edward Gage (Exact rank is important) ------ Dear General Gage:
Officer and Wife	Capt. and Mrs. Kurt Kunzman ------ Dear Capt. and Mrs. Kunzman:

❧ A Word on Style ❧

MAKE SURE OF FACTS

This is good advice not only for a newspaper reporter but also for a school administrator. To many parents, school is a place where children learn facts. It creates doubt about the educational enterprise when a school administrator makes factual errors.

If you use quotations in your letters, be sure you get them right. Look them up in Bartlett's *Familiar Quotations* or other standard sources. Also, make sure you attribute a quotation to the correct author. Some well-known quotes are so commonly misstated or misattributed that it really pays to check.

Index